The Future
of Eternity

The Future of Eternity

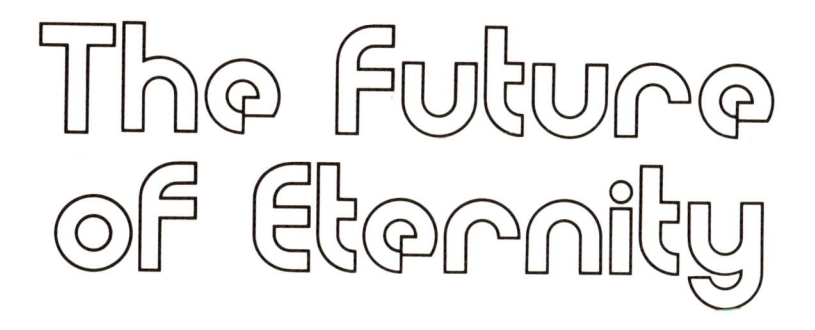

MYTHOLOGIES OF SCIENCE FICTION AND FANTASY

Casey Fredericks

INDIANA UNIVERSITY PRESS

Bloomington

Copyright © 1982 by Casey Fredericks
All rights reserved

No part of this book may be reproduced or utilized in any form or by any means, electronic or mechanical, including photocopying and recording, or by any information storage and retrieval system, without permission in writing from the publisher. The Association of American University Presses' Resolution on Permissions constitutes the only exception to this prohibition.

Manufactured in the United States of America

Library of Congress Cataloging in Publication Data

Fredericks, Casey, 1943-
   The future of eternity.

   Bibliography: p.
   Includes indexes.
     1. Science fiction—History and criticism. 2. Mythology in literature. 3. Fantastic fiction—History and criticism. I. Title.
PN3433.6.F7   809.3′876   81–47773
                                          AACR2

1 2 3 4 5 86 85 84 83 82

CL. ISBN 0-253-32530-7
PA. ISBN 0-253-20295-7

I Dedicate This Book
to
All My Student Friends
(1969–1979)

CONTENTS

Preface ix
Acknowledgments xv

1. Old and New Myths in Science Fiction 1
2. "Estrangement" in Myth and Science Fiction 34
3. The Big Time 65
4. In Defense of Heroic Fantasy 91
5. Men like Gods 121
6. The Return to the Primitive 149
7. The Future of Eternity:
   A Vision of Science-Fiction Myth-Making 170

Selected Bibliography 183
Notes 193
Index of Authors and Their Works 225
Index of Mythologies 229

PREFACE

The following comprehensive essay on science fiction and myth proceeds from an interest in both subjects that goes back some twenty years. It is based on a first intuition that while science fiction is somehow very important, yet it is far too soon to decide which stories of modern SF will turn out to be "classics" of literature. A second intuition is that science fiction is fundamentally involved with myths. The two have to be discussed together; without some understanding of how myths and science fiction are intimately connected, we cannot answer the question as to whether SF is or is not an important literature. This leads to the third intuition from which this study proceeds: that myths, ancient or modern, are still an unresolved problem for our time. Hence, we will often have to depart from the narrower interests of SF to make what are, I hope, revealing comparisons with other myth-based facets of our culture: film, philosophy, and popular cult as well as literature. Correspondingly, some strictly modern issues seem best clarified by a comparison with an ancient example. This essay, then, looks at manifestations of myth and science fiction in both modern and ancient culture and looks outward to other facets of modern and ancient culture to provide a comparative basis for the impact and importance of both SF and myth.

The work began in the summer of 1972 with quite a different purpose. I delivered a paper entitled "Patterns of Myth in Science Fiction and Fantasy" at the second annual conference on curricular innovation at Heidelberg College, directed by Frank Kramer of the Center for the Institute for Coordination of Ancient and Modern Studies. The paper was based on an experimental course of the same title that I had taught the previous semester at Indiana University in the College of Arts and Sciences Experimental Curriculum. In the course there was no doubt on my part that I was leading a group of enthusiastic students through some popular science-fiction narratives, some of which I was reading for the first time myself—I had chosen them because my students recommended them—and my special expertise was to offer interesting critical comment from my vantage point as a teacher of classical and comparative mythology. My enthusiasm for the course was totally natural since I had been a reader of myths since childhood, of science fiction since my early teens.

However, for a long time my attempts to be a critic of mythical SF got no further than simple declarative accounts of what ancient myths the modern SF writers used, how they changed an incident or character here and there, or how they created a modern analogue for an ancient mythical conception (e.g., atomic holocaust as the updating of the Eddic Ragnarok or superscientific gadgetry as a realization of age-old mythical wish-fulfillments).

The first challenge I have had to meet in writing this book, then, has been to respond to the modernity and contemporaneity of SF, and not to reduce it to its sources in classical and other myths. I am a professional classicist, and my specialist training has contributed substantially to this work. But I am even more a person of my own culture and time, which fact seems significant for both the conception and composition of this book.

A second challenge has been even harder to meet because it has arisen simultaneously with the composition of this book. I refer to the growing body of criticism on the SF narrative directed from solid bases in the academic community. When I began my study, there was little of value to me in the way of either theoretical or practical literary critical commentary on the authors and narratives I selected for this study. Though some useful books were scattered here and there—like J.O. Bailey's classic *Pilgrims Through Time and Space* or Kingsley Amis's *New Maps of Hell* or a helpful article here and there in Leland Sapiro's *Riverside Quarterly*, Thomas Clareson's *Extrapolation*, or the fine British journal *Foundation*—I began mostly on my own, rooting around like any other "fan" to discover interesting mythological SF narratives. Science-fiction criticism did not have a nineteenth century, and it is actually only since the early nineteen seventies that everything seems to have been getting done at once:

fundamental bibliographical work, including reliable indexes to SF magazines and paperback anthologies; solid basic essays on individual works and authors, such as the valuable essays in Thomas Clareson's recent edited collection, *Voices for the Future*, or David Ketterer's attractive *New Worlds for Old*; a first-rate "hard" academic journal, *Science-Fiction Studies*, edited ably by R.D. Mullen and Darko Suvin; valuable theoretical essays on the SF narrative, again by Darko Suvin, and by Robert Scholes in his *Structural Fabulation*. With the publication of Robert Scholes and Eric Rabkin's *Science Fiction: History, Science, Vision* by Oxford University Press in 1977, the field received a first-rate general academic essay on SF. I rest my case: SF criticism has come of age. (Darko Suvin's *Metamorphoses of Science Fiction* [Yale U. Press, 1979] appeared too recently for me to observe more than the following: the chapters of his book originally appeared as journal articles that I have considered in the discussion in chapter 2; and besides, his book is best taken as either an alternative or a supplement to my own, since Suvin doesn't deal with Anglo-American SF after Wells.)

Research on fantasy fiction has progressed even more rapidly, and within the last half-decade major book-length studies by Tzvetan Todorov, Colin Manlove, W.R. Irwin, and Eric Rabkin have turned this area into one of the most promising for the major literary theorists and critics of our time. But since I have already gone over this ground at length and in depth in a review-article ("Problems of Fantasy," *Science-Fiction Studies* 5[1978]:33–44) I will not repeat myself unnecessarily here. (Throughout this book "SF" is used to refer as broadly as possible to the modern popular literary form and is used for magazine "science fiction and fantasy," for "science fantasy," for what some critics call "speculative fiction" or even "speculative fantasy" [Alexei Panshin] or "structural fabulation" [Robert Scholes].)

I have tried to take into account as much of this recent criticism as possible, and I hope my notes are generous enough to the many SF scholars who have shaped my viewpoints. However, I have chosen to confine my more theoretical and academic arguments to chapter 2, since I thought it fair in my first chapter to let the authors speak for the genre through their stories. Thus, the overall approach in chapter 1 is inductive, that in chapter 2 deductive. In all the chapters, synchronic focus on structures is interlaced with brief lectures on diachronic aspects of the genre: this is not a literary history, though I have set myself the goal of understanding the genre's long and varied history. Besides, science itself is preeminently a historical phenomenon, and insofar as SF is involved with science, it must be considered in a historical context; however, even the older SF—that of Shelley, Verne, and Wells—appeals to contemporary readers as a real experience, so there must be some contemporary significance in such narratives—certainly they are more than antiquarian curiosities.

And it was equally my intention that any reader could read my essay without consulting the notes: they are potentially useful for the specialists or for in-depth research, but hardly necessary for a first reading.

I have aimed at a general reader as my audience, so no previous knowledge of either mythology or science fiction is required. On the other hand, this is supposed to be much more than an introduction to either subject, so aficionados in either area should find it a unique and informative addition to the pursuit of the comparative method—in literature, ideas, or mythology.

Every work of literary criticism shares some features with the genre it studies. I enthusiastically emulate science fiction and hope that my work reflects the imaginative freedom and inventiveness of that genre. Like the science-fiction authors themselves, I aim at being *intelligent and interesting*. In style and tone, I have allowed myself a certain amount of informality nor have I repressed my sense of humor: this is only in tune with the SF writers themselves; among critics Eric Rabkin has been successful with the freer style I'm trying to emulate here.

Perhaps I should also apologize for the number of "stories" retold in these chapters, but only some of my readers can be expected to be familiar with these tales. The *stories* of science fiction and fantasy are very often their most memorable characteristic, and I have tried to describe them briefly, accurately, and interestingly. I hope my readers will be enticed to look up many of them on their own, for I admit it is my desire to recruit new readers for the genre. Maybe some of the stories will be republished in more permanent and less obscure formats.

Preface [xiii]

My analyses of individual works vary anywhere from a few words, paragraphs, or pages to rather detailed, lengthy essays like that on Philip José Farmer's *Flesh* in chapter 6. David Ketterer in *New Worlds for Old* set a precedent for this approach, but the material itself practically demands it. Suppose yourself on a walk with a good amateur naturalist through an interesting forest. Sometimes you identify birds or insects, sometimes you look at wild flowers, plants, or trees. All of these involve different classification problems from a strictly "scientific" point of view, but on the walk the natural environment is so rich and varied, and your walk such a brief encounter with this world, that you have to observe, describe, and try to identify the individual plants and animals as you meet them. Yet you do come out of the woods with a more precise, even "scientific" understanding of this forest world and a heightened perception of its beauty and harmony. In the world of the imagination, science fiction and fantasy literature constitute just such a rich ecology, and one does not wish to miss the "bugs and birds" by paying attention only to the "trees." At least, it is my honest purpose in leading my reader on this trek through the forest of SF to raise his awareness about an entire system, not just one species or genus of literary fauna.

I have had to deal with many fields of knowledge, sometimes as a professional, more often as an amateur: not only classical and comparative mythology, myth theory, SF literature and criticism, but also the history and philosophy of science, fiction theory and mainstream literary criticism, structuralism, comparative religion, and psychology. It seems to me that SF and fantasy literature actually demand such a "horizontal" approach to knowledge. Usually, especially in American universities, we conceive of a field of knowledge as a vertical line: we start at the bottom, at an elementary level, and move up a stepladder into more sophisticated levels of the discipline; thus in math, we might move from arithmetic to algebra, then to geometry, trigonometry, and calculus, and then beyond to esoteric heights where only professional specialists go; the same might hold for a humanities discipline like foreign-language study, where one starts with elementary language acquisition, moves into author and genre courses in that language, and then reaches a level of "higher criticism" on very specialized problems of a historical or philological nature reserved for the professional Ph.D.'s. But SF narratives intersect these vertical axes at very many points in a perpendicular manner: the SF fable will touch on a great number of these fields—combining, say, psychology, politics, and cosmology—and integrate them into a higher system. Science fiction focuses on the interconnectedness of our varied knowledge systems and creates out of them a synthesis—a "system of systems" as Robert Scholes calls it in his *Structural Fabulation*. At some point in the "system," a writer may be strong in his research, but in another area weak or naive; yet, overall, SF writers show a strong awareness of the *relative interdependence* of our knowledge systems and their understanding of it is rich and sophisticated, even in the case of the juvenile authors. That is why I have examined the subject from several points of view, and in my interpretations of individual works I have tried to react to more than one dimension of either meaning or classification.

Since relatively few SF narratives have received any critical attention at all, I have deliberately avoided those that have already received enough attention in contemporary criticism (with the excusable exception of an old friend or two) and have instead concentrated on long-ignored or underrated works. Sometimes the conceptual formulations in these stories are their major source of interest or excellence, but in other cases I needed a lengthier, more detailed analysis to take into account the images or language texture of a specific tale. Again, I assume my readers will find this approach justified by the heightened interest and awareness of mythology and SF that it produces.

In sum, I have tried to produce a critical study that is new and different, and I have faith that readers will approach it anticipating fun and pleasure as well as intellectual edification—as both myth and SF certainly demand.

ACKNOWLEDGMENTS

Thanks are due to William Cagle, Librarian of the Lilly Library, Indiana University-Bloomington, for making Lilly's extensive resources in SF and fantasy available for this research and for encouraging me to pursue SF scholarship by inviting me to be the co-compiler of Lilly's 1975 Exhibition on Science Fiction and Fantasy and editor of the exhibition catalog; to Theodore Klein of Texas Tech University, for asking me to be associate editor of and reviewer for his interdisciplinary journal *Helios* (Journal of the Classical Association of the Southwest United States) and inviting me to speak at the Texas Tech Comparative Literature Symposium on "Mythology in Twentieth Century Literature and Thought" (January 1978); to Leland Sapiro, for helping me get started as a publishing SF critic, in his *Riverside Quarterly*; to Dale Mullen of Indiana State University, editor of *Science-Fiction Studies*, for inviting me to be a reviewer and an editorial consultant; to Darko Suvin of McGill University, the co-editor of *SFS*, for being the most challenging intellectual and demanding critic available to me as a new SF scholar; to Tom Clareson of Wooster College, Ohio, editor of *Extrapolation*, for encouraging my interest in SF; to SF writers Alex and Phyllis Eisenstein and classicists Betty Rose Nagle of Indiana University and William C. McDermott of the University of Pennsylvania; to William Orum of Smith College for his helpful critical reading of chapter 5. Needless to say, no one but me is responsible for any specific views espoused in this book, but I hope I have learned something from the efforts of all these intelligent and imaginative people. Special thanks are due to Deb Munson and Derek Vint for typing, gratis, the important first draft; and to Nan Miller of Indiana University Press for being the first to encourage me to turn the original Heidelberg College paper of 1972 into a full book-length study.

Finally, the ten years of work on this book required a number of preliminary studies, listed below. However, all of these analyses have been severely rethought and revised and placed in new contexts in the book.

"Revivals of Ancient Mythologies in Current Science Fiction and Fantasy," in Thomas Clareson's critical anthology, *Many Futures, Many Worlds: Theme and Form in Science Fiction* (Kent State University Press, 1977).

"Science Fiction and the World of Greek Myths," *Helios* N.S. 2 (1975):1–22.

Two encyclopedia articles (on Philip José Farmer's *Strange Relations* and L. Sprague de Camp and Fletcher Pratt's *The Incompleat Enchanter*) for *Survey of Science Fiction Literature*, 4 vols. (Pasadena, Calif.: Salem Press, 1979).

"Greek Mythology in Modern Science Fiction: Vision and Cognition," in Wendell Aycock and Theodore Klein (eds.), *Classical Mythology in Twentieth-Century Thought and Literature* (Proceedings of Comparative Literature Symposium, Texas Tech University, 1980).

The Future of Eternity

1 Old and New Myths in Science Fiction

My goal is to account for the impact of mythology on modern science fiction and fantasy, to study how the oldest form of the human imagination serves as an inspiration for the newest. The writers of science fiction and fantasy in their search for striking, new imaginative conceptions of alternate realities—meaning precisely worlds and societies that are *not* like ours—have discovered in the ancient myths ideas, themes, and characters that are stimuli for constructing fictive models of new realities. What is it in, or about, those ancient stories and their long outmoded interpretations of reality that modern writers have found so useful for their own purposes of taking us readers out of our "lived" reality and transporting us to an imaginary universe of possibility and potential?

In 1969, Robert Silverberg, a prolific writer by any sort of standard, published one of those little stories which indicate that mythology is, and will continue to be, a central interest of science-fiction writers. I have chosen it as the first story for detailed attention because it too asks why myths are so important, but does so indirectly, by starting from the make-believe viewpoint of a person who lives in a world where there are no myths.

"After the Myths Went Home"[1] is set in the middle centuries of the twelfth millenium of our era. Mankind has already long been bored with its technological power. For a century now these men for their own amusement have been able to call up from the past great figures of human history like Caesar and Cleopatra, or Freud and Marx. So Leor the inventor devises a new and more powerful machine that can recreate the great mythical personages of older mankind in physical form. Some of them are supposedly products of pure imagination, others are figures who were once real men but after their deaths were transfigured and assimilated to pre-existing archetypes and so became more than men. John Kennedy is one of the latter group, for his glorious young life and tragic early death caused him to fall into the same mythological category as Osiris, Attis, Adonis, and Baldur: he is a Dying God. Somehow, though, even those mythical beings who ought never to have existed in the real world at all (like the Biblical Adam or the Greek Pan) still have "the aura of humanity" about them because they are all the products of the men who imagined them. All the mythfolk were originally created by and for men; all display the mark of humanity, even the monsters.

Silverberg also plays with the paradise myth by altering the relationship between gods and men. This future Earth combines features of Eden (Eve says she feels right at home!), Olympus, and the Eddic Asgard—it is a tinseled playground in which men have finally become like gods, and Silverberg says specifically that in this future all men "live a myth of their own." So it is as second-class citizens that the various gods, heroes, and monsters move into this society of godlike men and are allowed a new lease on life. That is, as long as the mythfolk are entertaining, they survive, but soon men get bored again, and after half a century the mythfolk are gathered up one by one and stuffed inexorably back into the machine. Only Cassandra, the last to go, provides a prophetic comment:

> "You should have kept us," Cassandra said. "People who have no myths of their own would do well to borrow those of others, and not just as sport. Who will comfort your souls in the dark times ahead? Who will guide your spirits when the suffering begins? Who will explain the woe that will befall you? Woe! Woe!"

The unspecified first-person narrator of the story, a fellow-citizen of Leor, only replies: "The woes of Earth lie in Earth's past. We need

Old and New Myths in Science Fiction

no myths." This is where we need to remember our ancient Greek mythology, for in the *Iliad* Cassandra, daughter of the Trojan king Priam, was filled with the ecstasy of the god Apollo and always spoke true prophecies that no one ever believed—to their own tragic undoing. And so it happens for the race of Leor:

> Cassandra smiled and stepped into the machine. And was gone. And then the age of fire and turmoil opened, for when the myths went home, the invaders came, bursting from the sky. And our towers toppled and our moons fell. And the cold-eyed strangers went among us, doing as they wished.
> And those of us who survived cried out to the old gods, the vanished heroes.
> Loki, come!
> Achilles, defend us!
> Shiva, release us!
> Heracles! Thor! Gawain!
> But the gods are silent, and the heroes do not come.

Thus concludes this tale, where even in a technologically accomplished paradise of the far future, gods and demi-gods are a necessity. Why? Because the decadent race of Leor lacks imagination; these men have no sense of the "inner space" of the mind—they possess only sybaritic gadgets, games, sports, and amusements—the externals of the good life only. Because, in Cassandra's words, "they have no myths of their own," they have isolated themselves from a universe that still contains a large number of "unknowns"—like the invaders who unexpectedly bring them low. Myth lies between man and this unknown, and when his myths go home forever, he is truly left "alone," without imaginative resources. The loss of myth is equated with the loss of the ability to think creatively about the universe we live in. Thus the story does turn back to confront our own real world in a way that is simultaneously *indirect and didactic* (a characteristic SF shares with satire), for the narrator tells us that our era, the twentieth century, was "the end of the age of mythmaking." Silverberg is telling us it's up to us to keep the myths alive.

Silverberg's didacticism is also based on a solid, well-researched understanding of myth theory. He makes use of Carl Jung's concept of "archetypes," primal categories of the unconscious mind that structure our experience in the real world; James George Frazer's

Dying God from *The Golden Bough* (discussed further in chapter 6); and the neo-Kantian theme that the gods are "imaginary figures by means of whom the ancients attempted to give structure to the universe."[2] The story is so slickly produced that its subtlety and sophistication could go unnoticed. (Yet, what does Silverberg mean by the expression "moon*s* fell" in that final paragraph? That plural creates such ambiguity: are we on "another" earth or only on another *version* of the earth we know? What does it say about the imaginary world's relationship to our own?)

However, it isn't necessary to rely only on a fable like this one to assert that SF writers are, by and large, myth-lovers. A great many SF writers themselves admit the influence of myth over their lives as creative writers. Among those who have informed me of this in various more or less personal ways are Roger Zelazny, Ursula K. LeGuin, L. Sprague de Camp, Emil Petaja, Philip José Farmer, and Philip Klass ("William Tenn"). From the pervasiveness of famous myths throughout many of their works, the list could readily be expanded to include Poul Anderson, Ray Bradbury, Avram Davidson, Samuel R. Delany, Harlan Ellison, Michael Moorcock, André Norton, Robert Silverberg, Brian M. Stableford, and the late Thomas Burnett Swann. Myths are typically encountered early in life, even sooner than science fiction itself, and then typically remain an interest from this first encounter on.

It is no wonder then that for years an ever increasing number of writers, fans, and academic critics have been referring to science fiction as a "mythology" or "new mythology." In its most popular manifestations this means only that the imaginative paraphernalia of lasers/ray-guns/blasters, alien bug-eyed monsters, faster-than-light spaceships, and intelligent robots have replaced the older myths' magic weapons, monsters of divine origin, supernatural powers of flight, and servitor golems. The list could be multiplied endlessly. Indeed, it is in precisely such terms that the SF writer Fredric Brown has described the process of "rewriting" the Greek myth of Midas to turn it into a science-fiction narrative:

> Mr. Midas, who runs a Greek restaurant in the Bronx, happens to save the life of an extraterrestrial from a far planet who is living in New York anonymously as an observer for the Galactic Federation, to which Earth for obvious reasons is not yet ready to be admitted. Same offer of reward, same request. The extraterrestrial, who is master of sciences

far beyond ours, makes a machine which alters the molecular vibrations of Mr. Midas' body so his touch will have a transmuting effect upon other objects. And so on. It's a science fiction story, or could be made into one.[3]

Even this brief paragraph, however, is a masterful and sly little satire which assumes the reader is already acquainted with the story of the curse of the "golden touch." It is quite representative of Brown, who is widely known as an expert practitioner of the short short story. But it is true that for many fans and writers myths are nothing more than racy, imaginative tales to be rewritten with SF gizmos and speculations as replacements.

This very admission has led a number of contemporary SF critics to dismiss science fiction as being nothing more, in fact, than a rehash of *old* mythological themes, characters, and ideas. No matter how disguised, such SF to these critics is not a new literature, as SF ought to be, but a barely concealed displacement of archaic myths into phony scientific gadgets or even phonier pseudo-scientific epistemologies—like extrasensory perception or the concept of the "Force" in *Star Wars*. My second chapter is a detailed response to this attitude, but for the moment it is enough to insist that, if a critic eliminates myth from SF, he emasculates the genre and badly misreads the actual narratives.

That myths are as important to science-fiction writers as I claim seems undeniable from the entire history of the genre as well as from its immediate contemporary situation. A work as ancient as Lucian's *True History* of the second century A.D. combines a fictional treatment of both Greek science and myth with a satirical and critical view of man's knowledge of the universe.[4] Some, like James Gunn and L. Sprague de Camp, have gone even further back and identified Plato's Atlantis-fable (told in two versions in the dialogues *Timaeus* and *Critias*) as the first SF; and certainly the Atlantis tales show very close and explicit affinities with the older Greek myths.[5] (Along the way from classical antiquity to modern times, one has to recognize utopian fiction, the *conte philosophique*, Gothic fiction, the imaginary voyage [including the cosmic voyage], the Menippean satire, and the Tall Tale—all of which contributed something to the overall shape of modern SF and fantasy literature.)

However, historians of the genre like Brian Aldiss, Robert Scholes, and Eric Rabkin[6] date the origin of strictly *modern* SF to the early nineteenth century with the publication of that famous mutation of Gothic, *Frankenstein* by Mary Shelley, in its full title *Frankenstein; Or, The Modern Prometheus* (the first edition appeared in 1818, though the edition of 1831 is usually cited as standard).[7]

Prometheus, of course, in no way enters the story of *Frankenstein* directly, though the mere mention of his name in the title establishes certain patterns of thought that are brought to fulfillment later in the novel. Shelley provides a scientific displacement of Prometheus as creator when she has Victor Frankenstein, a young, intensely Faustian student of science use electricity to generate life in his created life-form, henceforth called a "Daemon." But Victor Frankenstein, the New Prometheus, unlike the providential champion of mankind in Aeschylus' tragedy, is repelled by his creature once he has made it. Rejected and isolated, the Daemon becomes a rebellious monster who methodically takes revenge on his own creator by killing all of Frankenstein's loved ones, thus rendering Frankenstein as isolated as the Daemon. Hence, as Muriel Spark has noticed, the Daemon also has some claim to being Prometheus:

> That casual alternative *Or* (in the title of the novel) is worth noting, for though at first Frankenstein is himself the Prometheus, the vital fire-endowing protagonist, the Monster, as soon as he is created, takes on the role. His solitary plight—". . . but am I not alone, miserably alone?" he cries—and more especially his revolt against his creator, establish his Promethean features. So, the title implies, the Monster is an alternative Frankenstein.[8]

Creator and the Monster are ambiguous mirrors of one another, and it is one of the abiding "classic" features of *Frankenstein* as a Gothic horror story that it becomes impossible to separate victim from victimizer. Finally, Shelley herself does not seem to make a clear distinction between the titanically creative rebel who is necessary for cultural and scientific progress and the Faustian mad scientist who creates only disaster by transgressing the laws of God and Nature. And indeed Scholes and Rabkin locate the origin of modern SF precisely in this essential feature of *Frankenstein*: moral ambiguity created in the face of speculative science.[9]

The Frankensteinian awareness of the ambiguous potential of science has never dropped out of SF. One need not appeal solely to the popular horror films of the thirties nor even to the ever-prevalent mad scientist theme. Critic Robert Philmus refers to it as the "Faustus Redivivus" archetype in his chapter on "New and Old Myths" in nineteenth-century SF; H. Bruce Franklin has noticed how prevalent it is in *American* science fiction of the nineteenth century (Hawthorne and Poe especially); and Eric Rabkin and Brian Aldiss have further confirmed that it is now endemic in modern SF.[10]

Realizing that the Frankensteinian consciousness of the demonic capacity of science has a long history, let us move to the other end of the historical spectrum, to see how it informs contemporary thought. One exemplary work which appeared recently is Brian W. Aldiss's *Frankenstein Unbound* (New York: Random House, 1973), published in the same year as his history of SF, *Billion Year Spree*. (The latter contains a half-satirical, self-effacing reference to Lucian's *True History* in its subtitle, "The True History of Science Fiction." Tellingly enough, Aldiss begins his history of modern SF proper with a consideration of Mary Shelley's classic. And the title of the novel alludes to both Mary Shelley's novel and her husband Percy Bysshe Shelley's famous poem, "Prometheus Unbound.") *Frankenstein Unbound*[11] describes a frightful breakdown in our sense of reality, due to the changes in our awareness that come from modern literature as well as science. All the boundaries of reality have become fluid, indistinct, fantastic: in the midst of a world developing "timeslips," or rifts in the fabric of space-time, a contemporary man finds himself hurled into the Europe of 1816, the year *Frankenstein* was written; however, that Europe is indistinguishable from the fictional world of the novel itself, so the modern protagonist, Joe Bodenland, has a series of escapades in which he meets the historical Mary Shelley and makes love to her as well as confronts and kills the fictional monster. The rift in our uncertainty extends beyond the rips in space-time to include the relationship of fiction to reality.

Without doubt, this Frankensteinian anxiety about the demonic and destructive potential of modern science is a basic belief-structure for many in our culture; it is just as definitely the twentieth-century offspring of the older Prometheus myth which was important to ancient Greek society and to nineteenth-century Romanticism. Aldiss's sophisticated fable emphasizes the disorientation of man's intellect and consciousness, but *The Prometheus Crisis*, a recent popular novel that was also made into a film, deals more closely with sociopolitical issues.

Greek myths seem peculiarly appropriate as archetypes and metaphors to be used in SF since they were developed in a rational and speculative culture. Ancient Greece gave Western culture its first theoretical philosophy and speculative science and, especially important, its first epistemology of science. We should not separate characters like Prometheus or Odysseus or the lesser heroes and monsters from the larger concerns of the culture which produced them. In the case of the Greeks these include our oldest developed consciousness of intelligence and many basic and rooted images of creativity, both human and divine. In their three-millenia history in Western culture, Greek myths have been the focus of significant movements in literature, art, and speculative ideas and now still have much to say about the basic concerns of contemporary culture, in SF no less than in movements like French existentialism (Albert Camus's *Sisyphus* or Jean-Paul Sartre's *Flies*) or Jungian psychology (Erich Neumann and Carl Kerényi among others) or structuralism (Claude Lévi-Strauss on Oedipus). The ancient Greeks were speculative and visionary in both their general culture and myths, so we should expect Greek myths to have some powerful associations for modern SF. In any case, Greek myths turn up everywhere in SF.

However, there are other literary and mythological affinities besides the Greek in the story of *Frankenstein*. Nelson Bond's "The Cunning of the Beast" (1942) is a well-crafted short story which exposes the other major ancient myth lurking behind the modern myth of *Frankenstein* (fortunately this story is available to today's readers in Mayo Mohs's popular and attractive anthology, *Other Worlds, Other Gods*[12]).

The Frankenstein imagery is obvious from the outset. Bond's narrator is an alien of the planet Kios who renders a very sympathetic account of the tragedy of Yawa Eloem, fellow Kiosan and fellow scientist, "who, delving into secrets better left unlearned, succeeded only in creating a monster mightier than its maker." From the outset, the first-person narration is a literary device which coaches us to view mankind as we often view the monsters of grade-B horror movies. We also recognize that the fallible creator-scientist is the God of the Old Testament whose two names in the original Hebrew are "Yahweh" and "Elohim."

Early in the story the narrator reveals that the Kiosans, despite magnificant intellectual and technological capacities, are physically the most vulnerable life-form on their world; all members of the Kiosan race are encased in metal containers which are their means of locomotion and which perform in all other physical capacities for them too. They even have to live in domes sequestered and protected from the natural elements of their own planet. It is to correct their own "angelic" failings that Yawa performs biological experiments in his laboratory, turning it into a "garden spot" and fashioning from the natural, lower life forms of Kios a pair of intelligent beings to act as his servants and lab assistants. They are not created, to be accurate, in his own natural image, but in the image of what a Kiosan might be if he had natural locomotion of his own—the beast is a Kiosan plus his artificial powers. But the narrator is simply horrified by the monster, the "cunning beast," that Yawa creates—here there is no sympathy, only loathing.

Yawa is really the wrecker of his own creation, however, especially when it comes to the She of the race, whom Yawa makes a dominant independent power in the microcosmic world of the garden and its beasts. The result is a series of murders and a reign of terror against the vulnerable Kiosans whose very existence as a species is threatened—until Yawa's beasts are revealed as the culprits. Poor Yawa is condemned by his own race to share the fate of his beasts: to be placed in a spacecraft, transported to the stars, banished forever from Kios. Yawa is doomed to co-exist eternally with his own traitorous, monstrous creations.

The Kiosan narrator palliates the horror of his tale, defending his friend against the charge of being a traitor to his race or a willful fiend:

> "That he sinned is undeniable, but his sin was only that of tampering with forces too great for him. For all we know, there are limits beyond which one is forbidden to probe. And they who seek to know, with gods, the secret of the creation of life are ever doomed to failure."

The story is a wonderful joke on Genesis and Frankenstein alike. God himself appears as a "mad scientist" in the grand literary tradition, and mankind is ranged on the monster-side of the ledger of creation. If Yawa is Frankenstein, we are the Daemon. In fact, if we take the alien narrator's point of view, we humans are a tragic, awesome mistake, in our very conception. The entirety of the Judeo-Christian account of the creation of man and his purpose in the world is turned into a mock horror story.

This story is also important because it hints at the very major role Biblical myths play in modern SF from Shelley to Aldiss—their popularity is at least equal to that of the Greek tales. David Ketterer has effectively brought out SF's frequent use of, and fascination with, Biblical myths in his *New Worlds for Old*, and of course his central critical concept of "Apocalypse" has Biblical roots.[13] But much more remains to be said about the Bible and SF, and "Genesis" is a Biblical metaphor for the world-creating dimension which is fundamental to all SF (this Biblical creation-metaphor is considered further in chapter 3, "The Big Time"). Since Man is not yet God, the creative powers of modern science are ambiguous: every Creation may also be a destruction, so the modern myth of Frankenstein is a justifiable reconsideration of the Biblical myth of Genesis.

Another advantage of our close look at Bond's tale is that it suggests how American SF of this period tended to create *games* with myths. The writers could assume their readers knew the tales and main characters (gods and heroes) well, so they could manipulate readers' expectations for almost any kind of effect. The only requirement here—to avoid Freudian and Jungian views of literature that would emphasize subconscious artistry and subconscious responses by readers—is that the reader have some knowledge of the myths beforehand; and here, of course, reader-competence will vary greatly. But there is no reason why SF should be different from other kinds of fiction, where readers range from sensitive professional critics to more naive readers who gain no more from a narrative than control of its plot and characters and see no more there than that—nor wish to. But those who do know their myths will have some other model against which they may read the literal narrative. And the relationships between the myth-structure and the main narrative may, again, vary greatly—from reinforcement to outright negation (the latter constituting an ironic relationship between the main and subsidiary, or mythical, structure).

Old and New Myths in Science Fiction

Charles L. Harness's novelette, "The New Reality" (no date),[14] is a literary game that conceals its mythical significance until the very conclusion, and the "mystery" format of this tale is obvious. Whereas Bond lets us in on the Edenic allusions right off, Harness withholds from the reader full awareness of the myth until it can be used for shock-effect.

The intellectual basis for this story is Immanuel Kant's distinction between the *noumena* (reality as it is in-itself; things as they really are; the *really* real) and the *phenomena* (reality as it appears to limited human knowers; things as they are perceived to be, as we know them from their surfaces only). In Harness's fictionalized version of this philosophy, men are not limited to knowing only the *phenomena* as Kant himself supposed; throughout his history, man has been developing progressively in the direction of full knowledge of the *noumena*, and in the world of the story he is at that critical point in time when his phenomenal universe may come to an end, through his own heightened awareness a *noumenal* one to begin.

Since the character of a noumenal universe is totally unknown, an "ontologist" (or "scientist of reality"—a fictitious profession) named Adam Prentiss is a special federal agent dispatched to prevent any experiments being done on reality that might alter its configurations. All of this is based on the fantastic premise that Kantian "metaphysics" can be identified with hard physical science and that a disruption in our philosophical understanding of the natural world is automatically *isomorphic* with a disruption in the fabric of nature itself. Changes in consciousness are real, they involve realistic effects, but never in the simple equation, "imagination is the same as reality." Kantian philosophy is not a physical science, but a mind game.

Prentiss fails in his mission. A malevolent scientist named Luce successfully performs the ultimate experiment on phenomenal reality by making a *single* photon of light reflect simultaneously in two opposite directions, thereby throwing the physical laws of our universe into abeyance. Luce becomes another Frankensteinian creator-destroyer, for as a result of the photon paradox, the phenomenal world does come to an end. Only three survivors make it to the brave new noumenal world, which turns out to be the Garden of Eden: Prentiss himself is Adam, Luce Satan in serpent form, and Prentiss's co-worker, named only "E" earlier in the narrative, is Eve.

And, of course, the reader's expectation of a "new reality" has been totally betrayed, the story from ironic title to mythical conclusion forming a joke on him.

An alert reader might have seen the end coming along much earlier in the story. "Luce" prefigures "Lucifer" in his name (as "E" does Eve); his estate—which ends up as the Garden in the noumenal world—is called "Snake-Eyes," which also refers to Luce's demonic facial expression. The idea of man's knowledge as the "forbidden fruit" which he tasted, leading to his expulsion from Eden, is alluded to by "E" early in the story. Any number of other minor "clues" point to the solution to the mystery of the new reality without giving it away completely.

Still a third literary game from generally this same period makes sure the reader knows the ancient myth as the modern story is occurring, yet all the while also betrays his expectations derived from the myth. This story is a novelette entitled "Medusa Was a Lady!" (1951), a comic science-fantasy adventure based on the ancient Greek myth of Perseus, slayer of the Gorgon Medusa.[15] Its author is William Tenn, well-known writer of satirical SF (Tenn is the pseudonym of Philip Klass, who is now an associate professor of English at Penn State University).

The complex and ironic idea that Tenn is trying to put across in this story requires lengthy exposition. The very nature of the imaginary world the author projects has to be re-evaluated constantly, only to have the tale ultimately circle back on itself and the "end" only be the same as the "beginning" from another perspective. Tenn is explicitly *not serious* and, though very funny, has no deep lesson to impart to his readers. But, still, it is a paradox game which requires intelligent reading and concentration, a worthy predecessor to the kinds of games with myths produced by John Barth (*Lost in the Funhouse, Chimera*) and John Gardner (*Grendel*).

Percy S. Yuss, a down-and-out young man of the Depression era who constantly berates himself for being a "sucker," comes upon a piece of unexpected luck—an apartment at a reasonable rate. In the apartment he finds a scrap of parchment with the legend of Perseus written on it, and from that moment on his fate is inseparable from the narrative events of the ancient myth—just as our own reading of the tale in terms of both form and meaning is inseparable from our acquaintance with this famous myth.

Old and New Myths in Science Fiction

First, Percy takes a bath and suddenly finds himself, tub and all, in a weird alternate universe that seems to be that of the ancient myth but often provides disturbing differences from the original. The ancient version says that King Acrisius was told by an oracle that his daughter Danae would give birth to a son who would kill him. To prevent this happening, the princess was locked in a bronze chamber, but Zeus the king of the gods came to her in a golden shower anyway. Mother and newborn babe were then sent away on the waves in a chest (Tenn's bathtub?) until they reached the island of Seriphus where a man named Dictys cared for them. This man's brother, Polydectes, however, fell in love with Danae and ultimately caused her son Perseus to go on a quest—seemingly impossible—for the Gorgon Medusa's head. Ultimately, of course, the young hero does succeed, even acquires a heroine named Andromeda by slaying a monster, and unfortunately also fulfills Acrisius' doom-laden oracle.[16]

Tenn's comical fantasia rings many different kinds of changes on the details of the original myth. Percy's Danae, for instance, is not his mother, but Mrs. Danner, the drunken old landlady who rented him the apartment and got him into this mess in the first place. There are Olympians—notably Hermes, the hero's patron—yet here they are not gods, but a cruel superscientific race from still another space-time universe; having run out of room on their own world, they need to conquer this alternate earth. Men are championed by the Gorgons, the Olympians' mortal enemies, who are imagined to be a species of intelligent reptile. Eons ago the Gorgons realized they were doomed to racial extinction, so they fostered a primate race which ultimately evolved into humanity in order to carry on the work of civilization.

Another world-perspective is offered when Percy finally meets Professor Gray, a comically displaced version of the Graiae, the three hags in the original tale who possessed the secret knowledge required by the hero to perform his task successfully. Gray not only half-explains the existence of this alternate universe and its partial relationship to the Perseus myth, but claims that he was the one who created it: it is psychic in origin, that is, a state of the professor's own imagination, resulting from an experiment with mental control of time which he conducted as head of his classics department. Gray is a comic version of the Frankensteinian world-creator, and Tenn directs a gentle satire against the old classicist whose idea of a "scientific cosmology" is utterly antiquated. Though the ancient Graiae were revered and feared as the repositories of special powerful wisdom, Gray is caricatured for being so out-of-date as to "create" a universe out of a speculation 2500 years old.

This radically different *cosmos* ("universe"), as Gray asserts, is based on the theories of the Greek pre-Socratic philosopher Anaximander (6th century B.C.) who posited an "Indefinite-Infinite" to conceptualize that original state of the universe out of which all actual and possible *cosmoi* developed. (Anaximander's *to apeiron* should not be confused with the mathematical concept of infinity. Debate among scholars of pre-Socratic philosophy still continues as to whether the term refers to the qualitative "indefiniteness" of the original primal substance out of which the *cosmos* arose, or whether it means "spatially indefinite.")[17]

Gray further insists that in this alternative space-time, "anything could happen," and only time would tell whether or not our myth of Perseus will recur or not. By reciting the legend of Perseus, Gray ended up here, just like Percy and just like Ann Drummond, another girl from the normal world, who plays Andromeda, heroine to Percy's Perseus.

Obviously, we share Percy's viewpoint and problem throughout this science-fiction narrative—which group do we side with in *this* "war of the worlds"? Is this the famous myth, in which case Percy must behead the Gorgon? Or is it different, in which case he must not be seduced into aiding the Olympians' cause?

It does not help that everyone in the story knows about the Perseus myth already, and narrative events are inseparable from all the characters' previous awareness of how things are supposed to turn out. For example, as soon as Percy reaches King Polydectes' island he is captured and at first mistaken for a sea-serpent; then he is arrested for "impersonating a hero" inasmuch as everyone knows a Perseus is on his way—but this loser can't be him! Even a talking sea-serpent knows the myth before it ever takes place.

One odd event intimates that still another loop is developing in the story. Just the same day another impersonator had shown up and Polydectes' men had captured him, ripped out his tongue when he tried to prove his identity, then had him boiled alive—but the story will return to this anomalous event later on.

Let us return to Percy's tale and take up events after his meeting with Gray, when against his better judgment he decides to heed the call of the original myth and side with the Olympians. Hermes fits our hero up with the proper superscientific hardware, and, drugged by the Olympian's *nectar* (really a hypnotic mickey finn), Percy does behead the Medusa, the last of her race, only to have her severed head address him in turn, telling him what a mistake he has made in slaying the "alma mater" of mankind. Momentarily the severed Medusa head accounts for the working out of the Perseus myth as a conspiracy of the Olympians, who "happened upon a superstitious myth-prophecy and decided to develop it into a fact." Thus, supposing Hermes had played him for a sucker, Percy does change his mind—and the myth; he beheads Hermes, steals the Medusa head, uses it against the Olympian invaders, and seals that universe off from theirs. Surely, the SF yarn is complete, the circuit of narrative events closed.

It isn't—at least not in the way we were expecting. The Gorgon gave Percy one last instruction: to recite the legend from the parchment once again. Supposedly, Percy will return to his starting point both in the myth and in the alternate universe and this time get it right—save Medusa, kill Hermes. Yes and No. By reciting the legend, he does end up in the *same* alternative universe again; and he does start the tale at the beginning. But he is not in the bathtub; he's on Polydectes' island, looking out at the sea where there is a young man floating in a tub.

Poor Percy never does realize that he's been played for a sucker again: he's the same man he saw earlier who was being boiled alive by Polydectes for impersonating a hero, who was without a tongue in that earlier scene and so unable to warn that version of Percy of his impending fate when the story would loop for the last time! Now the circuitry is complete, and the nasty end that awaits Percy is a grim joke on our expectations which were provoked by the presence of the ancient Greek hero myth, only to be betrayed.

James Blish has referred to fables like this as the "intensively recomplicated story," and has singled out Robert Heinlein's "All you Zombies" (*F&SF*, March 1959) as the most representative and perfectly executed example of the type.[18] The story is also important because it displays still another, even subtler use of traditional mythology than met with in the previous three writers (Bond, Harness, Tenn).

This sophisticated literary game elaborates the time-travel paradox tale about as far as it can be taken: through manipulations by a later version of himself from the future, a man becomes both his own mother and father; there is a trans-sexual operation along the way, too, so that he can become his own lover. Thus the man from the future, Pop, is both the beginning and end of himself—or rather, *neither*; there is only his own cyclical solipsism. His life story is like tracing your finger along a Möbius strip; trace it as you will, you always come back to your starting point. And it is all accomplished bewilderingly fast, in under 5000 words, with true economy and rigor.

Though the perfection of this circuity is withheld from the reader explicitly until the end of the story, implicit clues to it are strewn everywhere: like the song "I'm My Own Granpaw!" blaring on the jukebox in Pop's Place, and Pop's ring. The latter contains the central mythical symbol of cyclicality and temporal eternity without beginning or end, the ouroboros, which is represented as a serpent devouring his own tail. Whereas Tenn was about as explicit with a myth as one could be, Heinlein's allusion to myth here is obscure and indirect; the myth, i.e., image, acts as an implicit, largely unnoticed (at least by the conscious mind) reinforcement of the explicit content of the tale. Such images are a mythic dimension in SF which will often receive comment from here on, and they are especially important since at the least they so often turn up in SF fables which might otherwise seem to describe very un-supernatural worlds.

The critic and literary theorist Fredric Jameson has described another kind of manipulative game played by modern SF writers. By "generic discontinuity," he means that a reader involves himself with an imaginary narrative world only to have his expectations betrayed and the "world" turn out to be of an entirely different nature, another "genre" of SF.[19]

Robert Heinlein has mastered this technique of switching genres on his reader more than any other SF writer of the "classic" period. His novels are typically built out of two structures: an action/adventure tale which entices the reader into the narrative, then a moral/didactic section, composed in the form of a lecture or conversational essay, which so often reverses the norms and expectations established in the first part.

Old and New Myths in Science Fiction

In *Glory Road* (N.Y.: Avon, 1963)[20] Heinlein plays up every conventional attraction and adventure of the hero myth, only for the last third of the novel to alter the hero's understanding of his experience completely. Heinlein does not reproduce a specific myth as Tenn did with Perseus: the otherworldly adventures of Heinlein's hero are really more like the archetypal symbolic experiences described in Joseph Campbell's theory of the heroic monomyth in *The Hero With A Thousand Faces*.[21] These are universal in scope and include mating with a goddess, trials and tests, slaying monsters, and acquiring a magical talisman on a quest. With some justification, the SF community viewed *Glory Road* as a parody of sword-and-sorcery, for Oscar admits openly to modelling himself after s&s heroes like Conan (more will be said in chapter 4 about this genre, which uses the same common store of hero symbols, images and archetypes).

Young Oscar, age 21, is a bored Vietnam service vet who heeds what Campbell calls the heroic "call to adventure" and crosses a magical threshold into a wonderful alien world. He follows an incredibly beautiful woman named Star (who is often compared to Helen of Troy) and her clever old male companion, Rufo, into a weird parallel universe. From then on everything is pure fairy tale: the hero, now renamed "Scar," thinks of the place as "Valhalla," the afterlife for warrior-heroes in Scandinavian myth; Star always seductively calls Scar "my hero": and even the Road itself is the Yellow Brick one from Oz. Oscar never quite understands why *he* was chosen to fulfill the heroic quest, but there are just too many adventures for him or the reader to question this much. The trio slay a Golem ogre named Igli, have encounters with fire-belching dragons and the "Horned Ghosts," who are bipedal Minotaurs; and ultimately Oscar wins a fencing match to complete the quest for the enigmatic Egg of the Phoenix, located in the Mile-High Tower, which is also the Labyrinth of classical mythology and a Funhouse. None of it is quite serious and the tongue-in-cheek tone of a tall tale is maintained throughout the adventure. It's all just too good to be true, as when Oscar picks up a magical/superscientific bow-and-arrow and scores a perfect hit the very first time.

The reader, like Oscar, also gets sucked into the tale by all the free and easy sex everywhere, with Star and others. There is even an orgy-visit to a culture where promiscuity and mate-lending are the norm. The sexual episodes, like the racy action, are a kind of fantasy or daydream that gets exploded by the didactic revelations that occur in the last third of the novel.

Though Oscar has undergone his heroic trial and initiation successfully for his fairy princess, his sexual naivete is rudely shattered when he finally learns the whole hero business was a ruse. Every bit of the road adventure was artificial, somehow contrived for an effect on Oscar. He is as much a product as the Egg, which turns out to be a valuable artificial memory-bank. Queen Star is actually eons old and the grandmother of "old" Rufo. There are also a number of cynical revelations about civilization on planet Earth, including the solemn assertion that our world is the only place in the known universe where prostitution exists. So Oscar was important only on the Glory Road; otherwise, he has no role in Star's world except that of a fancy gigolo—heroes really weren't needed there any more than they are here. In the final pages of the novel, Oscar ends up in exile back on earth. His story is a satire on the hero myth and a joke on the reader (males especially) for being gullible enough to fall for the heroic fantasy in the first place.

However, the conclusion of the story is subtle and ambiguous, for Oscar is still dreaming of another road adventure and he eagerly waits for Rufo to come for him. Heinlein doesn't expect us to give up our hero fantasies that easily, even if they do amount only to sword-and-sorcery daydreams. Heinlein is well aware that the hero myth is still with us, that it is as much a *modern* myth as an ancient one.

The ironic treatment of the hero in *Glory Road* should be contrasted with another novel where mythical heroism is taken seriously in the context of a romance of the future. Harry Harrison's *Captive Universe* (N.Y.: Berkeley Medallion, 1969) also uses the technique of "generic discontinuity" described by Frederic Jameson. Though Harrison's attitude toward the hero is the more conventional one met in SF and is far from Heinlein's subtle and complex stance, this novel does achieve intellectual sophistication through the interplay of several common SF genres: the "spaceship as universe," dystopian (or "anti-utopian") sociopolitics, and the hero myth.

The story *apparently* begins in an Aztec universe with the fathering of a mysterious baby. The boy, Chimal, is the illegitimate child of a tabooed union of two Aztecs from two different villages; the young man's father is no longer alive; he was killed by Coatlicue, the hideous scorpion goddess, on the night of his son's conception.[22] The boy is a dangerous nonconformist and sacrilegious troublemaker in the eyes of the status-mongering priests in his own village, and so—as in a typical hero-tale—runs away to escape being executed for his antiauthoritarian behavior and beliefs.

At this point both the world of the Aztecs and their hideously inhumane gods—as well as Chimal's hero tale—turn into "another reality." The Aztecs' world turns out to be an artificial, enclosed one, and this is really an elaborately conceived and executed colony ship which is heading for a distant star and its planet. The villagers have been kept deliberately in the dark for many generations and have no knowlege that things are not what they seem. Only Chimal, since he combines genes from two villages and two types of mankind, is creative enough to figure out what has happened. Of course, the hero disrupts the entire working of this ship and its mindlessly obedient crew. The latter are really the "priesthood" of this ship and are in every way just as uncreative and dogmatic as the priesthood of the Aztec village.

"Captive Universe" means both the first-order enclosed world of the pseudo-Aztecs, but also the second-order enclosed world of the ship's crew, who are incapable of meeting the strange new requirements that are imposed on them by their journey. They can only react as always to the orders they were given by the cruel dictator who originated this colonial venture. At the end, only Chimal has the creative/heroic intelligence to realize that the ship is completely off its destined course, and that the flight has failed unless the colonist-Aztecs are set free and the entire experiment brought to its completion. Chimal is savior-hero of the ship-universe as well as of the captive Aztecs.

However, for all the apparent discontinuity in Harrison's shift from false Aztec universe to the spaceship universe, there are several underlying correspondances which suggest barely disguised analogies with myth: Chimal becomes known as the "First Arriver," the chief of the decadent ship-priests is the "Master Observer," and the ship itself bears the name Eros. The name of the evil Earth tyrant who started the experiment, the "Grand Designer," implies a connection between the Frankensteinian scientist-creator and dystopian politics. The demon-ridden world of the Aztecs is only a foreshadowing of the demonic society that created the spaceship. That science and technology may be put to tyrannous social uses by a political or bureaucratic elite is a common enough fear in our time.

A Maze of Death (N.Y.: Doubleday, 1970), written by Philip K. Dick, is another novel that raises fears of political conspiracy and psychological paranoia in the framework of a series of "false realities" and "artificial universes." Here, then, generic discontinuities multiply, for Dick carries the reader through a bewildering gamut of alternate realities that simultaneously represent a sequence of science-fiction genres. Thus the characters are precipitated from one nightmarish closed universe into another, only to leave the reader continually asking what kind of reality (and, therefore, what kind of science fiction) Dick is writing about. Like Harness's "New Reality," *Maze of Death* withholds full mythical significance until the apocalyptic conclusion.

Fourteen characters, all searching for a "new world" to relieve the boredom of their previous lives, find themselves on Delmak-O, a secluded colony world. The maze-like plot then involves the reader simultaneously in two different kinds of problems. The story is first of all an absorbing murder mystery in the "Ten Little Indians" style. Dick usually involves many characters in his plots, but in *Maze* he additionally has the entire narrative proceed as a series of "points of view" so that the reader always sees the action from the psychological perspective of one of the characters: anyone who gets isolated from the group is murdered. Then it also turns out that the colonists are isolated and confined on Delmak-O, a closed world where they feel they are the object of some sort of "plot" whose ultimate significance continues to elude them. One response to the "unknown" is to appeal to the supernatural, for the universe of Delmak-O does seem to possess a functional theology. The colonists pass through other explanations of their existence on the planet: they are prisoners of the Terran military authorities for the purpose of some unknown experiment (in which case the story is dystopian science fiction); or the experiment is some unannounced psychological one—and the possibilities of criminal insanity and mental "solipsism" are often raised, too, suggesting that the novel is speculative fiction dealing

Old and New Myths in Science Fiction

with the alternate realities of aberrational mental states. The question remains—what sort of alternate reality is this and what genre of science fiction is this? Dick's plot remains as much a plot against his reader as against his characters. Every "clue," either to the murder mystery or the reality mystery, turns out to be a false lead.

Then in chapter 13 the story shifts ground completely when it is assumed that none of the action has been taking place on Delmak-O after all, but on Earth, though the plot against the colonists remains a mystery still. Yet this too is another of the author's tricks, and the end of chapter 14 is more radical. There is literally an Apocalypse: the earth cracks open, the landscape melts away, and the last of the colonists are swallowed up. There is no one left to murder nor any world left to explain. Only in chapter 15 does the reader become aware that all that has preceded has been a communal dream, taking place in the fourteen characters' heads through the agency of a hypothetical science-fiction device, the "polyencephalic cylinder." In retrospect, the entire story has to be redefined as speculative fiction concerned with "inner space" where the sequence of dream murders is sure evidence of a progressive psychological implosion toward solipsism, the most thoroughly isolated mental universe.

Fredric Jameson has spoken quite rightly of Dick's thematic obsession with manipulation as a social phenomenon which can be correlated with the author's manipulation of the reader through his baffling narrative,[23] but in *A Maze of Death* Dick has formulated a more radical, cognitive-psychological variety of manipulation, *self-manipulation* of one's own mind through the dream (or the dream as nightmare) as an escape from a more horrible waking state. Consequently, this transformation of the narrative which culminates in our awareness that the story has been a dream all along is not the final word on its genre, either. The fourteen "colonists" of the dream are actually the crew of a ruined spaceship which is doomed to circle a star forever and the cylinder dreams are used as the one escape from the claustrophobic life on "the space ship as universe."

Finally, it seems as if every literary "apocalypse" (in David Ketterer's sense of the transformation of the meaning of a fictional reality taking place in a reader's head)[24] is obscured in the final pages of the novel (chapter 16). As early as their first appearance in chapter 2, it was clear that Seth and Mary Morley were differing character-types, the husband disposed to religious convictions about the universe, the wife to naive realism. This difference between the pair prefigures the bewildering conclusion of the novel when—incredibly—one of the supernatural beings derived from the totally artificial theology of the dream universe appears to Seth and then removes him from the ship. At least from all the empirical evidence that the reader has (and it comes from Mary) Seth has left the ship by completely inexplicable means. Mary herself rejoins the rest of the crew in a "new" dream which ironically begins again with Delmak-O, indicating that the polyencephalic cylinder will no longer be able to aid the crew against destructive boredom and eventual group solipsism; even the artificial dream worlds are now "closed" forever.

One approach to solving the meaning of Seth's ambiguous fate (rescue by the god or death in outer space) is available from the structuralist critic Tzvetan Todorov with his definition of the "fantastic" as an equilibrium between two ways of accounting for a seemingly irrational event: either there is a perfectly natural, empirical, or "scientific" explanation, but our present knowledge is incapable of providing it, or the supernatural exists and is the answer to the problematical phenomenon.[25] Dick's ending remains in the fantastic as such (the ambiguity remains unresolved). Still another approach —and this would relate the significance of the closed universe to the epistemological character of the science-fiction narrative itself—can be based on that fictional device which Morse Peckham in a public lecture called a "hermeneutic vacuum," meaning that an author deliberately sets up an irresolvable ambiguity in his narrative as a means of engaging the reader's active participation. In this individual case we are assured only that the closed universe of Dick's science fiction narrative remains obscurely "open" to more than one interpretation, thereby suggesting a correspondence between the form and content of the novel.

It is true that this complex, experimental narrative is far from any specific, explicit mythology, but the otherworldly atmosphere is there, especially in the mythical categories of "deity" and "the supernatural." Indeed, it is clear from this story—as well as from those by Silverberg, Aldiss, and Harrison described earlier—that Anglo-American SF over the decades has progressively involved itself with more complex and experimental "games" with myths, with ever more exotic mythologies beyond the traditional Graeco-Roman, Hebrew, or Norse, and with more thorough understanding of myth theory and researches. These four writers in particular—Dick, Silverberg, Aldiss, and Harrison—have been identified with a special movement, called "New Wave," within the SF writers' community during the last fifteen years or so.

"New Wave" began with Michael Moorcock at *New Worlds* magazine in 1964. As Scholes and Rabkin have observed, this movement in SF involves a twofold emphasis: (1) a new social consciousness, explicitly antiestablishment and iconoclastic in its thinking; and (2) a self-conscious attempt to make SF meet the same high standards of writing as other literature and to merge with the literary "mainstream."[26] Basically, New Wave SF wants to be more challenging and complex as literature for its reader than earlier, traditional SF (though this is a matter of degree rather than kind, as some of the "intensively recomplicated" stories indicate); and it has become ever more difficult to distinguish SF proper from contemporary mainstream literature since there has been so thorough a cross-pollination of literary conventions between them over the last fifteen years.

However, even beyond these political and literary issues, myth has been a central obsession of New Wave. Two exemplary writers in the movement in particular show that New Wave has as much to say about new and old myths in today's world as either traditional SF or the literary mainstream. The first story is a novella by the British founder of the movement which shockingly makes Jesus Christ into a sex pervert; the second is a short story by the ever-iconoclastic American writer and New Journalist, Harlan Ellison. Both involve their protagonists with insanity and hallucinations; in both, hopelessly incompetent and impotent modern social types merge identities with mythic prototypes; both tales are equally imbued with irony and ambiguity which reveal a complex attitude toward the myth.

Michael Moorcock's irreverent masterpiece, *Behold the Man* (1968), takes up the life and mission of Jesus Christ considered as a myth.[27] The hero, Karl Glogauer, is a psychiatrist manqué whose sexual biography from early childhood on forms the background to his story, and his checkered career is a textbook case-history in neurosis: it combines masturbatory fantasies, homosexual interludes, heterosexual love-hate relationships, a mother fixation, and an obsession with crosses; added to these are alcoholism, migraine headaches, and epileptic seizures until Christian mysticism and Jungian psychology complete the picture of this garbled personality. Glogauer is, on the one hand, an absolute masochist, and on the other, a would-be Messiah, who must suffer frustration in a world in which God is dead (as his mistress, a psychiatric social worker named Monica, keeps telling him). Whereas modern man to Glogauer's mind has destroyed "the myths that make the world go round," Glogauer wants the myths to be true; he needs God.

When Monica leaves him for another woman, masochist Glogauer's ego endures its last rebuff from the modern world, and he becomes a willing participant in a time-machine experiment conducted by one of his homosexual acquaintances, Sir James Headington. The machine itself, shaped like a womb and insulated with fluid to reduce the shock of travel, constitutes a second birth for the hero. He reaches the shores of the Dead Sea in A.D. 28 in time to join John the Baptist and his group of Essenes.

From this point on, all the themes coalesce perfectly as Glogauer, calling himself Emmanuel (Hebrew for "God is with us"—an ironic choice in view of Glogauer's fate), takes up a quest to locate the Christ who has provided the only meaning for his neurotic life. It is during one of his seizures that he wanders away from the Essenes through the desert and finally makes his way to Nazareth, only to discover things are not quite what he expected. He encounters Jesus as a congenital imbecile and Mary as a lusty, overweight wench who tries to seduce him. His god-seeking seems to have reached a dismal conclusion.

However, Glogauer despairs of faith only momentarily—after all, more than anything in the world he "wanted the New Testament to be true"—then he executes the mission of Christ himself, pretending he is Jesus the son of Mary and Joseph, preaching to the poor, healing the sick, performing the other miracles, and finally dying on the cross. This is a most successful, if perverted, *imitatio dei*.[28]

> But it was not his own life he would be leading now. He was bringing a myth to life, a generation before that myth would be born. He was completing a certain kind of psychic circuit.

The cycle is indeed perfect. In terms of the science-fiction theme of a time-loop paradox, Glogauer merely fulfills what will become history when he plays out the role of Jesus. It is psychiatrically complete, too, because he is by the time-loop the source of his own Christian neurosis which he resolves when he dies on the cross and satisfies his masochism.

In this perfect circle there is a potentially compelling statement about our myths, that even when they are inadequate models for reality, by wish-fulfillment we make them work anyway; or as Glogauer says, "Jung knew that the myth can also create the reality." Indeed, the irony of the novel may be summed up in the argument between Monica and Glogauer: "The *idea* preceded the *actuality* of Christ" (Glogauer); "The actuality of *Jesus* preceded the idea of *Christ*" (Monica). Given Moorcock's use of the time-paradox, both statements are accurate.

But there are still further sources of cyclicality. I have described Glogauer's story as if Moorcock told it in continuous narrative, and this is not the case. The narration begins with the protagonist inside the womblike time-machine, awaiting rebirth in another time, and from there the narration unfolds by turn in two directions: first, Glogauer's life-development since childhood, with particular emphasis on the sources of his masochistic sexuality; second, there is Glogauer's development as Christ in the past, culminating in crucifixion. There are no contexts for either narrative frame of reference, and no transitions from one to the other, Passages range variably from three or four-page descriptions, whose meaning is clear, to one or two-sentence comments, done in "stream-of-consciousness" style, which switch back and forth from one frame to the other. Thus in the final chapter, Glogauer keeps hearing Monica's aggressively critical words, browbeating him even though she is not even present, and other "voices" from the past; also he relives childhood feelings of impotence and again has a fleeting remembrance of the cross from his childhood.

By "intercutting" passages from the New Testament gospels and the Book of Job, plus citations from Jung and William Blake, Moorcock further confuses the relationships between the two narrative frames of reference and thus produces an effect of "narrative simultaneity." By this expression, I mean that neither of the two frames of reference is an absolute fixed point from which we can judge the veracity of the other; both are relative to one another. Sharon Spencer in *Space, Time, and Structure in the Modern Novel*[29] has suggested that such narrative techniques are the literary correlative of Einstein's theory of relativity in physics. William S. Burroughs's *Naked Lunch* was a classic experiment with narrative simultaneity, but without the SF genre of time-travel.

Ultimately, in fact, we cannot decide if the first story is only Glogauer's distorted *memory* of his own life, triggered by his traumatic experience in the time-machine. On the other hand, it is equally possible that the entire Christ episode may only be a delirious fantasy, none of it real because the time-experiment failed and killed the protagonist. This may only be an *apparent* time-travel story. The final paragraph of the novel raises this disturbing possibility. Supposedly, Glogauer has gasped out his last breath while Roman soldiers watched from the foot of the cross, but these are the final sentences of the book:

> Later, after his body was stolen by the servants of some doctors who believed it might be found to have special properties, there were rumors that he had not died. But the corpse was already rotting in the doctors' dissecting rooms, and would soon be destroyed.

Has Glogauer ever left the experimental station? Can "doctors' dissecting rooms" be anything but modern? Was his career as Christ all a sexual/religious fantasy which merely fulfills—and terminates— Glogauer's lifelong masochistic fantasies? Simultaneity, cyclicality, self-conscious manipulation of an SF genre (time-travel), and the inability to distinguish between abnormal mental states and normal reality—these characteristics certainly distinguish this brilliant novel as a classic example of "New Wave" technique. Add this careful attention to twentieth-century forms of narrative technique to a studied knowledge of psychiatric analysis and the Jungian theory of myth, and we have in this work one of the most intellectually ambitious SF narratives of the previous decade, and one that deserved the recognition it received from the Science Fiction Writers of America, which granted it the Nebula Award.

Many similar New Wave techniques are visible in Harlan Ellison's "The Place With No Name."[30] This short story creates a fantastic

Old and New Myths in Science Fiction

atmosphere in which we share with the fictional characters an uncertainty about what is or is not reality. In this science-fiction horror story hell is indistinguishable from heaven, and the ultimate pain of eternal suffering—the eternal pain of Prometheus being devoured by the bird of Zeus—is indistinguishable from the highest good of perfect Justice.

The tale which acts as Ellison's starting point is that of Norman Mogart, a pimp and cocaine addict who also becomes a murderer. Eluding the police, Mogart has a fantastic escapade, encountering a mysterious figure disguised as an old man who calls himself "Simon or Peter." We are never sure in this episode whether Mogart is in his right mind or not, whether the being he meets is natural or supernatural, human or alien, or whether he exists at all. Is Mogart going to hell to be punished for his crimes, or to heaven, opened by the legendary gatekeeper, Peter?

Mogart awakes in another world, with another identity, as Harry Timmons, Jr. Yet the more important change in identity belongs to the *narrative itself* rather than to any character: this second tale relates Timmons's painful, delirious search in the jungles of South America for the answer to an ancient Indian legend (precise locale uncertain, "fantastic," since its ultimate destination is specified only as "the place with no name"). Timmons/Mogart ultimately discovers the fantastic alien being who lies behind the truth of the Prometheus legend (and several other mythologies, Hindu and South American alike; as already noted, it is characteristic of New Wave SF to be concerned with non-Western mythologies and their points of view).

Finally the third shift in the tale comes when Timmons/Mogart replaces "Prometheus" in his chains, to suffer unlimited eternal torment, rather than the mercly limited, human torment he would have endured if caught by the police for murder. Yet he is happy with his lot, and the reader is left finally uncertain whether this adventure is anything more than a "masochism trip" or whether the reader can distinguish retribution, justice, charity, and benevolence.

Indeed, the story concludes in self-effacing ambivalence: the alien Prometheus had a mate who shared with him a perfect mutual love and a total love toward mankind. But their own race punished the homosexual pair with divine torment. Mogart, of course, takes the place of Prometheus; another human being is said to take the place of his partner. The latter is Christ, another benefactor of mankind who suffered divine torment (Ellison is again enigmatic and says only "when April came round again he would be given his crown of thorns").[31] Neither Prometheus nor Christ is rewarded for his benefaction. In this vision we see only pain and release from pain (and even this release comes at the cost of a cosmic scapegoat).

The story appeared in Ellison's extremely famous and popular collection *The Beast That Shouted Love at the Heart of the World* (1969), which also included "A Boy and His Dog," equally famous in its film version. In this collection and his *Deathbird Stories: A Pantheon of Modern Gods* (1975), Ellison envisions frightful new deities, projections of contemporary man's fears about his own terrifying new world of the present or near future and the torments he may suffer. Ellison is an urban visionary who sees a mythic, demonic dimension to contemporary man's life styles and beliefs which verges on supernatural horror. It is not even quite fair to call this dimension cosmic pessimism, because there is a grim humor in Ellison's metaphysics of pain which suggests that his work is a fictional correlative of the cartooning of Gahan Wilson, whose demonic caricatures are well known.

Though this chapter has ranged broadly over the modern history of science fiction, it has perhaps inadvertently given it a negative complexion. Mythology has been used for satire and irony, for cautionary speculation on world destruction and psychological aberration. New Wave writers in particular have a propensity for dystopian attitudes toward the future.[32] Yet most of us who were readers of SF from youth on associate it with more positive visions, and some justice should be done to the relationship between scientific optimism and mythology.

In 1968, right in the middle of the New Wave revolution, the prolific writer Poul Anderson, whose name is often associated with "conservative" political views, wrote a short story for juveniles, "The Faun." It appeared in the magazine of the Boy Scouts of America, *Boy's Life* (September 1968). It is a fable of the Promethean creative powers of modern science that depicts them as forces for good. We are introduced to a twelve-year-old boy who is the only humanoid in an idealized natural setting where he has been biologically adapted to fit the landscape perfectly. For all intents and purposes, the boy is a faun, a sylvan creature of ancient Roman mythology. Once, we are informed, he was a normal human being, but only at the climax of the tale do we discover the basis for this mythical, godlike act of physical and emotional re-creation: it was accomplished by the boy's own father, himself a famous and powerful scientist. To be sure, the tale is "juvenile" because the act of faith in science and in one's parent is too easy. We know that the biological altering of a human being to live *perfectly* in tune with any natural environment—let alone one alien to his species—is a difficult and dubious proposition: we could never be so confident of it as Anderson and his potential young readers. What is revealing is the broad educative and didactic purpose of the magazine in which Anderson published this story; *Boy's Life* is an excellent forum in which to tell a story while making a case for the authority of science; the theme is "science as god (creator) and parent."

American SF has always emphasized a spectrum of educative functions; the genre as a whole is loaded with didacticism: lectures, lessons, explanations, philosophical dialogue and critique, on almost any topic, not just science. Writers like Poul Anderson and Robert Heinlein write for youths as well as adults, and this very fact—that they are not afraid to preach their philosophies to the young in the form of engrossing or shocking stories—is why they have been a major shaper of youthful minds in our era. They make didacticism interesting and captivating.

This kind of tale has its roots in the magazine SF of the thirties, both in its literary conventions and underlying ideology. The use of a title based on Greek mythology as a metaphor for a speculative idea is still another special effect. Though the technique is as old as Mary Shelley's Promethean subtitle, Stanley Weinbaum's application of it became especially influential for all subsequent magazine writers.

Weinbaum's "A Martian Odyssey" (*Wonder Stories*, July 1934), gave American SF its first well-conceived example of alien intelligence, the bird-like character, Tweel. Written in the middle of the period that Jack Williamson has called "The Years of Wonder"—when American SF was being subjected to one literary revolution after another—this tale has been singled out as revolutionary by Isaac Asimov and others.[33] The story of First Contact on Mars is related in first-person narration by a realistic and credible narrator—an American space explorer. In his eyes, Tweel is a being whose precise physical and intellectual makeup remains largely unknown, yet the fact of his intelligence is indisputable (e.g., he carries a sophisticated weapon; he can communicate with the earthman more effectively than the earthman can with him). The speculation is solidly presented. However, though this short story deserves its place in SF's "Hall of Fame," it has its failings: the human characters are still anachronistic national stereotypes of the '30s—German, French, American; and there is a naïveté and adolescent quality in the attitudes toward human nature. Science fiction still had some decades of social and psychological maturation to experience.

Much the same is true of Weinbaum's second tale of alien intelligence, "The Lotus Eaters" (*Astounding Stories*, April 1935). The speculation is intelligently presented: an intellectually superior race of vegetables on Venus possesses spores that have a narcotic effect on consciousness, and they therefore are vulnerable to a fierce Venusian carnivore. These events are all well realized, with a touch of comedy too. Again, the shortcoming of the story lies in the relationship between the two human explorers, an American man and an English woman who are on their honeymoon—thus Weinbaum projects the particular marital and sexual mores of the thirties middle class onto humanity's interplanetary future.

Though we may remain critical of aspects of this fiction, as of other SF of the thirties and early forties, there is one further reason why Weinbaum's tales are so significant for the later history of SF. Homer's *Odyssey* provides the metaphorical titles of these two tales, "A Martian Odyssey" and "The Lotus Eaters," as well as of a third, "Proteus Island" (*Astounding Stories*, 1936, posthumous publication), which tells of an island where chromosome experiments have resulted in a riotous variety of mutated life-forms. The Odyssean metaphors imply that modern man's scientific adventures—other worlds, alternative life-forms and alien intelligence in alien environments—are the spiritual kindred of Odysseus' exotic adventures in the unknown.

Thus, in "A Martian Odyssey," the human hero, Jarvis, has suffered the wreck of his scout ship and must wander back as best he can to home base (so far this is an analogy with the hero's homeward journey in the ancient *Odyssey*). On the journey the hero must confront, and deal with, a series of unpredictable and unexpected lifeforms that inhabit the planet Mars, some harmless, others dangerous; some intelligent, others not. He even has one hazardous encounter with a Siren-like "dream-beast" that traps its victims by adopting the form of their private fantasies. Finally, beyond these thematic considerations, Jarvis is an Odyssean hero because he has to survive through the use of his wits and his ability to adapt to the strangest and most hostile of environments. And the plant Mars itself is a displacement in quasi-scientific terms of the fairy-tale lands visited by the ancient Odysseus.

In all three stories the mythological orientation should in no sense be considered a limitation, for it adds another intellectual dimension especially since each story is composed in the form of a mystery tale in which the goal is to discover the scientific principles that lie behind the outrageously unrealistic situations in which the heroes find themselves. The mythological titles—and the more or less limited mythological contents—foreshadow the answers to Weinbaum's scientific riddles; hence, the presence of mythological prefigurations promotes an active reading of the story.

Before Weinbaum, aliens were nothing more than Bug-Eyed Monsters, uniformly and predictably loathsome and hostile to the human race. Weinbaum made us aware of the positive creative potential in First Contact, and his long-term influence is evident in the recent popular film, *Close Encounters of the Third Kind*, where UFOs represent mankind's mystical and religious quest for alien humanity as well as man's most exhilarating adventure with the unknown from outer space. Also completely Odyssean in spirit are the episodes of *Star Trek*, with its optimistic belief in man's adventurous future: "To boldly go where no man has gone before" is the keynote of each episode.

Weinbaum died of cancer at the age of 33, but the few short stories he wrote have influenced so many writers that his fables are Odyssean in much more than a metaphorical sense. Thus, his works provide us with another mythical archetype from ancient Greek myth for modern SF. Odyssean SF emphasizes the openness of the universe to mankind's speculative intelligence. As science and allied modes of cognition modify our understanding of the universe, man will have the opportunity for greater and greater adventures. Philosophers of science like Robert Oppenheimer and Thomas Kuhn[34] have informed us that science is inherently self-improving and self-correcting; of all means of learning about reality, science alone seems concerned to make its earlier models, formulas, and even data obsolete by providing new, better, more powerful ones. This view of science, at least, is espoused by writers of Odyssean SF. One recent critic, John Huntington,[35] has actually gone so far as to suggest that science fiction provides imaginative freedom in a modern world which has become more and more determined by the sheer quantity of human knowledge and scientific research. In his essay on science in the modern world, Robert Oppenheimer confirms this intuition that extreme specialization in the sciences—which has by any estimate produced real results—has led to intellectual claustrophobia for many:[36] they feel "determined" by the dimensions and precision of the given scientific tradition because it puts intense limits on the imagination of any individual who would like to be creative or innovative. Odyssean SF, however, keeps the imaginative vision of a creative, nondetermined future open: science is here viewed as conducive to imaginative freedom. In its exuberant, optimistic attitude this kind of SF often seems too good to be true and is suggestive of dream or wish-fulfillment, yet it more accurately amounts to a different world-view, a different vision of man's future altogether.

It is remarkable how extensive and pervasive mythology is across *all* of modern SF; from Mary Shelley to the most recent (especially "New Wave") writers. The myths themselves are of many kinds, derived from the ancient cultures, yet completely modern in their thrust. Nor is the use of mythology limited to a few writers or to one kind of SF: myths are equally prevalent in nineteenth-century Gothic novels and the Scientific Romance, in American magazine (or "pulp") SF from the seventies to the present, in difficult New Wave writing, and in light juvenile fiction. The Silverberg fable that began this chapter was an accurate gauge of the plenitude of myths in this literature.

The myths are also associated with a broad variety of stylistic and narrative techniques—latent images, metaphorical titles, games, generic discontinuities—so the SF and fantasy stories engage the reader at more than one level simultaneously. But underlying any clever, engaging, and playful use of myth there is a deeper, more serious connection to the ancient myths: images like those of Prometheus/Frankenstein and Odysseus call into question the whole of creation by delineating our species' and planet's future in terms threatening or beckoning: they suggest, in fact, cultural archetypes which shape our entire world-views. Without myth, then, one might well not be able to have science fiction at all, certainly not science fiction as we know it. What remains in the chapter immediately following is to pin down some of the formal reasons for the strong, almost inevitable, affinity between myth and SF.

2 "Estrangement" in Mythology and Science Fiction

The role of ancient and other myths in modern culture remains a subject of much controversy. Often it is argued that, whatever myths might do, they *must* involve a return to outmoded thinking or social action. This supposed retrograde evolution caused by myth is then judged objectionable from the viewpoint of intellectual or social progress. For example, David Bidney, an important anthropological critic, charges that "the positive value of myth is affirmed by those who are skeptical of the power of reason to comprehend reality, . . . Myth must be taken seriously as a cultural force but it must be taken seriously precisely in order that it may be gradually superseded in the interests of the advancement of truth and growth of human intelligence."[1] This view is usually known as "scientific positivism," though fewer and fewer intellectuals in Western society these days show as much confidence in the powers of reason and science as Bidney's optimistic statement suggests. Eastern European thinkers like Stanislaw Lem and Darko Suvin still adhere strongly to the cause of rationalism, but as "Marxists" they explicitly reject positivism.

Sometimes, however, it must be admitted that the *defenders of myth* in the intellectual community do fear the future and prefer the security of the past. This criticism would seem especially appropriate in the face of Mircea Eliade's advice to contemporary Western man to abandon "the terror of history" (really "the fear of change") and return to a more archaic stratum of belief in supratemporal "archetypes," which are quasi-Platonic, static models of conduct represented in ancient myths and religions. By its own standards Eliade's system is thoroughly retrogressive, and he finds the modern worldview deplorable because it has substituted the process of history (a relativistic one at that) for a transcendental Judeo-Christian God and thereby created very real anxieties for modern man who must live in a universe without fixed meanings or absolute patterns of existence.[2] Eliade would replace today's world of "future shock" with a timeless and mythic world of the future which would be oriented only to the past and imaginative constructs from the past:

> . . . it is not inadmissible to think of an epoch, and an epoch not too far distant, when humanity, to ensure its survival, will find itself reduced to desisting from any further "making" of history in the sense in which it began to make it from the creation of the first empires, will confine itself to repeating prescribed archetypal gestures, and will strive to forget, as meaningless and dangerous, any spontaneous gesture which might entail "historical" consequences. It would even be interesting to compare the anhistorical solution of future societies with the paradisal or eschatological myths of the golden age of the beginning or the end of the world.[3]

If this is what we mean by "taking myth seriously," then indeed we must think badly of myth. Critic Philip Rahv has rightly insisted that modern man cannot depart, at least not authentically, from what he knows to be the truth of his condition in the world, even if that truth is unpleasant:

> The craze for myth is the fear of history. . . . The fear of history is at bottom the fear of the hazards of freedom. In so far as man can be said to be capable of self-determination, history is the sole sphere in which he can conceivably attain it. . . . In our time the historical process is marked far more by loss and extremity than growth and mastery, and this fact is interpreted by the spokesmen of traditionalism as completely justifying their position. The mythic principle appeals to them because of its fixity and profoundly conservative implications. But the hope of stability it offers is illusory. To look for deliverance from history is altogether futile.[4]

Thus, beyond the matter of not returning to primitive life-styles or world-views, Rahv points to a simpler and more universal kind of impossibility—the impossibility of recovering a lost mythical consciousness (if there ever was such a thing). Modern man's sensibility has been far too altered, far too many centuries, for any critic to ask him to react to the ancient myths with the same consciousness as possessed by his ancient predecessor. This much has been admitted by one of the most eloquent and imaginative defenders of the value of myths, Joseph Campbell:

> No one of adult mind today would turn to the Book of Genesis to learn of the origins of the earth, the plants, the beasts, and man. There was no flood, no tower of Babel, no first couple in paradise, and between the first known appearance of men on earth and the first buildings of cities, not one generation (Adam to Cain) but a good two million [sic] must have come into this world and passed along. Today we turn to science for our imagery of the past and of the structure of the world, and what the spinning demons of the atom and the galaxies of the telescope's eye reveal is a wonder that makes the babel of the Bible seem a toyland dream of the dear childhood of our brain.[5]

What this leaves is a recognition by almost all critics of myths, defenders as well as opponents, of both the power of myth and its universal appeal—though both of these may be deplored by certain critics. Without question, there are always atavistic movements like Nazism or pseudoscientific cults like Dianetics and Sun Moon's Universalist Church that involve mythic beliefs and structures. But the essential point is that this is only *one*, limited side of mythology. There is a much more liberal and liberating side to mythology than either the defenders or critics we've met so far would be willing to admit. One doesn't have to choose absolutely between Eliade on the one side or Bidney and Rahv on the other.

Mythology really does not create any issue of modern Western man abandoning the complex theoretical and analytical knowledge of his world that has accrued in logarithmic progression since the intellectual revolution of the Renaissance. If we are to defend the value of ancient myths for the modern mind, we have to presume from the outset two poles—a modern analytical mind, conscious of the principle of individuation and aware of the positive effect of specialization on almost every facet of modern existence, and an ancient myth—meaning a text or story (not art for the practical purposes of my study, though mythical art is also an appropriate subject for such critical scrutiny as follows). In fact, no educational or "cognitive" result is possible without recognizing, and even exploiting, this polarity; in it resides the whole reason for a modern mind to confront ancient myths.

It is possible to describe two values of ancient myths for modern culture: their ability to refine and extend imaginative thought and their ability to help human thinking focus on still *unknown* aspects of reality. The first suggests that myths somehow develop our creative intellectual capacities; the second that this developed capacity can be employed in dealing with reality itself. I therefore wish to undertake a more positive interpretation of the educative function of myth, and I will do so by introducing the notion of "estrangement" as the philosophical underpinning to a defense of myth as an authentic form of human intellection which does not presuppose cultural archaism, retrogression, or anachronism.

"Estrangement" was first proposed by the Russian Formalist Viktor Shklovsky in 1917 as a concept in literary criticism and later elaborated by Bertolt Brecht in his famous essay, "A Brief Organum for Theatre," whose title was inspired by Francis Bacon's *Novum Organum* and whose format is "scientific."[6] Brecht asserts that "a representation which estranges is one which allows us to recognize its subject but at the same time makes it seem unfamiliar."[7] In keeping with the general scientific cast of the "Brief Organum," and alluding to his own *Life of Galileo*, Brecht chose an illustration from the history of science, comparing the estrangement-effect (*Verfremdungseffekt*) to the visual detachment with which Galileo observed a swinging chandelier: "He (Galileo) was amazed by the pendulum motion as if he had not expected it and could not understand its occurring, and this enabled him to come at the rule by which it was governed."[8]

The concept of "estrangement," however, is too powerful to be confined to the literary theorizing for which it was originally formulated. It seems, rather, to refer most generally to the mind's ability to adjust itself to a new set of experiential or intellectual coordinates; we are thus speaking here not of new "facts" acquired atomistically, but of being shocked into whole new *systems* of thinking or experiencing. For example, among genetic psychologists like Jean Piaget, a cognate of "estrangement" has been in use for some time. This parallel term, "decentration," refers to one's surmounting of the tendency to fix his attention on a limited, superficial aspect of a stimulus.[9] Piaget himself gives two instances derived from different spheres. The process of decentration can be seen, first of all, in a small child where the development of the notion "brother" shows what an effort is required of a child who has a brother to understand that his brother also has a brother, that this concept refers to a reciprocal relationship and not to an absolute property. Or, second, we can consider what a giant feat of decentration was required for astronomical science to shift from the geocentric to heliocentric perspective.[10] It is easy to see, I believe, that in both of these cases we are not talking about estrangement or decentration as leading to the acquiring of new facts so much as to the acquiring of whole new systems of understanding, and thereby whole new worlds of perception are opened up. One need not stop with either literature or science: Morse Peckham in *Man's Rage for Chaos* describes much the same effect in the area of our experience of the visual arts, and he speaks of the artist presenting his recipient with "perceptual discontinuities" that challenge him to react to the new aesthetic work with a corresponding new sensibility which transcends earlier preconceptions about the possibilities of art.[11] In an article in *Classical World* for 1974 entitled "Vygotsky on Language Skills," I discussed decentration as an effect derived from the study of foreign languages, and what is at stake here is a fresh viewpoint on our understanding of language as such and a renewed comprehension of the possibilities and limitations of our own native language.[12] In a private correspondence, Professor David Samuelson has rightly suggested that Arthur Koestler's "creative act" and Thomas Kuhn's "paradigm-shift" in revolutionary science[13] are based upon much the same epistemological insight.

J.R.R. Tolkien, in a famous essay on the fairy tale, has written intelligently about this estrangement-effect in imaginative fiction, and in his use of the term "recovery" he puts the emphasis on what the reader gains after he returns to the normal world from the alternative universe experienced in an imaginative narrative:

> Recovery is re-gaining—regaining of a clear view.... We need to clean our windows; so that the things seen clearly may be freed from the drab blur of triteness or familiarity—from possessiveness. Of all faces those of our *familiares* are the ones most difficult to see with fresh attention, perceiving their likeness and unlikeness: that they are faces,

and yet unique faces.... We should look at green again, and be startled anew (but not blinded) by blue and yellow and red. We should meet the centaur and the dragon, and then perhaps suddenly behold, like the ancient shepherds, sheep, and dogs, and horses—and wolves.[14]

In his own famous *The Lord of the Rings* Tolkien provided an example of defamiliarization leading to recovery more impressive than "the centaur and the dragon." I refer to the Ents, a nearly extinct race of sentient, sapient, and mobile trees who appear in the second volume of the trilogy. Certainly there are many ways to learn to appreciate trees. I learned one way in the Boy Scouts when I earned a forestry merit badge; another in botany in high school when we learned about photosynthesis and made leaf collections; still a more sophisticated one in college biochemistry. It is saying the obvious to note that a logging expert, a paper mill owner, a forest ranger, a tree surgeon, and a landscape gardener—not to mention Joyce Kilmer—each have a different "appreciation" of the value of trees. But Tolkien's vision of the possibilities of trees is one that encourages us to react to them as beings complete and total in themselves, not just objects out there for us to expropriate for whatever technological or economic purposes we might have in mind—then otherwise forget. No, I do not believe in the least that there are or ever were trees which can walk, think, or talk: the Ents are impossible by any real-life standards and are a fantasy concept. Perhaps the recent issue of the possibility of plants "feeling" would just be so much pseudoscience if it were not for the fact that trees and other plants *are* sensitive to their environment, and we ourselves form a part of that environment. Tolkien's Ents raise just this issue, making us sensitive to the needs, habits, and distinctive beauty of trees as a life-form not like humans. The defamiliarizing effect of fantasy Ents enlivens, and deepens, our awareness of real-life trees. Thus, Tolkien's "recovery" hits on an important function of estrangement as something more than a confrontation with previously unknown systems of reference. Tolkien tells us that such dislocations can also impinge creatively on what we already know, making the familiar seem unfamiliar for a time, so we can come to know it anew and more fully.

It is also appropriate for this critical concept of "estrangement" to be extended to the educative function of myths. G.S. Kirk in his series of Sather Lectures on myth has already described the defamiliarizing effect of myths, and I therefore cite him at some length:

> Myths . . . make use of a special kind of imagination that I have called . . . "fantasy." Fantasy deals in events that are impossible by real-life standards; but in myths it tends to exceed the mere manipulation of the supernatural and *express itself in a strange dislocation of familiar and naturalistic connexions and associations* [my italics]. . . .The fantastic figures of myths tend to be giants, ogres, monsters, animals with supernatural powers . . . , heroes who can fly, or become invisible, or otherwise change their appearance, or climb up to the sky. To these must be added fantastic objects like magical rings, talismanic or doom-laden heirlooms, branches or brands that contain a man's soul, and natural phenomena full of mysterious power. . . . [But fantasy] includes more than causality; indeed *all* the rules of normal action, normal reasoning and normal relationships may be suspended or distorted. The hero suddenly becomes the villain or vice versa; minor actions turn out to have profound consequences; transformations of humans into trees, animals, natural substances or stars require no more explanation than, and seem just as arbitrary as, the sudden shifts in time and space.[15]

Kirk's words leave no doubt that he is explaining the wondrous ethos of myths in terms that do not differ materially from the idea of estrangement. Disorientation effects certainly won't distinguish myths from disorienting literary narratives; in fact, myths and science fiction and fantasy literature seem to have this feature in common. However, dislocations are essential to myths and without them we wouldn't think of the given narrative as a myth: in myths, abnormality is the expected, the universal given. Whereas in SF and fantasy the "abnormality" is often withheld from the reader until it can be used for a specific shock effect, in myths we expect to encounter an otherworldly atmosphere from the outset.

Beyond this, one can only say that the dislocations may be as varied as human experience itself. The diversity of Kirk's list is an indication that any number of persons, objects, or events may receive the estranging focus of myth. To be sure, some myths will also seem weirder, more abnormal than others. Thus archaic cosmologies like the Babylonian *Enuma Elish*, the Hittite-Hurrian epic of Kumarbi, or Hesiod's *Theogony*, dealing as they do with the original state of the entire universe, are bound to seem much more distant from the real world than, say, the heroic myths presented in ancient Greek epic or in Athenian tragedy where the protagonists are at least mortal like ourselves. Yet even in the latter group there are gods and monsters and estranged events that involve otherworldly dislocations of the familiar. As Kirk's list would imply, whether a tale is a legend, folktale, creation story, or dream it may be classified as a myth, based, really, on the number and degree of dislocations.[16] The word "myth" suggests that in the given tale or narrative there are more conceptions which are *more radically* distant from everyday norms than in other disorienting fictions. A "myth" may then be defined simply as a fiction whose entire narrative field is taken up with dislocation effects.

We can go further and pin down at least one recurrent characteristic of myth's dislocations: the strange worlds created are undefined or "undifferentiated." This fictive indefinite state is not merely poised between polarized alternatives, but encompasses the entire spectrum covered by those alternatives. The worlds of myths appear "undifferentiated" because they are inclusive and synthetic in those very qualities in which the normal "real" world is imagined to be analytical, exclusive, and defined. The ancient cosmological idea of chaos, common to Sumerians, Babylonians, Egyptians, Hebrews, and Greeks, is a ready illustration of the idea: chaos is seen as a primal state of indefiniteness, where nothing that exists *now* has yet come into being; all is without form or definition (equally the formula in the Hebrew *Genesis* or the Babylonian *Enuma Elish*).

Though their theory of myth is largely in disrepute among most scholars now,[17] the Jungians almost hit upon this essential characteristic of myth with their notion of the "coincidence of opposites": in myths we find dissolutions of antitheses normal to the real world, like the dichotomies between the living and the dead, animate and inanimate creation, male and female gender, animal nature and human culture, or human and divine, just to name a few of the possibilities. Sometimes, too, the oppositions are simply envisioned as complementary parts of, or processes of, a larger system, some larger, indefinite, monadic unity from which they may be derived.

The mythological figure known as the Trickster is the best illustration of the coincidence of opposites. Most readers will be familiar at least with classic mythological tricksters like the Greek Prometheus and Hermes or the Norse Loki—figures who are "non-systematic" in that they are sometimes good, sometimes evil, but who have the air of practical joker about them even when they are not particularly malicious. They are also always potentially dangerous to the *status quo* because their allegiances are never certain.[18] In Paul Radin's words, Trickster is "primarily an inchoate being of undetermined proportions," who is "at one and the same time creator and destroyer, giver and negator, . . . knows neither good nor evil yet he is responsible for both . . . possesses no values, moral or social, yet through his actions all values come into being."[19] Stanley Diamond notes that the Trickster is "the personification of ambivalence,"[20] and this quality more than anything else has attracted the attention of the Jungian critics. The Trickster represents a "coincidence of opposites," a single character in a myth who transcends the polarities of good and evil, creativity and destruction, or even male and female (Loki, for instance). A more impressive analysis of the Trickster figure has recently been offered by Claude Lévi-Strauss. Here Trickster is interpreted from his role in myths as an "anomaly" insofar as he cannot be reduced to either of any pair of oppositions, but always shares characteristics of both, and bridges both—thus illustrating his function as a *mediator* of oppositions.[21] In one single figure, we not only discover the presence of opposite qualities but also the possibility of the transformation of those opposing qualities into another. The Jungian term, *enantiadromia,* "conversion to the opposite," perhaps implies somewhat the same idea.

Jungians may not have provided a lasting satisfactory explanation of myth, but their approach does get one into a posture of experiencing myths, of being open to them, and this is a virtuous alternative to the strictly analytical approach. Even structuralists like Claude Lévi-Strauss feel the need to provide an explanation of subconscious operations underlying myths. There is always something in myths that eludes systematic analysis or taxonomizing: perhaps the theories overly specify myths, and so reduce their potential meaning and impact too severely. G.S. Kirk has commented on this obvious, but often overlooked, feature of myth scholarship: the inadequacy of universalist explanations and theories.[22] There is always something left over in myths that the given theory cannot quite account for.

Kirk also pinpoints another side of myths' indefiniteness when he observes that myths "are multiform, imaginative and loose in their details."[23] In other kinds of thinking, we are "system-bound" and "rule-bound"—this is usually what we mean by "logical" or "rational" thinking. We have to remain within one frame of reference; we are supposed to be consistent. Myths simply are not so rule-bound, and are commonly very inconsistent, even explicitly so. One can (1) connect items out of wildly different systems or (2) leap from system to system, pretty much at will. Examples of the first type are common transformations of human beings into plant and animal forms, and changes of sex. Instances of the second are the dissociations of body parts and organs which take on a life and personality of their own, and the continuity between the realms of life and death, where human passage either way is not interdicted.

But it must be made clear that estrangement-effects in myths are *semantic* in character and refer to possibilities of *meaning*. We probably have to think of myths as archaic, but the term "archaic" should not be taken to argue that myths are necessarily older in a true historical or genetic sense; they are logically or semantically archaic. Since typically myths posit a fictional time, antecedent to our own (the "Once Upon a Time" of the fairy tale or Mircea Eliade's "in illo tempore"), perhaps this best explains our feeling that myths must somehow be older chronologically even though they are archaic only morphologically. Then, why this common feeling that "myths are the *oldest* form of fiction-making"?

In a fascinating essay entitled "The Temporizing of Essence," the critic Kenneth Burke suggests that it is a universal principle of human thinking to try to explain the *essence* of a given phenomenon by discovering its *temporal origins*.[24] It is simply a commonplace habit of mind, and Burke himself demonstrates the principle with Sigmund Freud's description of the "primal horde" in *Totem and Taboo*, where the state of primitive man, the sons in competition with their father for women, can explain the anxiety-ridden character of modern family life with its Oedipal scenario. Even such influential and imposing intellectual structures as the contract theory of government and Darwin's theory of evolution, for all of their validity as moral or scientific blueprints, are still representative of this recurrent human desire to justify the reason for something which involves the "now" by explaining how it all began.[25] A "why" question is given a "then" answer. Indeed, this "prestige of origins" is only too well documented in the thought of archaic peoples who live in societies heavily oriented toward tradition, that is, the peoples we typically associate with myths. The English anthropologist Edmund Leach describes such peoples as "non-historical," meaning ones "who think of their own society as changeless and conceive of time present as a straightforward perpetuation of time past."[26] The myths of such peoples locate all significant primordial events, not in any real chronological time, but in an indefinite "in the beginning." Consequently in such societies there is a widespread interest in aetiologies, stories that explain the beginning of something, like the origin of the entire universe, of man, or of some object or institution of special cultural importance. For such peoples, as Mircea Eliade remarks: "*It is the first manifestation of a thing that is significant and valid* [his italics]."[27]

This confusion between the morphological and chronological implications of myths have particularly vexed myth theorists in the problem area of *the origin of myth* since the nineteenth century. A solution to this issue is far from apparent. The "origins" of myth have now been pushed back into "prehistoric" times, well before the invention of writing at the close of the Late Neolithic. Egypt and Sumer, the two most ancient literature cultures known, present us with mythological writings datable to the early Bronze Age (3000–2000 B.C.). Both already possessed sophisticated mythologies and the term "primitive" is not quite applicable in either case. The motifs and themes that appear in the mythological texts of both cultures have obviously already undergone considerable intellectual development and elaboration when we first encounter them in cuneiform and hieroglyphic writing. Even at this early date the origins of myth are long enshrouded in the dimmest antiquity, and one must resort to archaeological evidence and comparative anthropology to infer from what earlier prehistorical eras a belief or idea might derive.[28]

For Egypt, for instance, the creation stories from Heliopolis, Memphis, and Hermopolis—all ascribable in their main outlines to the third millennium B.C.—are complex theologies, elaborately conceived combinations of mythical themes and religious beliefs.[29] Behind them lie generations of priestly speculation about the emergence of the world from the primal waters, the divinity of the king and his kinship with the major gods, and the nature of the afterlife. That the theologies always interrelate these mythological issues is just one more evidence that tells against their being naive.

Sumer, too, discloses a complex system of motifs, each of which must have already experienced a long development. For example, a Third Millennium story, "Enki and Ninhursag in the Land of Dilmun," is a subtle combination of the motif of Paradise, its loss, and a death-rebirth pattern which is the solution to the tale.[30]

Claude Lévi-Strauss has provided another hypothesis: that the myth-making faculty originated in the Neolithic period (5000–3000 B.C.), a revolutionary period for man in so many other ways: at this time agriculture, turned pottery, weaving, and the domestication of animals came on the scene.[31] Yet this still remains mostly a speculation based on analogy, for we have no texts and the art, perhaps most likely religious, remains open to many interpretations. There is no reason to assume that mythic conceptions and images cannot have been created by people who could think in other, non-mythic ways equally well.

Archaeology and paleontology have combined researches to show that early man was a symbol-making creature, in art and in his conceptions of the "other worlds" of the gods and afterlife, for tens of millennia before even the Neolithic.[32] We might assume an archaeological metaphor for myth and begin to think of mythical ideas as having a long prehistory, with some ideas or themes or images belonging to much older strata than others. Thus one could speculate reasonably that the mythic-religious conception of the afterlife goes at least as far back as Neanderthal man (c. 40,000 B.C.)[33] whereas the Near Eastern myth of the universal deluge of mankind (to appear later in the Biblical story of Noah) derives from the late fourth millennium B.C.[34] The origin and history of myths and myth-making is no less complex and ambiguous than the origin and history of human intelligence and that even vaguer faculty, "consciousness."

The present stage of knowledge will not allow us to place the origin of myth at any stage in man's past, let alone the recent past, with adequate certainty. Nor can we hope to find it in alien "primitive" cultures of the present because those cultures, too, though simpler in some ways than ours, have been around as long as we have, and most have been much more dynamic and creative than Western man has been prepared to admit until very recently. Even granted contemporary archaic peoples' "anhistorical self-awareness" as described by Leach, it is no longer a popular practice to assume there was a "primitive mentality" behind the creation of myths, as earlier influential myth theorists like Lucien Lévy-Bruhl and Ernst Cassirer had supposed.[35] Of course, contemporary anthropologists regard all cultures as having undergone history, and even the term "primitive" is in eclipse because its meaning over the past has too often suggested that primitive societies contain "early man," *Homo sapiens* as he must have been just after he descended from the trees.[36] Current anthropological views would suggest that all groups of *Homo sapiens,* even those that still live in "stone age" cultures, are fully human; all of us are more or less equidistant from animal origins. Today's myth critics no longer expect to be able to find primitive societies whose myths are analogous to the ur-myths created by ur-man as he emerged from his animal origins. Myths seem to have undergone too much history to force this interpretation on them, and so have human beings.

Anthropologists and myth critics like Kirk no longer assume an isomorphism between myths and the minds that created them since even in their own native cultures myths now seem to be more estranged from normal conceptions about reality than was earlier realized. It may well be the case that myths represent non-naturalistic distorted worlds even for members of their own cultures and are no more to be considered realistic thought patterns and images than the "white tornado" and "helping hands" magic that appears in our TV fantasies could be considered our "reality."

In any case, we need not be concerned to describe the mental life of natives, but to demonstrate the value of modern people in our culture having their imaginative sensibilities altered by an encounter with a different system of conceptions given in a myth. Myths have a strong effect on the thinking of children, and on the imaginative lives of creative writers and many popular artists. Wherever myths came from, they still have their effect on us *now*. And they do this even in translations from strange, barely understood foreign languages. Unlike literature, myths are not so tied to specific verbal formulas and structures. Actually, they move easily from culture to culture, as myths like Noah's Flood or Atlantis show in their near world-wide popularity and distribution.

Indeed, there is a ready model for the protean character of modern culture's mythology in ancient Greek mythology. Many critics would disallow even the term "myth" for so historical and unprimitive a phenomenon as Greek mythology. Yet *mythos*, meaning "fable" most of the time, was a Greek word: all the many cognates and compounds of "myth" come from it. Are we really to deny the name "myth" to the very tales which gave rise to the whole question of mythology? Even before Plato, Sophists like Prodicus and Critias were laying the basis for the first philosophical myth-criticism, and Greek mythology was certainly the most universally popular and well known "mythology" in the West until the nineteenth century. In their thousand-year history in antiquity, these myths were primarily *aesthetic* in some cases (plastic art: myriad vases and statues); literary (Homeric and other epics), philosophical (Plato and pre-Socratics), or political (Athenian drama) in others; myths were central to eccentric, conservative religious cults like the Orphics or could serve a liberal democratic cause, as Aeschylus' drama *Prometheus Bound*. Myths are a historical phenomenon *par excellence:* they are metamorphotic, multivalent, plurisignative, and elusive. Given time, one variant can mean the opposite of its predecessor (Hesiod and Aeschylus on Prometheus, for instance).

I do not wish to leave the impression that myths are always and everywhere benign. In *Behold the Man,* Moorcock showed that myths can drive at least some of us crazy; myths suggest nightmare as much as they do dream. Myths can become dangerous, as when people invest completely in mythology and use their belief-code to justify repression or even worse treatment of outsiders (e.g., Nazism; some forms of Marxism, Christian fundamentalism, Zionism, and Islam). Othertimes, people just waste a lot of time, energy, and income when they impute powers to myths which just aren't there (as with cults of all sorts from UFOs to Big Foot, the Loch Ness monster, and Atlantis). Mainly, however, it is the low demands made on our critical faculties which make such cults and their beliefs undesirable from an intellectual standpoint.

Like all other human activity, myths may lead to improvement or deterioration in our condition, but myths *need not* necessarily lead to non-scientific or archaic postures toward the world. In confronting a myth we suspend our normal preconceptions about reality, about what the rules of the real universe are, and we think our way into an alien system of operations and relationships. We open up intellectually to new possibilities, even new impossibilities, and for a time abandon our awareness of normal human limitations. For a time the familiar seems unfamiliar to us, but this experience of estrangement can only impinge creatively on the real world we already know, aiding us to experience it anew and in greater depth. Once again Kirk may summarize the implications of this insight into myth:

> I suggest that the dislocation of everyday life is in itself life-enhancing and liberating . . . it is their [myths'] capacity to reveal fresh and otherwise unimagined possibilities of experience . . . and it seems plausible that the unconscious appeal of dislocation-fantasy might be no slighter, if different in quality, in the stratified and culture-bound circumstances of a traditional preliterate society.[37]

This view suggests that myth is dynamic in its function, not static and "archetypal" as Eliade's vision would insist.

In sum, too much discussion of the so-called problem of myth has centered on a two-part polarized relationship between "myth" and "reality," as if the two are mutually exclusive ways of looking at the world. My analysis of the problem proposes that we look at a three-term educative *process* of "myth," "sensibility," and "reality." The radical estrangements offered in myths can enrich our pool of imaginative resources, can stretch our intellectual potential, and then that sensibility—which, after all, can be educated by all kinds of experiences besides myths—can be deployed for dealing with reality. Myths need not require intellectual or educational monism, as its positivist and Marxist critics would have us believe.

Yet it is only in the context of preconceived hostility that the best SF critics have so far discussed the relationship between myth and SF literature. For example, in his recent popular book, *New Worlds for Old: The Apocalyptic Imagination, Science Fiction, and American Literature,* David Ketterer argues that instead of generating a "new mythology" which is *sui generis,* too many science fiction writers—like Samuel R. Delany and Roger Zelazny, whose works he singles out—are merely offering a "sterile revamping of the old," that is, they are merely rewriting old myths.[38] The influential literary theorist Fredric Jameson focuses the attack more specifically when he refers to "the so-called mythical SF which finds a spurious comfort in the predetermined unity of the myth or legend which serves it as an organizational device."[39] These two critics are alike in emphasizing the limits imposed on the creative writer who would choose an ancient myth as his inspiration. It is as if the myths set up a program which inhibits the creative writer from doing anything more than recapitulating the narrative form of his mythological source.

This attack on mythical SF really involves an *aesthetic* prejudice against rewriting "old stories" because it makes for banal fiction. It is an argument which is leveled specifically against SF because literary critics and scholars of all persuasions have identified several classics of mythifiction in the literary mainstream: James Joyce's *Ulysses,* Thomas Mann's *Joseph and His Brothers,* and Hermann Broch's *The Death of Vergil.* And a host of minor classics from Ross Lockridge's *Raintree County* and John Updike's *The Centaur* to the historical novels of Robert Graves and Mary Renault are taken seriously by a large intelligent readership. Is there really some precondition which makes it impossible for a serious mythical SF narrative to be written and then received intelligently by its readers and critics?

One side of the critics' attack against mythological SF has been clarified by John White's *Mythology in the Modern Novel.*[40] The answer resides in the subtitle of the book: "a study in *prefigurative* technique." By "prefiguration" White means that a myth stimulates a pattern of response in a knowledgeable reader, and in the course of a literary narrative the anticipations aroused by the myth's presence can be fulfilled or betrayed, or transformed in countless ways. "Prefiguration" as a term involves a secularized Biblical analogy: the early Christian Fathers of the Church regarded the Old Testament as a prophetic anticipation or *praefiguratio* of the New. The New Dispensation included the lessons of the Old but went beyond it; the New was more powerful and more authoritative than the Old.

An example from the literary mainstream that comes to mind immediately is John Barth's *Giles Goat-Boy* in which one set of possible responses by a reader is based upon the heroic initiation pattern described by Joseph Campbell in *The Hero With a Thousand Faces.* The complex monomythic ritual pattern of the hero's separation from society, his initiation as a world savior, and his return to the world, is fulfilled by Barth's Giles, who is clearly an "anti-hero" (cf. Oscar of Heinlein's *Glory Road* in chapter 1). Thus Barth's black humor parody of Campbell suggests that myths in fact do *not* establish patterns of universal validity for human moral action. The result of this literary transformation of a mythic pattern is, as it turns out, a completely contemporary and existentialist theme of an "anti-myth." Thus, as Robert Scholes has remarked on *Giles* in the final chapter of *The Fabulators:* "Myth tells us that we are all part of a great story. But the fabulators, so clearly aware of the difference between fact and fiction, are unwilling to accept the mythic view of life as completely valid. Against this view they balance one which I am calling the philosophical, which tells us that every man is unique, alone, poised over chaos."[41] Indeed, most of the SF and fantasy tales encountered in this study (many already encountered in chapter 1) illustrate this "anti-myth" and existential philosophy.

White's theory thus has the advantage of putting the accent on the creative literary work, without misconceiving the potential contribution of mythology to contemporary fiction, and it avoids the worst failing in most myth-criticism—the reduction of complex literary works to nothing more than illustrations of pre-existent archetypes or myth-and-ritual patterns. The modern work must not be reduced to its mythical basis, for in every case the modern work will have a meaning and interest that is both individualistic and contemporary, that will transcend its basis in myths.[42] Thus the novels of Roger Zelazny discussed in chapter 5 may be read quite satisfactorily as superman novels in the tradition of H.G. Wells, Stanley Weinbaum, and A.E. van Vogt, regardless of what a given reader may or may not know of Zelazny's recherché allusions to Greek, Hindu, and Egyptian mythlore. The modern work ought to be regarded as an extrapolation from the myth and a specification of its meaning, besides being readable narrative fiction in its own right for the many readers who know nothing about mythology or theory of myth. Mythical SF may involve new literary conceptions as well as be harmonious with the most up-to-date speculations of science and other cognitive disciplines.

Unlike Ketterer or Jameson, Darko Suvin, an influential SF critic

"Estrangement" in Mythology and Science Fiction

and co-editor of *Science-Fiction Studies,* does allow for White's type of criticism—and by extension my own—when he writes that *"fiction can be formally or morphologically analogous to myth, but it is not itself myth* [his italics]"; and later that "literary artefacts are not myths and yet . . . many of them are significantly marked by genetic and morphological connections with myths."[43] White equally allows for a more intimate, underlying connection between myth and some literary fictions than the rhetorical one of prefigurative technique though he chooses not to treat it in his book:

> One is often left uncertain whether the notion [of a "return to myth" by a modern creative writer] denotes a return to specific mythologies, such as Greek, Roman or Sumerian, or whether it refers to the revival of certain archaically mythical qualities in modern literature.[44]

The SF critics who dislike myths and mythification commonly tend to apply this second and more comprehensive of White's two definitions—"the revival of archaic qualities."

Thus a full discussion of "SF mythology" would have to include in its scope H.P. Lovecraft's alien demonology in his "Cthulhu-mythos," James Branch Cabell's pseudo-medieval Poictesme, and J.R.R. Tolkien's tragic cosmology in *Silmarillion*—even though these are "made-up" mythologies that revive the "archaic qualities" of myths rather than any earlier specific myth or mythology. The next four chapters of this book are actually intended to explore four specific types of such qualities in elaborate detail: creation, herohood, godhead, and archaic time. But it is important for immediate concerns to reiterate that myths themselves do not require philosophical anachronism, and so the attack on "archaic metaphysics" in literary fictions is even less fair to the intelligence of writers and readers alike.

Every work of literary art that we read with the consciousness that it is fiction presupposes an entirely different intellectual order of meaning from beliefs; one that does not necessarily include a system of beliefs or acceptance of a set metaphysical code. A work of fiction may offer us a set of values or perspectives on human nature or analyses of any facet of reality which are quite at odds with what we know or believe to be the truth, but even from fiction that is totally alien to our own most cherished values and attitudes we can always add fresh dimensions to our own intellects; attain new ways of focusing our attentions that we had perhaps not previously considered possible. There seems to me no way around the obvious conclusion that the serious pursuit of literature—old or new, good or bad—does continually alter our sensibilities, but that doesn't have to involve the inculcating of specific dogmas and beliefs in us.

Another reason to reject this notion that mythical SF requires archaism is that it just doesn't fit experience: SF writers are indeed myth-lovers (the results of chapter 1 are in mind), but these same authors are also notorious for their religious and intellectual nonconformism, nor can I see any of the transcendental absolutes or religious metaphysics Suvin does. This impresses me as a false problem.[45] There are a few writers who are orthodox Christians, such as fantasists Charles Williams and C.S. Lewis, but their literary works are anything but orthodox. Works like *All Hallows Eve*, the Perelandra trilogy, and the Narnia tales are much more noteworthy for being eccentric in their philosophy, bizarre and distinctive in their world-imaging, peculiar rather than conventional: they are, after all, fantasies. The critics usually have trouble agreeing on what Christian dogmas are being propounded, and the Christian fantasies of Williams, Lewis, and George Macdonald are too obscure and idiosyncratic to serve the narrow interests of *any* religious orthodoxy.

Let us look at one American SF writer more closely. The late William Anthony Parker White, known to fandom as "Anthony Boucher," was famous as an editor-founder of the *Magazine of Fantasy and Science Fiction* and a master of the science fantasy short story. He was a Roman Catholic, so apparently we should be on the alert in his work for fictionalized religious propaganda. But his two most famous short stories, now anthologized in Mayo Mohs's *Other Worlds, Other Gods*, betray this expectation.

"Balaam" (first anthologized in 1954) is wry and humorous in tone, open-ended in form and meaning. The Old Testament legend of the Midianite forced by the Lord to bless his enemies, the Israelites, told in Numbers 22–31, undergoes a reversal in this SF fable about mankind's first encounter with intelligent extraterrestrials: the aliens have a better claim than the earthlings to being the Chosen People who will colonize the New World of Mars, because the aliens are better adapted naturally to the environment on Mars, needing no artificial technology to adjust to its "alien" conditions. The human heroes—a Jewish chaplain and a Catholic chaplain—are aware of their mythlike roles, citations from the Bible abound, and a *partial* knowledge of the original legend is incorporated into the narrative. The Israeli Chaim is clearly the Balaam figure. Commanded by his captain to put a ritual curse on the aliens, Chaim decides to bless them instead, realizing that they have as much claim to being "men" as we do; the Catholic priest, an ex-football player nicknamed "The Mule," is a joke on the Biblical prefiguration—Balaam's portentous sidekick, the ass, an important figure in the original. In American magazine SF this kind of comic distortion is especially popular, but it aids the more serious purpose of undermining the applicability of the original tale. "Balaam" is open-ended because it terminates before the blessing and its potentially dire consequences. In Jesuitical fashion, the tale ends on a question that does not yet have an answer: how would the first alien encounter alter our definition of man? It is a tale delightful to readers of many religious persuasions, and it does not defend any specific dogmas.

"The Quest for St. Aquin" (which originally appeared in *F&SF*, January 1959) is a more explicitly Roman Catholic story, though it also raises a speculative question about the definition of Man, this time from the genre of robots and artificial intelligences. Boucher describes an imaginary future after a widespread atomic holocaust that brings the world back culturally to a New Middle Age, as in Walter M. Miller's classic, *A Canticle for Leibowitz* (1959). Because of the opposition of secular authorities (the "Technarchy," rule by technology), the Church has gone underground, returned to its primitive state as in the Catacombs period. The pope sends a priest named Thomas (same name as the Biblical doubter) to seek evidence of a legendary miracle-worker "St. Aquin"—prefigured by St. Thomas Aquinas, famous in Church history as Catholicism's most rational and convincing theologian and philosopher. On this quest-and-pilgrimage Thomas argues his faith with his android carrier, a "robass" or robot-ass, a very hard-nosed, skeptical, and persuasive atheist. Thomas discovers that the saint was an android, but one who preached Catholicism and converted multitudes to the faith because he could reason perfectly about theological matters. At the open-ended conclusion of this tale, the priest is left doubting his Catholic faith, wondering whether he could expand it to include artificial intelligent creations as part of Divine Providence: was "St. Aquin" hoax or holy?

In this second tale, in addition, psychic powers are highly regarded, and this is no recognizable part of Roman Catholic dogma or theology. Really, in both stories, Boucher is primarily an SF writer and the Catholicism is better taken as a hypothesis, or "as if," for an extrapolative fiction which is at once speculative and questioning of dogma.

Indeed, there is no reason why imaginative literature cannot discuss theological issues from Catholic, Jewish, or other religious points of view, but we should never forget that the theology is both speculative and fictional. Science fiction is didactic but not dogmatic, and reacting to it involves a large area of relativity: how a reader "takes" SF depends on the interaction of his experience and his education in the broadest sense of the word, beyond mere schooling.

Future criticism of the mythological literary narrative must begin from White's "Copernican revolution" and focus on the modernity of fiction rather than on the alleged archaism of myth. However, White is only a starting point because SF is a special kind of literature, requiring its own critical rules, and the contemporary critic of mythical SF has to adapt White somewhat as a critical model: his analyses are rhetorical and emphasize analogies between myths and contemporary experiences within the confines of the mainstream novel, the latter heavily indebted to a naturalistic perspective and psychological meanings, even in writers like Joyce, Broch, and Mann; analyses of mythical SF must emphasize relationships between the estranged worlds of myths and estranged worlds of SF narratives, the latter explicitly conceived as distinct from, and alternative to, the normal world. I believe the discussions of stories by Bond, Harness, Heinlein, Moorcock, and Weinbaum in chapter 1 illustrate White's methodology applied to specific SF narratives.

Contemporary science-fiction criticism has also made progress by abandoning traditional models of criticism, like the New Criticism, proposing instead that we look at science fiction as a "literature of ideas." This is how SF writer-critic James Gunn puts it in his recent popular book:

> In science fiction the idea became king; the situation, superior to the character; the character, a kind of purified vehicle for the idea. This

offends literary critics and literary readers; they are accustomed to reading about complex characters in familiar surroundings and to concerning themselves with the way these characters change or are revealed during the course of the narrative. In science fiction it has not mattered (until recently) how complex or how sensitive a character was if he was wrong in the eyes of the universe, if he held views that were in conflict with the physical laws governing the world we know; . . . Ultimately, of course, it is environment that matters to science fiction, to us, and to the human race.[46]

This emphasis on conceptual formulations, I should say, by no means eliminates aesthetic considerations or verbal sophistication, but it does mean that an aesthetic dimension in science fiction must be based on, and derived from, the control of cognitive elements, and words and style must subserve this same interest. For example, in *New Worlds for Old* David Ketterer has successfully analyzed image clusters and language texture in several science-fiction narratives while not ignoring their conceptual strengths (representative image studies are those of arabesques in Edgar Allan Poe, sexual innuendo in Stanislaw Lem's *Solaris*, spirals in Kurt Vonnegut's *Sirens of Titan*, and pins/brooches in Philip K. Dick's *The Man in the High Castle*).

This definition of SF as a cognitive literature is central to contemporary fictional theory, and credit should be given to its most eloquent proponent. In two of the most important theoretical articles on the SF narrative to appear so far, Darko Suvin has defined science fiction in generic terms as the "literature of cognitive estrangement."[47] In Suvin's terms, SF is "*a literary genre whose necessary and sufficient conditions are the presence and interaction of estrangement and cognition and whose main formal device is an imaginative framework alternative to the author's empirical environment.*"[48] This alternative environment, in turn, serves only as a fictional hypothesis, and the cognitive dimension of SF is involved with developing it with "extrapolating and totalizing ('scientific') rigor."[49] The intellectual distance—let us call it the "incredibility gap"—between the real world and the imagined universe diminishes in direct proportion with the author's skill in cogently and convincingly depicting the changes that will result from the researches and speculations of the physical and social sciences and other major intellectual disciplines of our times. Robert Scholes in *Structural Fabulation*, an essay on SF that should prove influential in the near future, has further confirmed

Suvin's view that SF is an estranged literature in which the bases of estrangement are conceptual rather than verbal.[50]

Structuralist-style criticism, which analyzes systems and processes, has been the most successful critical model for SF so far; Jameson, Scholes, Todorov, Suvin, Lem, Eric Rabkin, and Joanna Russ all approach the SF narrative as a fictional "interaction of systems;" and thus SF and structuralism share a fundamental likeness in their emphasis on explaining things as systems. However, in American SF this systematic side may proceed in part from the roots of the genre in popular-science magazines like Hugo Gernsback's *Science and Invention*.

We are still left with the fact that almost anything can act as a hypothesis for SF, and an answer to the aesthetic question of what makes good SF has to be broad and varied: It has to give credit to Lem's understanding of the history and philosophy of science in *Solaris*, to Philip José Farmer's comprehension of Freudian psychoanalysis and the power of wish-fulfillments, to Roger Zelazny's erudition in comparative literature and comparative mythology, and to the penetrating moral didacticism of the Swiftian satire of Kurt Vonnegut.

This is where myth again enters the picture. Insofar as a given science-fiction narrative is meant to envision the most radical transformation of man and/or his universe, in time and/or space, the imagined vision may recede far enough from present norms that the conceptions will fit in well with myths and the kinds of estranged events that appear in myths. If they are not recognizable as myths we already know, they will have a "mythlike" quality about them. This very tendency of science fiction narratives to appear the more mythical the more estranged they are is what Northrop Frye was getting at as long ago as 1957 when he defined science fiction as a "mode of romance with a strong inherent tendency to myth."[51] What Frye means by "myth" is a trans-human level of action and potency, a fictive environment where the issues of the beginning and end of man and the world are raised—in another context Frye speaks of "the outer limits of Heaven and Hell."

One might therefore speak of science fiction "domesticating the unknown." While working away from our naturalistic norms (which Suvin and Lem call the "zero world" or normal verifiable experience)[52] in the direction of further and further estrangement, science fiction narratives also provide a rationale—some interacting system of scientific explanations and speculations—which will make that new non-naturalistic set of norms "naturalistic." That is, what we now consider impossible in the real world may appear as part of the normal empirical environment in the new imaginative framework. As Suvin writes in his latest study:

> SF should not be seen in terms of science, the future, or any other element of its potentially unlimited thematic field. Rather, it should be defined as a fictional tale determined by the hegemonic literary device of a *locus* and/or *dramatis personae* that (1) are *radically or at least significantly different from the empirical times, places, and characters* of "mimetic" or "naturalist" fiction, but (2) are nonetheless—to the extent that SF differs from other "fantastic" genres, that is, ensembles of fictional tales without empirical validation—simultaneously perceived as *not impossible* within the cognitive (cosmological and anthropological) norms of the author's epoch. Basically, SF is a developed oxymoron, a realistic irreality, with humanized nonhumans, this-worldly Other Worlds, and so forth. Which means that it is—potentially—the space of a potent *estrangement*, validated by the pathos and prestige of the basic cognitive norms of our times.[53]

However, it is also true that as the SF narrative reaches out further from present norms, we discover the imaginative conceptions becoming bolder and bolder even as it becomes progressively more difficult to construct satisfying cognitive rationales. In terms of the insight recently offered by the structuralist critic Tzvetan Todorov, the estranged universe becomes "fantastic"—meaning it becomes progressively more difficult to explain events systematically at all.[54] In the "fantastic," the distinction between a naturalistic/scientific/empirical explanation and a supernatural one breaks down (cf. Dick's *Maze of Death* in chapter 1). Robert Scholes also confirms that our ability to distinguish between the natural and the supernatural diminishes as we move further away from our normal world and delve more deeply into the "unknown" in either time or space.[55]

Eric Rabkin has rightly identified a very broad genre of fantasy whose narrative world is entirely taken up with the fantastic.[56] The worlds and conceptions of fantasy are, simply, *impossible* by present norms. Fantasy can be every bit as systematic as SF proper, but the former's worlds are an "anti-system" to a contemporary system of world conceptions that are normally taken as "real" and "true." Fantasy undermines our present conventional sense of reality, extends our overall sense of reality with its new fictive one, but does not need scientific speculations, nor even rational forms of cognition at all, to posit its alternate realities. In fantasy fiction, for example, worlds met in dreams are typically taken as real as the one of the waking state. Thus SF proper is better regarded as a special kind of fantasy narrative, one which, as Suvin suggests, uses both speculative and systematic "science" in the broadest sense to account for the alternate reality's relation to the "zero world." Science fiction needs to posit its narrative worlds as at least potentially or arguably *empirical* ones, fantasy doesn't. Sharing this non-empirical and "anti-systematic" formulation, fantasy fiction and myths are bound to seem similar. All fantasy fiction also presupposes a mythic potential insofar as it creates an imaginary alternative to our present conception of reality.

In the first chapter, I identified a short story by Silverberg as my inspiration for an insight into the plenitude of mythical SF; in this chapter, too, one narrative in particular sums up my view that mythic and scientific forms of understanding may meet at a fictional interface, the SF narrative, especially if they imply a transcendence of present norms so large that it constitutes a complete new understanding of human nature and/or the cosmos. Winner of the Nebula Award, Samuel R. Delany's *The Einstein Intersection* (Ace, 1967), is explicit, even obvious, in its allusions to well-known myths and myth-theories.[57] In his own voice, in fact, the author tells us that "the central subject of the book is myth" (p. 71—this and all other page references are to the edition cited). In addition, Delany's work is highly illustrative of the mythic themes of estrangement, nondifferentiation, Jungian archetypes, and *coincidentia oppositorum* also encountered in this chapter.

Though I shrink from the onus of defending any recent SF narrative as a "classic" in the full elitist and hierarchical sense of that word, I think *Einstein* is at least a truly innovative statement about myth and it is well worth the attention of serious myth students and scholars. Many academic readers have expressed a dislike for the book: perhaps it is the style, full of popular culture elements and written in the "street people" idiom; or perhaps it is the world-view,

"Estrangement" in Mythology and Science Fiction

depicting a future that belongs to music, not literature, and remembers our time mainly for the Beatles and Great Rock-and-Roll. Yet this anti-mythic fable is complex and challenging, and it demands and deserves intelligent reading.

The story is set in a phase of earth's history that is discontinuous with our own. Perhaps the time is some future post-catastrophic world, for the gene pool of this future race has been permanently damaged: there are three sexes—male, female, and hermaphrodite—and two genetic types—functionals (or normals) and nonfunctionals; only the normals lead real lives while the mutant nonfunctionals are locked up in an electronically fenced area.

The book is so structured that the problem it raises—the relationship between being "human" and the great myths of mankind—becomes only partially clear at the end of the novel, and there is no complete resolution. The title itself is problematical enough, but in simple terms it means the world described by Einstein's cosmology—a world of rational science pushed by the analytical side of human intelligence beyond its limits—has been superseded by an irrational and unpredictable world of unlimited possibility described by Gödel's theorem. Jacob Bronowski, popular as a historian of science for his "The Ascent of Man" television series, offers the following explanation:

> It was shown by Gödel in 1931 that even in a purely abstract system of axioms like Euclid's there arise perfectly reasonable questions which have no answers. That is, even in such a tight, tidy, logical, and as it were entirely arithmetical system, it is possible to formulate theorems which cannot be shown to be either true or false. . . . There are theorems which may or may not be true; and there are states which might or might not be reached; the mathematics can never decide. And this is in a world without microscopes, matter, and indeterminancy, in a world of pure logic. It is indeed a remarkable landslide, this rift in certainty; and its implications will become clear to experimental scientists only slowly, as they learn that a geological fault has been opened up in the strata of logic itself.[58]

After the "Einstein Intersection" as fact of cosmology and history, these creatures have abandoned the recognizable world of our humanity altogether, and the populace of this new Gödelian universe is a different species. One evidence of this is that the normal categories of "physical" and "spiritual" no longer retain their original meaning, and even the distinction between life and death is ambivalent because some characters can conditionally be returned to life after they have been killed. Another evidence is that our own kind of humanity is one of this future species' myths.

The problem for the quest-hero of the novel, a male normal named Lo Lobey, is to find out *what* he is. In his intellectual odyssey through this world, it is the great myths of mankind that help him achieve, not just a sense of self-identity, but in fact a sense of the real. From our world, our only legacy to this new post-human race of creatures is myth. And it is reasonable, given the presuppositions of this world—its radical "difference" (a key word repeated in the novel) from ours—that only myths could be useful to them because only myths are free and uncategorical enough ("undifferentiated" enough) for a world that operates under laws that are distinct from ("estranged" from) our own.

Delany's attempt to explore the function of mythology may also explain why several myths appear either in clusters or in what Freud called "condensations." To give a few specific examples, Lo Lobey is in some sense Orpheus because he plays a flute that has power over nature and in fact—as we find out in the course of the novel—over life and death, too. But the flute, representing a Jungian "coincidence of opposites" (combining good and evil, creativity and destruction) is also a machete, a valuable weapon. In one of the first of Lo Lobey's confrontations with his heroic destiny he is likened to Theseus and defeats a mutant, minotaurlike bull in the labyrinthine source-caves beneath the surface of the earth; at this point he receives further knowledge from a computer there called PHAEDRA— Psychic Harmony Entanglements and Deranged Response Associations—which once belonged to the old humanity. The confrontation in the caverns with a minotaur and the computer is also the hero's descent into the Underworld to experience old humanity's Collective Unconscious (another Jungian theme). Other examples include Kid Death who is at once Hades, Satan, and Billy the Kid; the four-armed dragon-master, Spider, who is both Pat Garrett and Judas Iscariot; Green Eye, a transmutated Christ; Le Dove (a hermaphrodite), who combines Jean Harlow, the Great Mother archetype, and the Holy Ghost. In all of this is the basic idea that only

"Estrangement" in Mythology and Science Fiction

by living out myths can this ghostly and unreal race of post-human creatures become *real*, yet in this universe, because it operates under irrational, unpredictable Gödelian laws and not under rational Einsteinian ones, there will be differences; the reality that will ensue for Lo Lobey and his comrades will be a different world.

The final two revivals of mythical scenarios at the end of the story indicate the general direction of this perplexing book. Here the crucifixion of Christ/Green-Eye by Spider/Judas (an evil moment) is interwoven with the killing of Kid-Death/Billy-the-Kid by Spider/Pat Garrett (an optimistic scene). And just as Lo Lobey's Orphic quest for his beloved La Friza is left uncompleted, so is the question of Green-Eye's resurrection left open because this new universe and its populace—for all its debt to us and our myths—will not repeat our experience in any one-for-one correspondence. In Spider's words:

> Lobey, everything changes. The labyrinth today does not follow the same path it did at Knossos fifty thousand years ago. You may be Orpheus; you may be someone else, who dares death and succeeds. Green-eye may go to the tree this evening, hand there, rot, and never come down. The world is not the same. . . . It's different. (p. 119)

I am grateful to Mr. Douglas Barbour, SF poet and critic, for informing me—at second hand from the author himself—that Delany originally had entitled the work "A fabulous formless chaos" after a line from W.B. Yeats, and I report it as one important evidence that "myth" in this novel means a search for form in a chaotic world, though Lo Lobey's quest remains inconclusive.

Finally, I should single out one formal technique of composition that places this book in the "New Wave" category. Delany intersperses his narrative of Lo Lobey's quest with pages from his own autobiographical diary on his travels, many episodes of which take place in Greece. There is more than a hint that Delany as narrator is identifying himself with his fictional hero, but the deliberate disruption of the science fiction story by this nonfictional commentary forces upon every reader a less naive, more active involvement with the science-fiction fable, too. Since every one of the author's personal comments about himself may be juxtaposed to some event in the science-fiction narrative, there is an overall significance behind the author's "antinovelist" statement that "endings to be useful must be inconclusive" (p. 125) because Delany's universe is open conceptually as well as structurally: its relationship to our world is never fully explained; its future and the future of the book's protagonist, Lo Lobey, are totally indefinite; and even its nature in its own space-time frame—that is, synchronically as opposed to diachronically—is largely indeterminate. This universe is so radically estranged from our own normal world that the most disturbing speculations of modern science—Einstein's relativity and Gödel's theorem—have reached that conceptual limit which I have termed mythical estrangement, where the distinction between myth and science is blurred.

The strong meta-fictional dimension in *The Einstein Intersection* suggests that we are dealing with a seriously intended theory of myth couched in fictional form. It belongs generically to the "functionalist" mode of interpretation, but because myths are of relative value and do not presuppose absolute and fixed functions or meanings, Delany's futuristic universe is an authentically science-fictional one; it is dynamic, process-oriented, and open-ended in the face of both science and myth. Delany's SF "archetypes" are quite distinct in their implications from Jung's or Eliade's archetypes.

Consequently, the mythical SF narrative (at the hands of Silverberg, Moorcock, Delany, and many others) and contemporary SF criticism with its notion of "cognitive estrangement" have an important contribution to make concerning our awareness of the role of myth in the modern imagination. Science fiction taken as a genre, its explicitly mythical subgenre included, is concerned with new forms of cognition and speculation, not the sciences exclusively, which can help man to deal imaginatively with frontiers of the unknown, including, of course, the future. As science grows and with its tests and experiments extends reality through knowledge, SF analogously extends our consciousness through speculation, and since Mary Shelley's *Frankenstein* it has performed the critical service of testing modern science's effects on consciousness. As SF historians Scholes and Rabkin have observed: "For a century and a half, science fiction has been making a serious and dedicated effort to create a modern conscience for the human race."[59]

The significance of SF, then, lies in its attempt to deal with human knowledge and consciousness, especially to react to the explosive side-effects from the geometric growth in research that has taken place within the last century and a half. In his popular nonfiction history, Brian Aldiss has reconfirmed his Frankenstein fable (ch. 1) and defined SF as *"a search for a definition of man and his status in the universe which will stand in our advanced but confused state of knowledge."*[60] As Aldiss suggests, science fiction is not just concerned with man's relationship to the universe—almost all literature studies that—but with man's unstable relationship to his own ever increasing knowledge, the primary disturber of his condition in the world. Thus the same era that saw science fiction develop as a huge, independent body of literature—mainly since the epochal works of Jules Verne and H.G. Wells, who are popularly considered the twin founders of the modern form—has also been witness to unbelievable advances in both scientific and humanistic disciplines, a cultural development for which Alvin Toffler's phrase, "future shock," is more than appropriate. The growth of science fiction and the growth of its popularity go hand in hand with the knowledge and research explosion of our time.

It is precisely into such an unstable intellectual environment as our own that ancient myth would interact with contemporary SF without necessarily destroying *cognitive* potential. For as what we conventionally call "reality" recedes further and further from our everyday norms (as it must by means of concepts in physics like Einstein's relativity, Heisenberg's indeterminacy, and Gödel's theorem), as "reality" in and of itself becomes an *unknown*, ancient myths provide us with the outer limits of our visionary capacities. With their blurring of the distinction—or at least the boundary—between life and death, between man as we know him empirically and man as possessing ever greater transcendent powers in the heroes of legend and the gods of cosmology, we stretch our potential to conceive, and we expand our intellectual sensibilities so that we can react with comprehension and empathy to a maximal range of conceptions. In Alvin Toffler's words:

> Today as never before we need a multiplicity of visions, dreams and prophecies—images of potential tomorrows. Before we can rationally decide which alternative pathways to choose, which cultural styles to pursue, we must first ascertain which are possible. Conjecture, speculation and the visionary view thus become as coldly practical a necessity as feet-on-the-floor "realism" was in an earlier time.[61]

Perhaps in their original state myths were only impossible wish-fulfillments—dreams, daydreams, and desires; yearnings for a higher reality and a more perfect and incorruptible existence or fears about a more horrifying one (Northrop Frye's "outer limits of Heaven and Hell"). But modern science fiction demonstrates that at least some of the estranged territory between reality and dream can be explored cognitively. Modern man can speculate on those mythical dreams and nightmares. At minimum he can gain a critical self-knowledge, specifically about the range, limits, and history of his own mental products and processes. More importantly, myths can lend a direction and purpose to the more organized, "scientific" facet of his intellect as he questions what is most desirable or dreadful in his potential future. We can still count on myths and their radically estranged contents as an abiding resource of intellectual freedom, as an alternative for the mind when it becomes too preoccupied with other ways of thinking and comes to the one-dimensional belief that narrow, specialized research is the only worthwhile universe of discourse. The old myths still remain a viable mode of energizing and organizing our thoughts toward an as yet unrealized potential in man. In Ray Bradbury's poetic words, "fact circling dream and dream circling fact, Man, not the one thing but many, will continue his journey out of the Garden, on his way to becoming a thing he cannot now name nor know nor guess, but only wish upon."[62] But this vision of Creation carries us over to the next chapter.

3 The Big Time

With justification, writers, fans, and academic critics have referred to science fiction as a new mythology because it does share some features with all varieties of myths, even the most archaic ones. Like every other mythology, SF asks ultimate questions about the limits of humanity and all the imaginative extensions of humanity to the conceivable ends of time and space. Speculations of this order still demand the full resources of our imaginative capacities, from dream and nightmare and wish-fulfillment, as well as their more formal systematizations in myth, religion, and theology.

In a sense, all SF and fantasy narratives are related to cosmological genesis. Insofar as SF and fantasy require that the imaginative writer conceive of other worlds, alternative to our own "real" one, they also presuppose a visionary dimension that encompasses that new world as a total creation. In his four-volume *Masks of God* Joseph Campbell continually refers to one of the four basic functions of myth as "the rendering of a cosmology"; that is, all myth-making involves the creation of a totally structured and ordered world-picture. Creation stories in the narrow sense, like Hesiod's *Theogony*, the Babylonian *Enuma Elish*, or the Old Testament Book of Genesis, of course, expose this dimension of myth explicitly and purposefully. But all myths presuppose some degree of world-creation, for when we encounter a myth-world we expect it to be a world radically different from the one we inhabit in our normal lives and we get distinct feelings of "otherworldliness" when we enter, in our imaginations, a myth-world.

However, even though SF asks the same questions as myth about the beginnings and ends of our race, our world, finally our entire universe, it identifies and confirms the mythopoeic qualities of the speculations of modern science. Although the two dimensions of myth and science, of vision and cognition, are certainly variables, many critics have argued that the most convincing and significant SF successfully uses well-researched and carefully structured insights of science to fill in the conceptual ground between our world and that new, altered world envisioned by the SF writer. It is not necessary for SF to reproduce any particular research or speculation of modern science (though it may certainly do so), but we do expect SF to assume science's ways of looking at reality—and at knowledge itself, the greatest cause of change in our understanding. All the "geneses" of science fiction are typically intellective (Ketterer's "worlds of mind") and point to the intimate connection between consciousness and cosmology.

In modern SF, consequently, cosmology transcends history, and this transcendence is to be taken as an act of intellection, an apocalyptic transformation in consciousness. For the basic critical concerns of this chapter, one narrative is particularly representative; its title is the chapter title. In *The Big Time*, myth, dream, the supernatural, and the afterlife are all indistinguishable and undifferentiated from one another and constitute a mode of transcending the real facts of human history with cosmic-scale consciousness. The tragedy of war and the destruction of civilizations here assume an opposite, optimistic meaning because the *possible* is a fantastically greater universe than the actual.

In the Hugo-Award-winning novel of 1958,[1] *The Big Time*, Fritz Leiber pictures a transcendental bar-lounge outside conventional space-time where a number of superbeings who have escaped natural time-binding party and rest up from their participation in the Change-War. This "war" is conducted up and down the line of Time by altering the events of the human history we know and creating in its place any number of alternative possible histories. The scale of

The Big Time

operations is cosmic in its proportions: ". . . the Spiders are conducting operations on billions, trillions of planets and inhabited gas clouds through millions of ages. . ." (p. 84).

The Change-War involves the Spiders and the Snakes, two super-races who are also called "Demons" and who can range at will throughout time and space, within or without the normal human cosmos. Demons, in turn, are men who have been taken up into a higher state of evolution through the process of Resurrection (which the Spider high command calls "Recruitment"). Instead of being time-binders (those who unify temporal events through memory) as they were earlier in their merely human existence, "Demons . . . are possibility-binders—they can make all of what might be part of what is, and that is their evolutionary function. Resurrection is like the metamorphosis of a caterpillar into a butterfly: a third-order being breaks out of the chrysalis of its lifeline into fourth-order life. . . . The Change World is the core of meaning behind the many myths of immortality" (p. 168). Leiber further specifies that Adam, Eve, Lilith, and Cain were the first Demons, because he regards mythological beings as humanity's oldest means of conceiving *the possible*.

This evolutionary scheme is also a metaphor for growth in consciousness since evolution through Resurrection really belongs to the order of *mind* and is a mental awakening to a higher reality: "All fourth-order beings [i.e., Demons] live inside and outside all minds, throughout the whole cosmos. Even this Place is, after its fashion, a giant brain: its floor is the Brainpan, the boundary of the Void is the cortex of gray matter" (pp. 168–69). Inner and Outer space are mutually interpenetrated; human evolution to the far reaches of cosmic time and space involves an evolution of imagination, an extension of the inner cosmos of the mind.

In this concentration on the Big Time as the source of an evolution in imaginative terms—however appropriate this connection—we must not lose track of Leiber's central image, the Big Time as party, as much revel as revelation ("The Big Time isn't the little time"). Leiber develops this second sense for his title when he sets his narrative totally in the Place, a Spider way-station and center for recreation and recuperation. The Place is simply a timeless night club on the edge of the Void, where Soldiers and Entertainers have one endless hell-of-a-good-time drinking, making love, brawling, dueling, and philosophizing. Like the *Odyssey*, *The Big Time* is a cosmic comedy.

Superadded to this remarkable vision of Eternity are the bizarre characters who frequent the Place: a Nazi soldier, a Roman legionary, a British poet who died in World War One, a female warrior who fought for the Great Mother in prehistoric Crete, a barkeep from Shakespearian London, and a Red Cross girl. The sweep of *The Big Time* even includes two extraterrestrials, one from a billion years in the future, one from a billion years in the past—the outer limits of the finite scale of time. This cosmology of possibility has room for everybody. The first-person narrator, in fact, proves the point comically: she was a Hoosier, and if someone from Indiana can make it to the Big Time, anybody can; now she's the "hostess" of the Place. Leiber's optimistic cosmology evokes the supernatural, dream, myths; it is cognitively solid in its overall sense of world history and in particular details.

Imaginative transcendence of presently conceived cosmological limitations has a long history in Western culture, and it is a theme which is as common to, say, pre-Socratic philosophy, Platonic mythology, and Judeo-Christian eschatology as it is to SF.[2] Though SF is certainly not dominated by any one orthodox creed or belief, it expresses a thirst—very old and widespread among human beings—for election to, and understanding of, a higher state of power, existence, or consciousness. The urge to "get to heaven" and participate in eternity thus remains a powerful one with roots in the mythico-religious ideas of pre-Christian antiquity.

Though the sources and modality of the otherworldliness of SF are typically described as "cognitive," if not specifically "scientific," yet the creation of a science-fiction universe implicitly involves the writer in myth-making of the cosmological sort. Like myth, SF attempts to depict an alternative world at some remove from our own in space or time or both and involving some radical transformation of it. In his *New Worlds For Old*, a study of SF as "apocalyptic" literature, David Ketterer develops cosmological imagery into a critical metaphor for SF as a whole:

> The destruction of an old world, generally of mind, is set against the writer's establishment of a new world, again generally of mind. . . .

The Big Time

> Apocalyptic literature is concerned with the creation of other worlds which exist, on the literal level, in a credible relationship (whether on the basis of rational extrapolation and analogy or of religious belief) with the "real" world, thereby causing a metaphorical destruction of that "real" world, in the reader's head. The apocalyptic imagination may finally be defined in terms of its philosophical preoccupation with that moment of juxtaposition and consequent transformation or transfiguration when an old world of mind discovers a believable new world of mind, which either nullifies and destroys the old system entirely or, less likely, makes it part of a larger design.[3]

The cosmological metaphors of world-destruction and world-creation are unmistakable in Ketterer's formulation. J. R. R. Tolkien proposed much the same view for fantasy literature in his famous critical essay, "On Fairy-Stories," referring to the art of "sub-creation" in the rendering of "secondary worlds."[4] In modern SF and fantasy, each writer is the author of his own Genesis, one that alters our previous conception of Creation.

In terms of the overall project of developing a modern consciousness (noted by Scholes and Rabkin), SF has contributed greatly in an area where science proper has become progressively more esoteric and opaque to all but an elite few, and it is clearly an area where other kinds of fiction have had less to say.[5] The cosmological dimension has not proved very important in mainstream literature whereas it is essential to SF.

Once again Mary Shelley has to be credited as the creator of a new fictional genre. Her long novel, *The Last Man* (1826), though less successful and famous than *Frankenstein*, is still the seminal example of the "world-catastrophe" story, a type now known everywhere.[6] Like *Frankenstein*, this novel seems another transmutation of Gothic, emphasizing the isolation and loneliness of the last man. Romantic politics and characters are projected almost allegorically onto the twenty-first century, when a plague ultimately wipes out humanity. Shelley's idea of world cataclysm was more significant than her portrait of the future, and it was left to H. G. Wells to completely identify the mythic potential of world-end with a plausible and convincing scientific/empirical account of such a dramatic event. *The Time Machine* is well known and is as popular today as any narrative ever produced in all the history of SF.

The Time Machine (1895)[7] produced a temporal extrapolation on a scale previously unrealized, from the present to the far future where the world is dying and man as we know him has disappeared. As J.O. Bailey has noted, the work was also important for its literary exploration of the science-fiction device of time travel and was *the* seminal novel on this theme. *The Time Machine* brought "a cosmic perspective to science fiction; and [the book] dealt with *areas of imagination* that properly belong to no other kinds of fiction."[8] The whole field of imaginative play was greatly enlarged from then on.

Above all, *The Time Machine* raises haunting questions about the identity of *Homo sapiens* when the fate of the species is considered in a cosmological framework. Here we deal not with the traditional religious issue of individual mortality, nor with the mortality of the human race as determined by a personal God, but with the end of both man and Earth as determined by the theory of evolution and an *impersonal* physical law of *entropy*:

> *The Time Machine* is not about a lost Eden; it is—passionately and tragically—about the Three Laws of Thermodynamics, especially the second. The slow cooling of the sun in "the Farther Vision" foreshadows the heat-death of the universe. In fact, the novella is a series of deaths; individual death (as exemplified by Weena's presumed death and the threat to the Time Traveler himself from the Morlocks) is bad enough; the "wilderness of rotting paper" in the Palace of Green Porcelain, and abandoned museum, is perhaps worse; the complete disappearance of mind in humanity's remote descendants (the kangaroo-like animals) is horrible; but the death of absolutely everything, the physical degradation of the entire universe, is a Götterdammerung earlier views of the nature of the universe could hardly conceive—let alone prove. As the Time Traveler says after leaving "that remote and awful twilight," "I'm sorry to have brought you out here in the cold."[9]

Since the Copernican revolution in astronomy in the sixteenth century, humanity's continually expanding sense of physical time and space has led to widespread anxiety and insecurity. For this reason, the most significant myth in *The Time Machine* is that of the Sphinx. In the original Greek legend, this monster, part-lion/part-human, asked the Theban hero Oedipus a riddle whose answer was "man." When Wells's time-traveler reaches the world of the Eloi and Morlocks over 800,000 years in the future, he parks his machine beside a gigantic Sphinx monument: the Morlocks at one point in the story steal the machine and hide it inside the Sphinx. The Sphinx is the conjunction of the upper world of the childlike, but helpless, Eloi and the subterranean world of the degenerate, cannibalistic Morlocks; it is equally the conjunction along the time axis of the future and the past as embodied in the time-traveler himself. All along Wells poses the question, "what is man?"—are either of the degenerate future races "human"?[10] The Morlocks suggest retrograde evolution to the simian subhuman, the Eloi a betrayed Garden of Eden. Played out on the scale depicted by Wells, "man" is itself the twentieth century's riddle of the Sphinx and not the answer to her question as it was in the ancient legend.

The time-travel device allowed Wells to redefine Social Darwinism and the theory of evolution in terms of the far reaches of the cosmic perspective. Since *The Time Machine* it has remained common and popular in SF to juxtapose the scale of humanity (and the limited range of our species' existence) against the much greater magnitudes of the cosmic scale. The incommensurability between the two orders of magnitude often produces an ironic perspective on the human race.

However, the tragic entropy hypothesis projected by Wells isn't uniquely the cosmology of modern SF. Here we have the opportunity to contrast Wells's idea with that of Frenchman Jules Verne, who is often regarded as the other influential writer of "scientific romances" anticipating the twentieth century Anglo-American genre. Usually we identify Verne with near-future predictive fiction and not with large mythic issues. But at least in the case of this one important work, our understanding of human nature is altered apocalyptically by a new temporal framework that is cyclical in character, cosmic in scope. That is, time on the largest scale moves eternally in cyclical patterns, which Mircea Eliade has called "The Myth of the Eternal Return," though humans in their more limited viewpoint may think it moves otherwise.

In "The Eternal Adam" (1905),[11] Jules Verne's last story (as far as is known) and perhaps his best short tale, both the Biblical myth of man's origin in Genesis and the modern myth of progress are treated ironically by being placed in the context of a cyclical cosmology. Social Darwinists and historicist philosophers disclose the nineteenth century's naïve belief in the inevitability of progress as a law of nature. In discrediting this view, Verne seems to have been influenced by the growing skepticism over scientific rationalism and its corollary, technological "progress," which had received its classic and mythic formulation in Mary Shelley's *Frankenstein*. Another of Verne's later creations, the evil scientist-villain, "Robur the Conqueror," was also a Frankensteinian creator.

Verne envisions earth in the future, twenty thousand years after a deluge has wiped out all known land masses and thrust up only one new continent from the ocean's depths where the scant remnants of mankind had gathered and begun history all over again. After aeons of ignorance, savagery, and warfare, the continent has finally achieved an industrial age culture comparable to our own at the beginning of this century. The scientist Sofr, an optimistic believer in scientific progress, formulates a theory of evolution and proves his case with evidence drawn from the brand-new sciences of paleontology, geology, biology, and botany, though the general masses remain content with their myths and legends: "Explaining one mystery by another mystery, they traced the origin of man back to the interference of what they called a Higher Will. One day, this unearthly Power had created out of nothing, and for no apparent reason, *Hedom* and *Hiva,* the first man and first woman, whose descendants had peopled this world."

Yet Sofr uncovers an even more startling version of the truth than his scientific one when his archaeological excavations uncover a manuscript written by one twentieth-century survivor of the Deluge who explains the entire story of the end of his world. Here Verne adds an ironic leitmotif: the catastrophe occurs precisely at a moment when the narrator and his friends are arguing the question of social and scientific progress in the enlightened world of the new twentieth century. The narrator, a proponent of Darwinian evolution, is, like Sofr, a believer in modern man's mystique of progress: "We joined in composing a genuine dithyramb to Progress, and I confess to contributing my share. We were agreed on the point that humanity had reached an intellectual peak unknown before our era, and that we were authorized to believe in our eventual victory over nature."

Opposition stems from Mendoza, not only a believer in God and the Edenic version of the creation of man, but one who appeals to a succession of ages in which cultures—Lost Atlantis being a case in point—had reached tremendous intellectual and technological heights only to be overwhelmed by the forces of nature so that man had to start all over again with an Adamic *tabula rasa*.

Then, of course, Nature strikes, and our world ends. Rescued by the only surviving ship, the last men wander the faceless oceanic world for months before locating the new continent that has emerged. Its ruins reveal that it is indeed none other than the Atlantis that had sunk ages ago.

Sofr, both enlightened and terror-struck by the pre-diluvian testimony, no longer allows himself a simple-minded assumption of unchallenged human progress and ascendancy over nature: "Hedom, Eddem, Adam: here was the perpetual symbol of the first man—but it stood likewise for mankind's successive reappearances on earth. . . . The Truth would prove to be the endless ordeal of regeneration." Progress is a *cultural* process that takes place within the rhythms of human time and the human imagination, and it simply is not the same thing as the natural Law of Evolution.[12] "The true superiority of man lies not in dominating or vanquishing nature. Rather, for the reflective man, it lies in comprehending, in containing, the immense universe in the microcosm of his mind." Verne tells us cosmology is a significant form of consciousness because cosmology is the ultimate yardstick against which human activity will be judged; the myth of progress is subject to a severely limited human perception.

As a title, "The Eternal Adam" suggests a new cosmic context—the cyclical myth of the Eternal Return—for the Biblical story of the first man, thereby altering the significance of both an old and a new myth of mankind's place in universe-time. Unlike Wells's *Time Machine,* whose overall speculations carefully conformed to the best contemporary science, Verne's cosmology is completely fantastic, especially in its Atlantean formulations, and its main cognitive dimension lies in its critique of the myth of progress.

This cyclical image of cosmic time is a very basic, even archetypal one which at the least goes as far back as ancient Greek philosophers like Empedocles and Plato. The original Atlantis, imagined by Plato, was subject to a cyclical pattern of the rise and fall of human civilizations. The individual species or society meets extinction, but underneath the catastrophe there remains a comforting and reassuring image of the rebirth of a new society/civilization and a new, or "renewed," humanity.

Without doubt, the Atlantean "lost continent" formula or the Norse Ragnarok are archaic, but cyclical cosmologies with stronger cognitive and astronomical appeal have not been lacking in twentieth century American and British SF. Famous narratives might include Isaac Asimov's "Nightfall" (1941; published in Silverberg's *SF Hall of Fame I*); Walter M. Miller's *A Canticle for Leibowitz* (1959); James Blish's *Cities in Flight* (1969); and the New Wave short stories of J. G. Ballard's *Voices of Time* (1962). In chapter 1 we already observed the obsession with loops and cycles in Tenn's *Medusa,* Harness's "New Reality," and Heinlein's "All You Zombies"; and cyclical cosmologies with a death-rebirth pattern can be expected to turn up commonly. A recent astronomical show at the Adler Planetarium in Chicago, in fact, portrays the entire history of the known cosmos from beginning to end (using the "Big Bang" theory of an expanding universe), only to speculate finally on the rebirth of a new universe out of the death of our own.

At the other end of the literary spectrum covered by imaginative literature lies the genre of fantasy, whose hypotheses are impossible by any but the most fantastic assumptions. Here, too, the cosmic scale is significant and endemic, but it is important to distinguish fantasy's more heavily fantastic appeal to myth from SF narratives like Wells's and Verne's. One exemplary work especially offers revealing comparisons and contrasts: like "The Eternal Adam," it uses an archaic, specifically anachronistic, and mythic world-view; but like *The Time Machine,* the story contains a solidly presented scientific speculation with world-shattering implications. Like both earlier SF authors, the author of this fantasy story places the scientific theory of evolution in a new, ironic context that entirely alters its meaning, and the mythological cosmology is presented as a large-magnitude structure that completely transforms the meaning of human history and civilization.

Eden Phillpotts's novella *The Miniature* (1926) is a satirical mythological fantasia recently rescued from long and undeserved obscurity by anthology editor Lin Carter (who included it in *Discoveries in Fantasy,* Ballantine Books, 1972).[13] The title refers to mankind as viewed from the majestic perspective of the Olympian gods of ancient Greek mythology. Phillpotts derived his basic theme specifically from Homer himself, in the *Iliad*, where the ancient poet continually underscores the distinction between gods and men. Serenity and immortality characterize the former, whereas the human heroes who people the epic are bound over to suffering and inescapable mortality. As the Greek scholar Hugh Lloyd-Jones has remarked on the contrast: "Between men and gods there is no comparison in point of beauty, happiness and power. The gods live forever, and meet with little but good fortune; men meet with nothing but ill fortune or at best are given a mixed lot; . . . the gods look on men with disdain mingled with slight pity."[14]

To entertain his fellow Olympians, Zeus places on earth the "seed" for a race of beings who are miniature likenesses of the gods themselves. As quarrelsome, brilliant, and beautiful as Homer depicted them, the gods visit earth from time to time to observe human evolution, from the era of the first anthropoids, through the Paleolithic and Neolithic periods (note the scientific format here), to the Golden Age of Man, the era of the Greek myths and heroic legends. In the Golden Age the gods move frequently and freely among men, meddle in their affairs, often mate with them, and in general foster this most vital and creative period of mankind's history—the only era according to Phillpotts's interpretation in which men recognize the gods for what they really are and yet do not overlook the limitations of their own ephemeral human nature. After this, degeneration sets in; men turn to false gods like Jahweh of the Hebrews and Christians, then to agnosticism, and finally to modern scientific rationalism. The Olympians become progressively more displeased and bored as men try to believe they are immortal or otherwise made in the image of their false gods and anti-gods.

So human evolution ends as it began, as an entertainment for the gods, and Zeus invites his children out on the heavenly veranda to watch the final scenario, the extinction of man, just one cosmic flash in the heavens when man cataclysmically destroys his own world by splitting the atom. Mankind, although it was created in the image of the gods, is too circumscribed by its own minuscule dimensions to see the cynical truth of its own miniature origins and miniature destiny.

An additional irony that permeates the story is Phillpotts's handling of Darwin's theory of evolution. Rather than reject it or overlook it, Phillpotts places it in a new fantastic context that radically alters its significance. After the "seed" is planted, man does develop in the evolutionary way, but even the Darwinian theory is only a temporal miniature, a limited interpretation of man's origins and destiny that is swallowed up in the divine scale of reality. The pagan Greek gods are thus used by Phillpotts as a didactic warning in the Frankensteinian tradition that humans should be aware of their own limits in the face of potential scientific realities like atomic power— this warning, of course, was written nearly twenty years before Hiroshima, but nearly forty years after Hiroshima we are no more confident about our ability to control nuclear weapons and nuclear power and a major debate is still building in our society as of this writing. Phillpotts's Homeric mythology may only be playful and funny theology, but fear of what men might do without a critical sense of their own nature is anything but dated.

So far we have ranged broadly over the first hundred years of the history of modern SF, but it remained for writers on both sides of the Atlantic in the innovative 1930s to fix the twin mythical emphases in Wells's cosmic vision: (1) an "origin of species" transposed, in reverse temporal order, on the future—the end of man; and (2) a Genesis-in-reverse for the entire universe—an end to time (entropy) or an end with a new beginning (death-rebirth cycle). Further, these writers managed to develop Wells's cosmic-scale vision into a complex and elaborate "future history" of the universe. What was earlier a grand vision now emerges as an entire system.

Donald Wollheim, editor of the first paperback anthology of SF, who is known now for the DAW Books series, wrote a popular fan history entitled *The Universe Makers,* in which he tried to reproduce the composite results from many writers in an 8-stage "consensus" Future History: (1) man reaches the other worlds of this solar system; (2) man breaks through to the stars; (3) the rise of the galactic empire; (4) galactic empire in full maturity; (5) decline and fall of galactic empire; (6) interregnum; (7) rebirth, resurrection of galactic civilization; (8) challenge to God—merging with divine impulse behind all creation or the end of all time. Rebirth, Recreation?[15]

On the British side, Sam Moskowitz has singled out the two science-fiction cosmologies of Olaf Stapledon, *Last and First Men*

(1931) and *Star Maker* (1937) as epoch-making.[16] *Last and First Men* is a futuristic version of the "Ages of Man" myth, exemplified in Hesiod's *Works and Days,* an ancient Greek didactic poem of the seventh century B.C. Stapledon imagines eighteen distinct species of humanity, ultimately ending his tale nearly a billion years in the future where men have finally migrated to Neptune and the extinction of the race seems certain. The technique is to start out fairly close to the contemporary world and its history (the "zero world") and then move progressively to larger and larger scales of time in the distant future. Thus the later races, though comprising by far the larger time-space, receive the least detailed descriptions, and their fate is treated more and more cursorily. Brian Aldiss in mock horror has called these two novels of Stapledon's "the holy writ of SF," while Robert Scholes has described them as paradigms of modern SF, a kind of "perfect" SF which can be equalled but not really bettered.[17] Both critics have fairly observed a "coldness" in Stapledon's visions; like Wells he did dispassionately question the fate of intelligence and intelligent life in a universe whose ultimate extinction seemed certain. No one, not even Wells, thought out the problem of the end of man so thoroughly on so extended a temporal range as Stapledon.

The theme of imaginative awakening to cosmic-scale consciousness must receive its most thorough exploration in the breathless mind-travelling odyssey of the first-person narrator in Stapledon's *Star Maker.* The speaker first moves from a humble terrestrial perspective to other worlds where he makes contact with, and becomes united with, other minds at once "human" (because they have the powers of conception and self-consciousness) and alien (in origin they are variously mammals, nautiloids, arthropods, plants, and other forms of life). This composite mind then continues to grow in time and space, awakened to ever higher realities, "from the simple individual to the world-mind, and from the world-mind to the galactic mind, and thence to the abortively cosmical...."—abortive because this finite cosmical mind only at its death finally achieves the ultimate vision of fourth-dimension perfection, its Creator the Star Maker, "the eternal and perfect spirit which comprises all things and all times, and contemplates timelessly the infinitely diverse host which it comprises."[18] Finite and infinite are finally envisioned as mutually harmonious aspects of the one and same eternity.

In America, the thirties were the time when the SF genre was maturing rapidly in the specialty magazines like *Astounding, Wonder Stories, Amazing,* and *Unknown,* and the cosmology of the future played a great part. With the title of his history of SF, *Billion Year Spree,* Brian Aldiss suggests the presence of a cosmic, mythic dimension to all SF, and he intends the extravagant metaphor of a billion years to apply to the entire modern history of the genre, although he makes it clear that the image of a cosmic "spree" is especially and narrowly applicable to American SF of the thirties: the galactic empires and superscience of E. E. "Doc" Smith, Edmund Hamilton, and John W. Campbell.[19]

Campbell's *The Mightiest Machine* (1935) might be considered a typical representative of this broad subgenre of American SF: futuristic human superscience is brought to bear on a war to extinction in another solar system between another race of humans originally derived from our stock here on earth and the Teff-Hellani, a repulsive race of devil-like beings who also once lived on earth and have been the enemies of humanity from primordial times (myths about devils and demons are our race memory of the Teff-Hellani and the sound of their name conjures up "devils" and "hell"). Campbell uses a version of the Atlantis myth and the race-memory theory of myth: the sinking of the host continent sent the Devils to outer space along with the other half of our human race; in alien sun systems, civilization grew again, so did our alien enemies, and the two human races are reunited against their primeval foes in an all-out battle-to-the-death.[20]

A political interpretation would look to the Depression and the spectre of Fascism to explain some features of this space-opera genre, such as the emphasis on war and extermination of the other side who are identified as "devils," accompanied by power-fantasies justified on the basis of scientific technologies. We should also remember that more recent popular space opera from *Star Trek* to *Star Wars* and *Battlestar Galactica* are equally the descendants of these thirties war-and-power romances, but it's mostly the superscience gadgets and concepts that have remained, while the ideologies have altered.

It is debatable whether John W. Campbell was really as conservative as his reputation today would suggest, but his Arne Munro stories are definitely optimistic war (and war supertechnology) novels, a type of story viewed with distaste by most of today's readers.[21] However, Campbell did produce other narratives which show a more liberal side to his views and which contain fewer anachronistic elements than the space operas. Two famous ones were produced under the pseudonym Don A. Stuart.

Campbell's two classic short stories on entropy are worthy successors to Wells: "Twilight" (*Astounding Stories*, November 1934) is a powerful environmental fable whose cautionary messages are still valid for contemporary readers about a possible future, seven million years hence, where all life forms except humanity have been obliterated; "Night" (*Astounding Stories*, October 1935) goes even further into the future, beyond the extinction of man, where machines go blindly and mindlessly about the tasks set them by a now extinct race, and where all is blackness and cold—a frightening vision of a world where all the energy has been used up and another cautionary fable with contemporary impact.[22]

The cosmic vision and the Future History and the space-opera have remained a key focus in SF and fantasy over the last forty years and it would be hard to identify any of the better known writers of the "classic" years who didn't appeal to the cosmic scale as a mode of imaginative transcendence. It's there in Heinlein, Isaac Asimov, Fredric Brown, and Lester del Rey to a major degree, for example.

However, it seems fair to distinguish British writer and scientist Arthur C. Clarke for a number of reasons: he is widely popular and influential on both sides of the Atlantic; he has a large and various following among intellectuals as well as among SF fandom (two groups that often overlap); and while he is a practicing scientist, myths are an explicit part of his peculiar awareness of the universe—his visions of mankind's extraterrestrial future transcend both conventional science and orthodox religion in the interest of a new imaginative unity. His style is impersonal, and he views man dispassionately in the manner of Wells and Stapledon.

"The Star" originally appeared in *Infinity Science Fiction*, November 1955; it won the Hugo Award for best short story in 1956 and is often reprinted.[23] It describes the end of civilization on another planet, not our own. It is told in first-person narration by a Jesuit astrophysicist aboard a starship investigating a distant sun that ages ago became a nova. It turns out that the quasi-human civilization that was destroyed in the catastrophe did leave detailed records of its culture and history. As the Catholic priest desperately tries to affirm his faith in God and the meaning of the universe in the face of the horrible revelation of a disaster seemingly so arbitrary, the awe-inspiring and perhaps even terrifying coda of the story is that this nova shone brilliantly in our own atmosphere as the famous "star over Bethlehem" as described in the Gospels (Matthew 2:2) when Christ was born.[24] The end of an alien race of intelligent beings was, ironically enough, understood in completely different terms by our own ancestors. Clearly the cosmic dimension involves a transformation in the meaning of a critical event in the history of human self-awareness. This apocalypse (David Ketterer's sense) comes close to being an allegory of the very function of science fiction because the *revolution* in significance that takes place in the priest's head surely must correspond to that in the reader's, and that meaning is purely *secular,* purely *naturalistic.* However, it portends a conversion as great as St. Augustine's, a potential change of faith that Clarke leaves open. Clarke is every bit intelligent about Catholicism as Anthony Boucher, also founds his story on Jesuitical doubt, and always keeps the overall impact *humanistic,* focused on human meanings in the face of so un-human a universe. In Clarke's SF, the more man uses scientific knowledge and investigation to understand the universe, the more he also realizes that in many ways the universe wasn't built for man and that man as he is now constituted is a cosmic anomaly and curiosity.

Another of Clarke's short stories, "The Nine Billion Names of God" (1953),[25] is almost a satire on Western technological consciousness from the Oriental religious consciousness. American technology makes possible a computer program whose read-out completes the religious "program" of Tibetan monks who wish to satisfy the ultimate yearnings for Nirvana, the extinction of the human spirit in the ineffable, by exhausting the nine billion names of God; the program succeeds, the divine essence is totally described in reciting the list of names—and the stars begin to wink out because it is the end of the world.

We know that all logical entities (names of God or prayers included) can be multiplied indefinitely, so the computer program

The Big Time [81]

would have to go on infinitely, and the central hypothesis of the story is impossible and illogical. But the tale does slyly inculcate a respect for the ideas of Eastern humanity. Clarke's protagonists, two Americans who run the program far up in the Himalayas, are cleverly satirized as interested only in the money they make and the accoutrements of the soft life made possible by modern Western society: their lack of any real moral commitment, scientific curiosity, or any other sign of active intelligence is ironically juxtaposed with the selflessness of the monks who are willing to dedicate their lives to a task 15,000 years long (how long the "program" would take if worked at only by humans and no computer). East definitely understands West better than West understands East: this is made clear in the opening scene of the story, where a lama from the Tibetan monastery is comfortable both with Manhattan and with the science of cybernetics, but the Americans are unable to adapt to the Tibetan world. Besides, there is much to suggest that the end of the stars is a miraculous, optimistic event: in scientific terms, how many novas of distant stars, and how far away in light years, for all their last flickers to reach our eyes on this planet simultaneously?

Clarke appealed to the Jungian collective unconscious in *Childhood's End* (1953) where the alien Overlords are shockingly similar to devils in appearance because their presence on earth means the end of man as we know him, a bit of knowledge we have always carried in our unconscious mind as the fearsome image of Satan.[26] Clarke's narrative does not exactly posit the extinction of man, but a dramatic evolution in which the last generation of *Homo sapiens* joins the cosmic mind.

This conclusion is quite analogous to the destiny of the astronaut at the end of *2001: A Space Odyssey* (novel version, 1968), where he is reborn as a cosmic starchild and this event is evaluated as the next stage of human evolution. In the film version by Stanley Kubrick, no verbal rationales are provided: after a wild light show, followed by a series of aging and time transformations for the astronaut hero, the visual field is filled by a giant baby inside a luminous spherical bubble hovering outside another bright sphere seen in part (Jupiter).[27] This imagistic implication of birth and creation is reinforced by the music, the Creation episode from Richard Strauss's *Also Sprach Zarathustra*. Both *2001* and *Childhood's End* posit a quantum-leap in human psychic evolution well beyond today's normative science, and both openly admit the limits of twentieth-century man, a being not made for the stars as he is now constituted. For Clarke, human evolution is not yet completed but remains an open-ended task.

The cosmic perspective remains as central to the creative vision of science fiction—and its vision of creation—as ever. Not only do contemporary fans, if not all SF readers, feel that this cosmic subgenre is typical of the whole SF genre, but they also think of it as inherently mythical.

For example, even in the works of an author like Isaac Asimov who is a professional scientist and a writer of "hard" SF, the mythic potential becomes unmistakably clear. His important recent novel, *The Gods Themselves* (New York: Doubleday, 1972; winner of the Nebula Award), describes our entropic universe's contact with, and energy exchange with, a counter-entropic universe in another time-space. In this other cosmos there exists a larval form consisting of three distinct sexual beings: a left, middle, and right; respectively, a material, a passionate, and an intellectual component, on the Platonic model of a three-part soul. At adulthood, this triadic creature melts sexually, permanently, into a new unified adult. The plot moves back and forth from our cosmos to that one while scientists on both sides try to prevent the energy exchange from destroying both universes. The solution is found in a "cosmeg-Universe," a cosmic egg which is the source of other universes. This image of an egg for the birth of the universe is extremely ancient, going back through Greece (e.g., the Orphics) to the theology of the priests at Hermopolis in Egypt.[28]

Consciouness-altering, mythically transforming, the cosmic vision turns up everywhere in the long, rich history of SF: it is there in works of solid "scientific" speculation (Wells, Asimov) as well as in completely fantastic depictions (like Phillpotts and space opera). The very presence and popularity of so rich a field of narratives indicate how tellingly the theory of evolution and our ever increasing knowledge of an expanded universe have affected twentieth-century humanity's self-awareness, its awareness of the interdependence of all humans, and its previous unawareness of human interdependence with the non-human biosphere of this planet. Our new, transformed sense of "outer space" continues to alter the landscape of "inner space."

The Big Time

Finally, it is important to note that the visions of contemporary SF are often optimistic and counter-entropic, like Leiber's *Big Time* or Isaac Asimov's *Gods* or Clarke's *2001:* somehow the human mind will grow/evolve/expand and locate a powerful rebirth to outwit universal death and the end of time. I have therefore chosen to conclude this third chapter with an important contemporary work that reveals a solid, close understanding of the SF genre and is an optimistic reply to Wells, Stapledon, and even Clarke. The subtle use of Homeric mythology, in contrast with Phillpotts's explicitness, makes the latter's technique seem both too direct and too simple.

The *Dies Irae* trilogy (all three volumes published in 1971 by Ace Books) of Britisher Brian M. Stableford is an imaginative summation of the traditions begun in the Thirties and reveals both sides of the tradition superbly: the philosophical vision of Stapledon is played off against the action-warfare style of John W. Campbell. This is a grand and sophisticated space opera in a "New Wave" vein.

Stableford's trilogy explores the cosmological dimension of time and space through an imaginative and sophisticated rewriting of Homer. However, "rewriting" must here be taken in a very special sense because Stableford's appeal to Homer involves displacements. With one exception (Calypso in the second volume) none of the characters bear the names of their Homeric prototypes, and the third volume of the trilogy abandons its Homeric mold entirely and develops the strictly SF implications of the first two volumes. Even with these provisos, the trilogy is a paradigm of the mythological SF novel of the seventies.

Stableford fires off an allusion to the first line of the *Iliad* ("the anger of Achilles") in the very first paragraph (entitled "theme") of *The Days of Glory:* "This book tells the story of the anger of Richard Stormwind and its consequences." So begins Stableford's *Iliad,* which chronicles the causes of the galactic war between Beasts ("Achaeans") and Men ("Trojans"), two races of humans that are really more alike than different, yet are provoked to all-out war through the passions of the great heroes on both sides. Readers vary in their reaction to subtle, displaced allusions to earlier "classics" and, depending on their acquaintance with the Homeric original, some may or may not identify Homeric prototypes for the main heroes: Stableford does not reproduce the original Greek names, though the prototypes are always obvious; instead, the names of violent lords of Beasts and

Men always crackle with the names of the elements, creatures, and forces of nature in their simplest direct Anglo-Saxon: Stormwind–Achilles; Eagleheart–Agamemnon; Deathdancer–Diomedes; Blackstar–Hector; Mark Chaos–Odysseus; Slavesdream–Patroclus.

But since the *personalities and passions* of the heroes are most important, the names are near-allegories in many cases. "Eagleheart" best describes the gnawing visionary ambitions of the chief beast leader, passionate rather than calculating by nature; "Stormwind" not only denotes the awesome physical prowess and capacities of the greatest Beast warrior, but also the unfortunate vanity that undermines his intellect; "Slavesdream" points to the tragic surrogate existence lived out by the Patroclus-figure: who in his finest hour is only a mimesis of his stronger friend, and of course that hour leads to both their deaths; all the members of the ruling house on Home are "stars" in the seventies' sense of the winning and ruling elite of our culture, though Blackstar's name clearly marks out his ill fate in the war. The nomenclature in this trilogy is one of its finest touches, and Stableford is equal to the best SF writers in this regard.

With minor exceptions, the basic story is also the story of the *Iliad:* offended by Eagleheart, Stormwind withdraws from the Beast war, causing his shadowy alter ego, Slavesdream (Patroclus), to fight in his stead in order to save the Beast fleet; when Blackstar kills Slavesdream, Stormwind re-enters the conflict and destroys the Human leader before he himself is killed by Starbird. Whole scenes, too, are based on Homeric precursors: the inconclusive duel between Skywolf and Starbird recapitulates that between Menelaus and Paris in the *Iliad;* the wrestling match between Hornwing (Ajax) and Blackstar, the final contest between Stormwind and Blackstar, and the battle fury of Deathdancer are similar cases in point.

However, with the plot as with the characters, Stableford does much more than simply imitate Homer. His plotting is complex and New Wave: the narrative is broken up into a large number of very short chapters (one to five pages); some tell events in third-person past-tense narration, but the others size up the personalities of the heroes in third-person *present-tense* narration. The contexts of time and place are always considered, and every character in this fictive cosmic history is constantly re-evaluated from a relative frame of reference: later events, in another place, may dictate that an earlier good act or person may turn out to have evil consequences, and vice versa. Ultimately, these individual human personalities will affect the history of an entire galaxy.

The Homeric world is also transcended in the graphic descriptions of violence and death by fantastic means that are, happily, not yet possible in present time. There is more than just your Buck Rogers ray-gun stuff in *Dies Irae:* the weapon, in a detailed description, burns away a young human woman's face as the first act of brutal racial violence which commences the war. In the climactic combat scene of the first novel, Stormwind and Blackstar rip and tear one another with steel-clawed dueling gloves: halfway through the fight Blackstar is completely blinded and must blunder his way to death. In the final volume of the trilogy, one follows the progressive dismemberment of Judson Deathdancer as he struggles to save his warship from the Toys: he too becomes the burned-flesh victim of a blaster. The violence is individual and pathetic, yet somehow just as unreal as the formulaic descriptions in the Homeric original.

If in Homer the theft of a woman and misguided human passions like pride, vanity, jealousy, and hatred could ultimately lead to the destruction of a powerful city and to the extermination of the entire population of Troy and the house of Priam, then in Stableford this entire process is viewed anew from a cosmological perspective. Every emotion, every "human" act, becomes far more significant in its scale and will ultimately bring about the collapse of a galactic civilization that has endured for ten thousand years with two races co-existing peacefully. For in almost all respects the Beasts are only men, although they were in origin artificially created from the flesh of animals to further the Human project of colonizing the stars. Thus it is the root passions of heroes, Human and Beasts alike, that alter the history of an entire galaxy—Stormwind's anger, Eagleheart's lust for conquest, Starbird's refusal to give up a woman not rightfully his. It all begins with issues of individual honor and racial pride; it was to be a limited war fought only for glory—but even twisted human feelings have consequences far more drastic, for it will turn out that more than twenty thousand years of Human-Beast history will take a new turn with the death of Alexander Blackstar. When the House of Stars is exterminated and the Human race is nearly annihilated, too, the galactic empire falls to the Beast lords, and the Kingdom of the Beasts begins.

There have been any number of literary narratives, from

Phillpotts's "The Miniature" to Anthony Burgess's anti-war novel, *A Vision of Battlements*, that use Homeric prefigurations. Stableford is unique in modern fiction for attempting a rewrite of the original on an epic scale, yet within that enlarged magnification of scale he keeps a Homeric interpretation of human nature. "It is not simply that Stableford is borrowing from Greek epics, but that he is *writing* them—as the Greeks would have known them: heroic, stately, noble, filled with a grandeur that modern realism cannot grasp. And this is something that is not being done by any other writer today."[29]

In the Kingdom of the Beasts is Stableford's *Odyssey*; it traces the wanderings of Mark Chaos after the fall of the Human empire, though the plot of this second novel is not so close to the original Homer as *The Days of Glory* was. The hero's physical homeward journey is also a symbolic and psychological quest, for "home" means the recovery of his memories and the recognition of an identity that had eluded him his whole life. Most of the narration takes place in the first person; Chaos recounts his adventures to his rescuer, Yvaine (the Nausicaä of this *Odyssey*), as a therapeutic means of recovering the personality he had misplaced while out wandering among the stars. Yet his psychological restoration necessarily involves the revelation that he is not the same man he was but an initiate who is born anew: "He was a different man, a new man" (p. 187). Chaos's initiation is, in fact, cosmological in dimension, and the success of his journey has as much to do with the cosmological order of reality as it does with the psychological, for his wanderings lead up to a climax where his previously limited mind can experience hyperspace, the higher order of magnitude in time and space in which the galaxy exists. Chaos is reborn with cosmic consciousness, but it gives him no godlike powers or delusions: rather, he has a broader and deeper sympathy for all the humanoids and their myriad worlds. Chaos's *rite du passage* results in ethical maturity.

After the massacre of the House of Stars on Home (Earth), the Beast lords return to their own worlds, but Chaos's fleet gets lost in the Time Gap—a warp in hyperspace caused by the intrusion of a foreign body into our galaxy (this turns out later to be the planet Despair, an interloper from the future and an intelligent being that contacts Chaos in hyperspace). In its stars, the Devil's Tresses, Chaos travels through a wonderland in many ways like the fantastic lands visited by the original Odysseus. Here the hero encounters strange planets, alternate societies, hideous monsters, and captivating women, and finally realizes why the Beast war took place and what agents were behind it. In terms of their powers and activities, these agents appear as mysterious higher beings, but they too are only fallible mortal human beings who in our galaxy are more properly anomalies because they come from ten thousand years in the future, a future which no longer exists because its past has now been altered irrevocably by the Beast war.

The first of these time-manipulators is Heljanita the Toymaker, who loathed the perfect, changeless utopia of his own time and so sapped the total energy of his own world in order to reach the past. Once there, he provoked the Beast war in order to reduce the universe to chaos and prevent the future he escaped from ever coming to pass:

> He looked *through* the machine, and saw a thousand dying suns waning dim red amid the leaden gray skies of a thousand dead planets whose lands were coal black with age and decay. It was his dream, the dreams of Heljanita, architect of dreams. [*Days of Glory*, p. 15]

Heljanita's dream, like the name "Hell" lurking in his name, suggests that he is a mythic underworld figure, a king of the dead who can rule only over the lifeless Toys, an army of metallic automatons he has created. Heljanita also has "the crooked wheel," a hypnotic device in which men can see their own dreams of power and glory and be persuaded wrongly that they can be fulfilled. Heljanita possesses an even more dangerous weapon, Chaos himself, the name symbolizing that he is an agent of galactic chaos, for the real secret of Mark Chaos's identity is that he is a hybrid Beast-Human whose entire past has been manufactured artificially by the Toymaker.

Chaos also meets Heljanita's opponent, Darkscar of Despair, an agent of the future utopia who pursued his enemy into the past only to find the future sealed behind him forever. Darkscar intends to fight the Toymaker and create a utopian paradise in the present galaxy using the remnants of the Beast war—a prospect no more attractive than Heljanita's. Darkscar is another king of the dead who has at least a partial mythological prototype in Hades, king of the Underworld, perhaps ironic for a man from the future. Of mythological relevance is what Chaos experiences because of him: the equivalent of the *Nekuia*, or "visit to the Underworld," in book 11 of the *Odyssey*. Darkscar is "the collector" who gathers the minds of the dead by tapping the Time Wave and projecting their personalities onto metal plates, available for recall at will. Chaos addresses not only his former comrades in the war, but also men dead ten thousand years—Adam December, the Human creator of the first Beasts, and Moonglow of Amia, the Beasts' first great leader and prophet.

The Mark Chaos who finally arrives home is not destined to stay there long because he is now the fully initiated hero, the Cosmic Man, who knows the lost future and how it has meddled in the past, who has spoken to the dead men who made his own civilization, who has survived a vision of hyperspace and communicated with the Being who lives by its trans-human rhythms. Chaos is, after his wanderings, a man of two dimensions, the human and the cosmic, and it will be left to him in the third volume of the trilogy to choose between two alternate realities, Darkscar's stagnant utopia or Heljanita's cruel chaos.

With minor exceptions *Day of Wrath* transcends the Homeric models and is concerned with the resolution of the paradoxical relationship between the two temporal frameworks that Stableford respectively calls "pulse-rotation" time, that of human existence, and "hyperspace," or galactic time, which is beyond human experience until Chaos survives a look into naked hyperspace ("A mind that spanned both space and hyperspace would be a strange mind indeed," p. 71). The initiated mind of Chaos is the focus for the resolution of the human and the cosmic dimensions that have been juxtaposed throughout the trilogy.

At the human level, the action-filled plot of *Day of Wrath* portrays the final battle between Heljanita's army of Toys and Darkscar's allies, the Beast confederacy now joined by the remnant of the Human forces. The two races of men win a surprising victory because of unpredictable ("human") elements beyond the control of the Toys' cybernetic science, especially when a small ghost-fleet commanded by an alternate Stormwind turns up as an equal-and-opposite reaction to all the time-meddlings and then the great warrior runs amok through the Toy fleet before he is taken back into nonexistence.

The Big Time

Chaos ultimately has to kill Darkscar and is about to die with Heljanita before he is saved by Despair (the Toymaker isn't). Strictly *human* history is now back in the hands of the two races of men.

Heljanita's meddling in time has even further fouled up the workings of galactic time, causing a massive distortion in the Time Wave, which brings the Planet Despair to action or, rather, to an equal-and-opposite reaction. A composite mind is formed with Despair as the galactic component, but including four human agents—a passage, by the way, which has a predecessor in one of Henry Kuttner's books, *The Time Axis* (1948). The four are Chaos, the hybrid man who has all along been the center of Human-Beast history, Dawnstar (Stableford's Cassandra), a visionary terrified of her own native ability to see the Time Wave, Adam December, the Human creator, and Moonglow, the Beast civilizer. This Being achieves a vision of the entire galaxy in space (p. 166, in Chaos's eyes): "I saw every world in the galaxy, every continent on every world, every desert and plain, every mountain and river, every ocean and island, every rain cloud and road, every house and tree, every man and every woman.... I could see it all at once, and I could understand all of it, as a single, working entity."

Then Mark Chaos envisions all the alternate possibilities in Time, too—not only Heljanita's world, or Darkscar's, but every manifold potential reality inherent in Time itself. The final choice of just one real set of events in the myriad proliferations of Time is Chaos's, the decision of a man who was always indecisive, yet here Chaos's selection is both perfect and paradoxical: *to do nothing*. In choosing to let happen what did happen, and in refusing to play god, Chaos reasserts the primacy of the human dimension over the cosmic, and he has Despair put the galaxy back together exactly as it was in the instant when time went mad (p. 173). Reminding us of events in the first volume of the trilogy, Chaos accepts what Beast and Human did as *real*.

Though dissatisfied with the human interpretation of the universe, Despair returns Chaos to the human world and to Yvaine. The time distortion ends, and both Beast and Human are left with an open future that need not entail either Heljanita's vision of reality nor Darkscar's.

Clearly this powerful narrative is only a recent one in a long tradition which belies David Ketterer's unqualified assertion that "the cosmic scope of science fiction and the magnitude of the events or phenomena it treats causes the individual human being to shrink from view."[30] On the contrary, the cosmic scope can challenge the individual man to greater feats of competence. The galactic future of man may again require passionate, self-assertive Homeric heroes. No one would dispute that cosmic science fiction *can* belittle the individual, but it simply need not always do so. By casting his grand romance onto a new Heroic Age in the galactic future, Stableford asserts that Homeric man's passion, tragic energy, and willful desire will still be around in our future; and the cosmic-wide, cosmic-consciousness-achieving adventures of Mark Chaos reinforce the confidence that our human minds and spirit are ready for, "up for," the experience. But this question of individual human power and competence is a very controversial one which takes us over to the next chapter, on Heroism.

4. In Defense of Heroic Fantasy

For well over a half century mainstream literature has been dominated by the central fictional concept of the "anti-hero." Northrop Frye identified the "anti-hero" in terms of his *powerlessness* in his environment, which acts as a scene of bondage and a source of frustration of action.[1] The anti-hero is characterized as inferior to the fictive environment of the narrative world, and by extension the anti-hero is also inferior to the "real" world ("zero world"). Frye further characterizes the mode of literature that deals with the anti-hero as "ironic," a term that emphasizes the incongruity between hero/agent and his scene.[2]

Obviously the literature of the anti-hero is quite extensive in mainstream fiction, but one novel published a decade ago is an especially thorough critical and satirical treatment of this overworked literary modality by an academic who had published scholarly work in medieval studies before he became a famous contemporary novelist. This meta-fictional narrative will nicely put the issue of the hero-in-fiction in perspective as a prelude to seeing how SF writers have variously reacted to it.

John C. Gardner's *Grendel* (1971)[3] is a wildly funny parody of the Beowulf legend, told completely in first-person narrative form, this time from the monster's point of view and with his voice. This ironic fable is best regarded as an extension of that type of fiction termed "fabulist" by Robert Scholes.[4] Fabulist narratives point the reader in two directions at once, on the one hand to modernity and contemporaneity—or the contingent aspects of our contemporary life—and on the other, to a more universal and timeless reality, which can be variously termed (depending on the specific author) allegory, fantasy, myth, romance, or epic. The narrative oscillates between the modes of realism and fancy, so the two distort one another for deliberate effect. In works by John Barth, Anthony Burgess, Kurt Vonnegut, J.P. Donleavy, Bruce J. Friedman, Peter De Vries, and Joseph Heller, the dimension of non-realism is a secondary one adumbrated ambiguously and mainly by implication. In Gardner's novel, however, one finds these two frames of reference reversed: the universal and fantastic dimension of myth is explicit and primary, that of modernity implicit, developed for the most part by deliberate anachronisms in the idiom of its characters (linguistic anachronism) and the philosophical issues in the work (thematic anachronism).

Grendel is an existential anti-hero, and through his eyes—those of a creature lost, alone, and turned into a gruesome fiend out of his own loneliness—men appear to be the real monsters. As he remarks about his loathing of man at first sight:

> Some of them had shiny domes (as it seemed to me then) with horns coming out, like the bull's. They were small, these creatures, with dead-looking eyes and gray-white faces, and yet in some ways they were like us, except ridiculous and, at the same time, mysteriously irritating, like rats. [p. 18]

As a corollary to the shift in perspective, what were heroes in *Beowulf* become swinish, drunken thugs in *Grendel* where men are crueler to one another than animals could ever be (p. 27), crueler even than the monster who devours them half in sport. But can we trust what a monster tells us? Isn't he, to borrow a slur from critic Wayne Booth, an "unreliable narrator?" On the one part we can sympathize with the monster's misery, on the other we can't quite accept the monster's black-humor portrait of human beings as fair and accurate. If Grendel is a monster at the primary level of the story as a myth, in the second-order, meta-fictional world of self-conscious narration he is the anti-hero, the hipster anarchist who viciously satirizes his own futile role. In the latter case, he is ambivalently human and of a kind with ourselves.

It is the word "hero" that is most irritating to Grendel, for a poet named Shaper is always singing illusions and altering events to make meaningless and arbitrary acts of stupidity and villainy into ones of glory and valor. Grendel loathes the transformational power of poetic song (p. 9) as much as he does Shaper.

Thus the monster conducts a personal vendetta, lasting twelve horrible years, against the Scyldings and their king Hrothgar, in order to destroy human society and to prove to men that there are no heroes. Grendel, a creature born of torment and chaos, despises the order of human society and aims to show mankind that its every belief, custom, wish, or habit is pure illusion:

> I understood that the world was nothing: a mechanical chaos of casual, brute enmity on which we stupidly impose our hopes and fears. I understood that, finally and absolutely, I alone exist. (p. 16)[5]

Indeed most of the novel is Grendel's pursuit of his nihilistic quest-ideal: his humiliation of the would-be hero, Unferth, in chapter 6, his destruction of the ideal of beauty with his assault on the lovely young queen, Wealtheow, in chapter 7, his ridicule of the priests and their belief in the gods in chapter 9. For Grendel, who was born in a cavern and still lives there with the elemental forces and his gruesome mother, knows that beneath the illusions that men so dearly love there lies only the ineffable, uncomprehending, impersonal Unconscious.

However, there is a world-weary dragon who is momentarily Grendel's teacher and, although he is too much disposed to preach like a modern academic professor of philosophy, he correctly defines the role of the monster as a worthy opponent of man, however much Grendel chooses not to believe him:

> "You improve them, my boy! Can't you see that yourself? You stimulate them! You make them think and scheme. You drive them to poetry, science, religion, all that makes them what they are for as long as they last. You are, so to speak, the brute existent by which they learn to define themselves. The exile, captivity, death they shrink from—the blunt facts of their mortality, their abandonment—that's what you

make them recognize, embrace! You *are* mankind, or man's condition: inseparable as the mountain-climber and the mountain. If you withdraw, you'll instantly be replaced." (p. 62)[6]

The ending of this story which has so much of the atmosphere of black humor about it moves off even further into ambiguity and self-enclosed irony. A "stranger" (who is never named) arrives (chs. 11 and 12), no ordinary man as Grendel comes to admit, for the monster must acknowledge that he has finally encountered an authentic hero who can break his arm and tear it off at the shoulder and, even more important, can make Grendel do what he hates most—sing illusions as Shaper did! (p. 150). The words of the dragon come true, the illusions of men are all the truths that there are and the hero does exist:

Heroism is more than noble language, dignity. Except in the life of the hero the whole world's meaningless. [p. 143; cf. 76 and 77]

If *Grendel* is the ultimate statement of the anti-heroic perspective and of the jaundiced perspective that accompanies it in the monster's outlook on life, then I believe Gardner has taken the concept of anti-hero to the point where it becomes inverted and returns to the original image of herohood. In Grendel's final dismemberment, there is defiance, but also perhaps joy and a sense of belonging ("*Is it joy I feel?*" p. 152). The inverted perspective has been carried to a conclusion where, with Northrop Frye at the end of his essay on irony and satire in *Anatomy of Criticism*, we "pass a dead center, and finally see the gentlemanly Prince of Darkness bottom side up."[7] This myth of an anti-anti-hero ambiguously restores the world of proper heroism, as Grendel knows from the hero's whispering:

Though you murder the world, turn plains to stone, transmogrify life into I and it, strong searching roots will crack your cave and rain will cleanse it: The world will burn green, sperm build again. My promise. Time is the mind, the hand that makes (fingers on harpstrings, hero-swords, the acts, the eyes of queens). By that I kill you. [pp. 149–150]

"Green sperm builds" has implications of a death-rebirth pattern which looks beyond the monster-ruined world of the Scyldings to the second-order, meta-fictional landscape of literature itself where the possibility of heroism is reborn.[8] Gardner himself seems to recognize the paradoxical duality of twentieth-century man's attitude: his need for heroes and for the meaning and structure heroes provide to human experience; and the fatalistic recognition that heroes don't exist anymore, that they are, properly, fantastic and impossible. Grendel remains, after all, a very funny, thought-provoking black-humor novel: we may be waiting for Beowulf to come, but we know for sure that at the moment we're like Grendel!

Obviously, SF has not ignored the anti-heroical consciousness which characterizes twentieth-century man in general: we have already encountered Percy S. Yuss in Tenn's "Medusa" and O/Scar of Heinlein's *Glory Road*. But with the advent of New Wave in the mid-1960s, it could be truly said that SF developed its own literature of the anti-hero and the ironic mode. Moorcock's Karl Glogauer and Ellison's Norman Mogart are convincing, grittily realistic character portraits sketched against a fantastic backdrop. Here again, we might single out one narrative, this time a short story, to typify the New Wave attitude toward heroism.

J.G. Ballard's "The Drowned Giant" (1964)[9] is a masterpiece of understatement. The completely dispassionate tone of the reportage reinforces the complete lack of interest by the other human beings in the story about a remarkable and fantastic event. A drowned giant human being of whale-like dimensions is washed up on the English shore. Now, in our world, this would be something astounding, but the fact, though known at once by all kinds of people, rouses little interest, let alone the incredulity we might have expected (a lot less, in fact, than a beached dying whale would provoke today in the real world).

By far the most interest in the Giant is shown by the first-person narrator, a *librarian* who pursues the story from the beginning to beyond the end. Yet he too evinces but idle curiosity (his library colleagues aren't even interested enough to want to see for themselves; they're happy to delegate the narrator), and when the huge body has finally been dismembered and disposed of piecemeal, the narrator long later follows up reports and tales of the few scattered remnants, not with the intention of doing anything, but as with any scholarly interest. No one ever sees the Giant as a Wonder!

On the one hand, the Giant is likened by the narrator to a denizen out of Greek legend who even in death "still retained his magnificent Homeric stature"; the figure was more exquisite, more beautiful than the normal human, "a more authentic image of one of the drowned Argonauts or heroes of the Odyssey than the conventional human-sized portrait previously in my mind." The narrator continually recalls the graceful lines of the Giant's torso and the delicacy of his features before decay set in.

On the other, there is grim near-humor in the fate of the huge corpse which registers an anatomy of present civilization: most of him ends as fertilizer, but the thigh bones are put up as a gateway, a mummified hand ends up in a carnival float, the jaw goes to a museum, and the penis ends up in a circus novelty act; all in all, he's chopped, burned, stolen, played on — and somehow, through it all, ignored. Northrop Frye associates this ritualistic dismemberment, known by its ancient Greek name *sparagmos*, a "rendering," with the anti-hero and the ironic mode.[10] What happens to the Giant in Ballard's story is a mirror of what has happened to the idea of the hero in modern life and literature. Like Gardner, Ballard identifies the disappearance of the hero with the disappearance of our sense of wonder.

The ironic world-view and anti-heroic consciousness remain dominant in our culture. Science fiction and fantasy have, of course, produced a tremendously broad subgenre where heroism lives on. This narrative type is commonly known as heroic fantasy, and it remains the subject of much controversy among critics and writers alike because it is so often charged with being simple-minded and "escapist." However, in all heroic fantasy the worlds, characters, and events portrayed are supposed to offer a hypothetical contrast with the real world where heroics are known to be incredible, fantastic, and all but impossible: in this kind of fiction, the heroic is self-consciously countercultural and a wish-fulfillment.

Recently Eric Rabkin and W.R. Irvin have written at length on how fantasy narratives react critically to the normative sensibilities of their times and cultures. Fantasy, including heroic fantasy, erects an anti-system to prevalent cultural beliefs and codes, thus questioning their validity and rigidity.[11] In heroic fantasy, the imaginary anti-system to modern life and times is known as the "Heroic Age."

The Heroic Age is a mythical interpretation of time that

presupposes as its most important characteristic a contrast between two eras of mankind. The later, more civilized, socialized, and complex age looks back with nostalgia on the earlier race of men who are believed to have lived in simpler, less civilized times, times which were also more individualistic, adventuresome, and—more brutal. To the imagination of later men, their glorious ancestors were figures larger than life.[12]

> .... heroes are simple men, versed in the activities of common life—hunting, law, farming and cooking; they are leaders not through class status or wealth or even birth, but through the excellencies of heart and mind and hands. Their motives are linked with the practical necessities of life, and they share a tragic view of existence, through which they and the reader are constantly made aware of the instability of earthly things and the inevitability of man's fate.
>
> * * * * * * * * * * * * * *
>
> The world inhabited by the hero is basically a tormented battle ground, a darkling plain in which confused armies clash by night and in which there is no assurance that God has taken sides at all, in which evil must be combatted simply because it is a part of the heroic code to do so, and in which, although the hero may gain a temporary victory, his eventual defeat is both expected and acknowledged.[13]

Two of the most popular and important fantasy authors, E. R. Eddison and J.R.R. Tolkien, depicted exemplary Heroic Ages without resorting to specific ancient myths except for a detail here and there. Their works are therefore best characterized as personal mythologies, taking place in distinctive imaginary universes, but appealing to the idea of a Heroic Age in the abstract. Both authors extrapolated new and contrasting fantasy conceptions which indicate that the Heroic Age is as central to modern imaginative literature as it was to pre-modern epics, sagas, and legends.

E. R. Eddison's *The Worm Ouroboros* (1926)[14] depicts a quasi-medieval heroic age, involved in a decisive world-conflict between the Demons, a race of noble warriors, and their more thaumaturgically gifted opponents, the Witches, themselves no mean fighters. Within this staging of the ultimate war for mutual destruction (indeed the races are as equally matched as the Trojans and the Achaeans in the *Iliad*), a primary narrative focus is a quest myth which transforms the homeward journey of the hero in the fundamental quest myth of our culture, the *Odyssey*: in *Worm*, the three warlords of Demonland must go on a quest to recover their greatest captain, Goldry Bluszco, and deliver him from the Witch-king's powerful enchantment. The work is plotted on a broad, lavish scale and written in a distinctive archaic English that intensifies the fantastic atmosphere of a never-never land where the heroes are too noble to be true.

Perhaps one element that should be singled out is the unique ending that Eddison constructed for his story. The Witches are ruined, their empire destroyed, and their stronghold overthrown by their enemies as drastically as was Homer's Troy. But Eddison does not wish his Heroic Age to end, so he wilfully perpetuates it: Queen Sophonisba pronounces a benediction, and the entire cosmos of Demons and Witches is reborn, fresh for further exotic and splendid combat. The eternal recurrence of this Heroic Age is symbolized by the ouroboros, the world-serpent who binds the planet by biting his own tail and who therefore represents the cyclical eternity of all existence, of death that ever leads to rebirth.[15] If we find fault with Eddison's ending, because it is not commensurate with the preceding story of tragic necessity, at least we cannot miss his meaning, especially since Eddison's own nostalgia for the lost world of heroes has already received enough comment from his critics.[16] For example, under the influence of William Morris, who was also attracted by Scandinavian heroic literature, Eddison composed a historical romance, *Styrbiorn the Strong* (1926), which is set in the Viking Heroic Age of the tenth century; despite the entrance of the god Odin in a supernatural, apocalyptic coda and other mythological lore derived from Snorri Sturluson's *Prose Edda*[17] in the final chapter, "Valhalla," the work is primarily a historical novel. Some few years later, Eddison also published a translation of *Egil's Saga* from the Icelandic (1930). We can also recognize a very famous precedent for Eddison's ending in both the *Prose Edda* and in the "Sybil's Song" from the Old Norse *Poetic Edda* where the All-Father recreates the nine worlds of the known universe after the apocalyptic end of time known as Ragnarok.[18]

The pattern of sacrificial death-and-resurrection in *Worm* equally raises the suggestion of Valhalla, the palace for the Viking heroes who died in combat ("with a sword in their hands"), created by Odin in Asgard: after much feasting and drinking every day the heroes ride out with the king of the gods, to do battle and die, only to be resurrected the next day for more of the same.[19] However, Eddison's characters and his world landscape owe much to Spenser's *Faerie Queene* and other chivalric fantasy, with a touch of the allegory of Bunyan's *Pilgrim's Progress*. His works do not advocate a return to primitivism or barbarism, a charge often made against all heroic fantasy, but an extreme intensity in life coupled with a chivalric moral code, which suggests the literary genres of the idyll and the pastoral as much as epic or saga. Like other modern fantasists, Eddison propounded ideals and ideas so individualistic, personal—and idiosyncratic by contemporary social norms—that his fiction cannot be identified with any recognizable political ideology or program, despite the definite conservative ring to his grand saga.

Eddison's *Worm* is not set in our mythical past but on a fantasized version of the planet Mercury, and this is just one indication of the fantasy writer's greater freedom in manipulating his ideas. Heroic Ages can appear with equal success in the past or the future; in our world, on another planet, or in parallel universes. Ursula K. Le Guin, for example, has depicted a Heroic Age on another planet in our own distant future in *Rocannon's World* (1966), a novel outstanding for its anthropological verisimilitude alone.

Eddison was clearly a man who felt powerless and repressed in the face of the increasing bureaucratization of modern life, and like William Morris before him, he offered his epic fantasy as an imaginative alternative to normative reality, especially in its social and economic relations. Some three decades later, however, the immensely popular J.R.R. Tolkien saw a different threat developing in the mid-twentieth century: the uncontrollable growth of power ideologies and institutions, the unshakable thirst for control and dominance. Tolkien counters with a unique (inverted) version of the heroic quest myth which includes a deep concern for increased environmental sensitivity (see the discussion of the Ents in chapter 2).

In his monumental trilogy, *The Lord of the Rings* (1954),[20] Tolkien describes the imaginary world of Middle Earth, now nearing the close of its Third Age, a period of cataclysmic upheavals as the forces of good and evil prepare for the ultimate clash of arms and test of moral wills. In the midst of an awesome play of magical and preternatural forces, the hero Frodo—an insignificant member of a lowly race, the Hobbits—pursues his quest-in-reverse, trying to throw away and destroy the Great Ring of Power which Sauron, the majestically malevolent Dark Lord, can use to achieve his aims in Middle Earth. Tolkien makes the understated heroism of his humble protagonist very clear when he provides him with a foil in Boromir, a typical human "hero" in the tradition of Homeric and Scandinavian saga—a man of grand passions and an accomplished warrior who is tempted by the power of the Ring and meets his doom. Even Frodo, despite the formal success of his mission, cannot undo the pernicious effect of the Ring on himself, and he is unable to return fully to his former Hobbit nature. Middle Earth is also changed irrevocably, and the destruction of the Ring signals the end of the Third Age and the eventual disappearance of the non-human races who populate it: Elves, Dwarves, Hobbits, and Wizards alike. The next age will belong to men.[21]

In contrast to Eddison's wishful cyclicality, Tolkien's fictive history in *Lord of the Rings*, as in the cosmology *Silmarillion*, is ultimately tragic and pagan. In both works one is left with a sense of loss, of beautiful beings and artifacts which might have been immortal but for the lust for power which was their ruin. Medievalist and fantasy critic Charles Moorman states this best:

> In spite of Tolkien's own implication in "On Fairy-Stories" that *The Lord of the Rings*, ending as it does in a "sudden, joyous 'turn'" (and surely no one would deny that it does so end), possesses eucatastrophe and is hence by extension both optimistic and Christian, I would maintain that the book itself does not bear out this view and that it reflects the attitudes and interests of Tolkien the student of *Beowulf* rather than those of Tolkien the Christian.[22]

Lord of the Rings integrates several other heroic myths besides Frodo's: (1) there is the "return of the king" myth, where the shadowy ranger named "Strider" ultimately reveals his truer identity as high king of the Dunedain; (2) there is a parallel version for the Wizard Gandalf the Grey, who undergoes a trial of death and resurrection at the hands of an agent of Mordor and emerges as Gandalf the White, an even more mysterious and wiser figure than before; (3) there are the heroic maturation tales of the young hobbits Pippin and Merry in the Ent Fable in *The Two Towers* when they are separated from the main group. There are also feminine parallels for both Aragorn and Faramir, the "good" brother of Boromir, and doublet-figures abound everywhere: e.g., Gollum and Sam Gamgee for Frodo, or Saruman the White for Gandalf. In the case of all these heroic myths, too, the powerless, the insignificant, the underdogs end up the winners while those who are too quick to grasp at easy power are the corrupted villains, whose tragic fall from nobility and grace is chronicled here as in *Silmarillion*.

It is probably not by accident that the popularity of the trilogy came only a decade after first publication, in 1965, with the appearance of an unauthorized paperback edition by Ace Books.[23] The trilogy almost singlehandedly made SF and fantasy more popular and intellectually acceptable than ever before and was long the single most popular fictional narrative on American college campuses. The indirect, estranged conceptions of this English storyteller fit many concerns of the Vietnam era and the American New Left and their political progeny: the Hobbit heroes express perfectly the "small is better" philosophy often associated with opposition to nuclear power and advocacy of solar energy, natural foods, environmental protection, and animal rights. One cannot really isolate an explicit political line in the Hobbit fantasies, but in contrast to Eddison the viewpoints are liberal by today's standards.

Of all the works of modern fantasy fiction, *Lord of the Rings* best combines admirable skills in storytelling; well-researched, yet thoroughly digested, researches into mythlore; and an authentic and intelligent moral concern for the quality of modern living conditions, planetary environment, and life-forms other than the human. Yet, without doubt, the work is heroic fantasy.

Tolkien's understated approach to heroism contrasts strongly with one popular subgenre of heroic fantasy which is perhaps the most universally despised and denigrated by critics of many persuasions. Sword-and-sorcery was a name coined by Fritz Leiber in 1961, according to Lin Carter.[24] In this instance, the imaginary setting provides a background for a swashbuckling hero and his companions to confront preternatural forces, usually represented by sorcerers and their allies. Like other heroic age fantasies, sword-and-sorcery stories revolve around combat and quest, the two traditional activities of heroes, though it is important to note that the divine machinery of the epic has definitely been replaced by the forces of magic and its practitioners.

Robert E. Howard, who began the famous Conan stories, is given credit for originating this story type common to the pulp magazines from the thirties on, and insofar as the stories tend to form series—not even necessarily by the same author as the number of Conan writers attests—sword-and-sorcery works are typical of modern popular culture. The Kothar novels of Gardner F. Fox, Lin Carter's Thongor series, and John Jakes's Brak the Barbarian also attest to the broad contemporary popularity of the genre, which invokes a fantastic image of personal power for an anti-heroic world.

Recent fan histories by L. Sprague de Camp and Lin Carter (see note 14 to this chapter), would make it easy to chronicle the history of the form, but this process would not be very revealing. Instead, in the following pages, I intend to start from the point of view of its strongest and most hostile opponents and proceed from there to discuss some positive features of s&s which make it an interesting literature for our time. The first enemy to speak is a master parodist from the New Wave camp.

A literary parody is, of course, valuable and illuminating because it isolates the most glaring conventional features of the genre it mimics and heightens these to make them look ludicrous and unintelligent. However, in this particular case, it would appear that the parody *uses* the conventions of s&s to make a statement about political ideology (Nazism) as much as about a literary form.

Norman Spinrad in *The Iron Dream* (Avon, 1972) has recently produced the ultimate ironic version of sword-and-sorcery.[25] To begin with, Spinrad claims he is presenting Adolf Hitler's classic science-fiction thriller, *The Lord of the Swastika*, which won its author a posthumous Hugo Award in 1955!

Hitler's science fantasy is placed in a future world still suffering the after-effects of atomic cataclysm. Radiation has produced several races of aberrant mutants: Blueskins, Parrotfaces, Eggheads, Lizardmen, and many more. However, the most important race of mutants are the Dominators, who rule the large empire of Zind and who have the telepathic ability to throw out mental patterns that can control others' thoughts; and who use great swarms of genetically altered monsters to fight in their armies. In opposition to them—on the "Sword" side instead of the Dominators' "Sorcery" forces—are the Truemen, blond, blue-eyed, genotypically pure humans as yet uncontaminated by the age-old radiation in the earth. The contest is nothing less than one for mastery of the entire earth and one which will decide whether the Truemen will remain the master race and exterminate the mutants in toto, especially the Dominators; or whether the contaminated hoards of Zind will overrun the world and make protoplasmic monstrosities the norm.

The "hero" of the piece is Feric Jaggar, a Trueman who was born in exile but returns home to the human Fatherland, the High Republic of Heldon, acquires possession and mastery of the Great Truncheon, once a royal scepter, but also a magical weapon which is a symbol of the power of pure humanity. From the sheer energy of his own racial purity and the uncontaminated force of his own vision Feric becomes leader of the Party and finally Commander of the entire Domain of Held. In the all-out war for racial mastery which then ensues, Feric liquidates all the other mutated races entirely. On the verge of complete extinction, the Dominators set off an atom bomb left over from the previous Great War, and its effect is a radiation disease that ruins the gene pool of all Truemen, even Jaggar's; the germ plasm of all humanity will now produce only mutants. The Helder scientists, however, come up with a solution: Jaggar's *somatic* plasm is cloned and all humanity is sterilized to get rid of any contaminated germ plasm. Hence, a race of genetic pure-breeds arise after the Commander's own genes and the final chapter of *Lord of the Swastika* finds cloned blond, blue-eyed giants after Jaggar's model entering spaceships to carry the "perfection" of the master race to other worlds!

Spinrad concludes the book with an interpretative essay by Professor Homer Whipple of New York University. His combination of psychoanalytical and sociological literary criticism is a gem of a parody in its own right, even without its bitterly ironic conclusion on the last page that "in an absolute sense we are fortunate that a monster like Feric Jaggar will forever remain confined to the pages of science fantasy, the fever dream of a neurotic science-fiction writer named Adolf Hitler."

In fact, this story is in great part an ironic reformulation of

William L. Shirer's popular history of Nazi Germany, *The Rise and Fall of the Third Reich* (New York: Simon and Schuster, 1960): Hitler's paranoiac vision and the horrifying Nazi Weltanschauung are converted into engrossing, if ironic and unbelievable, sword-and-sorcery heroics by being projected into the fantasy world of a post-Doomsday world with opponents, the Dominators, who have preternatural mind-powers.

Spinrad brought out his conviction that s&s is fascistic explicitly in a recent letter to the journal *Science-Fiction Studies* (5[1978]:p. 198); the New Wave writer highly praised a ferocious critical attack on heroic fantasy by the West German SF writer, editor, and critic, Hans Joachim Alpers ("Loincloth, Double Ax, and Magic: 'Heroic Fantasy' and Related Genres"). Alpers's charges are summed up as follows:

> The ideologies propagated [by s&s] are: magic-mystic understanding of the world, i.e., mystification of relationships that could be grasped by the intellect; right of the stronger as the principle of societal organization; glorification of violence, particularly killing; oppression of women; emphasis on the racial superiority of the Nordic (Aryan) type; fatalism toward hierarchic structures and their consequences, such as wars; the *fuehrer* principle: the greatest butcher of them all shall determine our fate; imperialistic policy; and antiintellectualism.
> What is, then, being glorified by HF? There is but one word that sufficiently sums up all these ideological elements: fascism.[26]

Now, first of all, Alpers's entire essay, though well versed in the many writers and works of s&s, fails to like anything in any of it. He justifies this by confusing the fictive alternate universe, which is intended by its author as an estranging-device, with a literal-minded nonfictional construct of some sort, which of course it isn't. Basically, it is true that a wish-fulfillment that reverses the time-clock of civilization, and not a scientific speculation, lies at the heart of s&s. The anti-system known as the Heroic Age is as much emotional as intellectual, representing a powerful desire that is known to be unachievable and unrealistic. The complex and paradoxical feeling that results from this conflict between the desirable and the impossible is usually given the undignified name "escapism." It isn't my intention to deny that most s&s stories are light reading, entertaining narratives strong in *story* value. If one does not enter into s&s in the spirit of fun (Alpers certainly doesn't), one cannot hope to do justice to what merits are actually present. Besides, escapist literature has co-existed with more "normal" or elitist forms throughout the entire Western literary experience, always garnering new readers who find it a fresh and liberating literature. No one has ever been able to prove that escapism is bad in and of itself, only that a steady diet of it, isolated from other experiences, would have undesirable effects; it is also debatable at what point readers should be involved with more challenging narratives.

Still, it would be a mistake to take s&s too seriously: Spinrad and Alpers, like many others, overemphasize the fantasy metaphysics of the imaginary world and neglect the light touches. Above all, in dealing with this subgenre, one has to have a sense of humor and allow for it in the writer. In the hands of capable writers, s&s has a tendency to become irony, satire, and the picaresque. Instead of taking either the hero or the Heroic Age at face value, many an author puts distance between himself and his readers on one side and his heroic subject matter on the other. Fritz Leiber's Nehwon-mythos with its ironically comical heroes, Fafhrd and Grey Mouser, is just one major testimony to what, after critic Kenneth Burke, I would term "perspectives by incongruity": as readers, we identify with, but feel ambivalent toward, less than ideal heroes operating in a less than ideal scene. Nehwon is clearly a decadent universe but it is just as clearly and obviously a satiric distortion of our own world.

It has been noted that Michael Moorcock's two popular s&s series, "Elric" and "Dorian Hawkmoon," suggest irony and self-parody when viewed against the more conventional Howardian type.[27] For neither murderous hero is the individualistic freebooter idealized by the creator of Conan: the first is ruled by a vicious passion for killing indwelling in his talismanic sword, Stormbringer; the second has a jewel implanted in his skull which makes him a pawn in a game played by other men. In either case, heroism is wryly undermined. And the ideological problems proposed by s&s are certainly further confounded by Moorcock's very real and popular success in it since he is one of the major originators of the New Wave movement and is unlikely to have sold out his liberal philosophy for an alleged fascist literary market. But if there are great loads of neo-Nazis out there buying Moorcock's bloody tales, they won't understand Moorcock's subtle anti-heroic reversal anyway since their problem isn't just what they read, but also *how* they read anything.

I have here provided a more detailed investigation of this double picaresque irony—ironic heroes in ironic Heroic Ages—in the Harold Shea stories of L. Sprague de Camp and Fletcher Pratt, which are set in the preconceived imaginary universes of famous myths; yet it is the comic distortion of the myths that convert the mythical scenery into a picaresque landscape.

There are actually five tales in the Harold Shea series, but it is the first two, known collectively as *The Incomplete Enchanter,* which have remained classics of comic sword-and-sorcery since their first appearance in the magazine *Unknown* in May and August of 1940.[28] The expected swordplay and adventures are certainly present, plus plenty of fantastic creatures and concepts, but Pratt and de Camp provide many special touches of fantasy genius: a wacky sense of humor which is often reminiscent of the bizarre illogic of Lewis Carroll's Alice books; deft satirical sketches of single persons or whole cultures and historical eras; eccentric, yet thought-provoking, speculations on cosmology and epistemology. Both authors were solid amateur historians with many nonfiction titles to their credit, and their fantasy worlds always reveal a concern for concrete, detailed research which makes them seem convincing and realistic.

Harold Shea, the hero of the series, is a bored young research psychologist working at the Garaden Institute in Ohio with Reed Chalmers, an older scientist who is head of the institute. The experiment being conducted is based on Chalmers's theory that there are an infinite number of possible universes that exist parallel with our own, and the differences between them are based on their inhabitants' prior assumptions about reality. Chalmers is trying to find a proper formula in symbolic logic (Shea jokingly calls it a "syllogismobile") that will allow someone from our modern world to travel back and forth among these multiple universes. (In fact, symbolic logic is strictly a conceptual science and it cannot produce any of the visible world-altering effects envisioned by the authors. The travel to other worlds is strictly a mind-game, played for fun, and the so-called "laws of magical universes" are not intended to be taken seriously.)

Tired of the humdrumness of the modern world, Shea anticipates his boss and takes it on himself to recite the latest version of the formula they have been working on, hoping thereby to locate worlds that are more interesting and adventuresome. More importantly, Shea hopes to escape the romantic overtures of his domineering co-worker, Gertrude Mugler, and find a more desirable mate.

Shea had planned well and intended to land in the world of Irish mythology, but ends up by mistake in that of the Old Norse gods. This is only the first of the goof-ups with Chalmers's new world-creating logic. Somehow, throughout the series, the magical formulas are never better than *almost* correct, and the mistakes are always hilarious in the tradition of "The Sorcerer's Apprentice." An attempt to conjure a mythical unicorn instead produces a befuddled rhinoceros; instead of one firebreathing dragon, a hundred flower-munching ones answer the wizard's call; an attempt by Chalmers to repeat Jesus' miracle of transforming water into wine produces Scotch whisky and a drunken brawl ensues.

The title of "The Roaring Trumpet" refers to the horn of the Viking god, Heimdall, guardian of Bifrost, the rainbow bridge which leads to Asgard, home of the gods. It is into this god's hands that Shea falls as a slave, and he ends up with far more adventures than he bargained for back home in Ohio. The gods are close to mortal combat with their cosmic foes, the giants; the fate of all nine inhabited worlds of the Eddas hangs in the balance, for it is the time of Ragnarok, the apocalyptic last battle that will destroy all creation.

At the end of the first novella Shea does manage to escape back to his own world before the final cataclysm, but before that the feckless Mid-American anti-hero has to change his status and emerge as a true hero. He goes on quest to Jotunheim, Giant Land, with the deities of Asgard and learns expert swordsmanship on the way. At the same time, one of the authors' cleverest touches is that this journey is a subtly disguised retelling of Snorri Sturluson's *Prose Edda*, a thirteenth-century handbook for poets which is the single most famous source for Scandinavian mythology. Snorri's half-comic tale of Thor fishing for the Midgard Serpent in a boat with the Giant Hymir is represented as the god's own story on himself—as a fish-story about the Big One That Got Away! In Snorri's version there are three contests at a banquet given by the giant Utgardloki in Jotunheim where elemental forces in magical disguises are more powerful than the Aesir Thor, Tjalfi, and Loki; but in the modern sword-and-sorcery tale these deceptions do not fool Shea at all and he sees the true nature of these beings because his modern mind has been trained to equate magic with illusion and deception.

In an autobiographical remark, de Camp gives Pratt credit for the thoroughness of their research into Norse myth for this story, yet the sense of humor here and elsewhere is of a kind familiar to readers of de Camp. By having the Giants speak Chicago gangster lingo, for example, the authors turn the coarseness and deformity of the Giants into a satire against an excessive stupidity which makes civilization impossible—a perspective and technique typical of many de Camp fables.

With comedy and wit the authors are always questioning the relative merits of our culture versus others in a manner that clearly echoes Mark Twain's *Connecticut Yankee*. For the most part the modern man and modern intelligence come out on top, and this sounds a note that ironically undermines the typical (e.g., Robert E. Howard's Conan) sword-and-sorcery attitude. Usually the hero in this genre is a rebel against, and escapee from, the confinements and decadence of modern civilization, but none of the alternate universes in the Shea stories are romanticized or idealized. Primitivism is definitely satirized in "The Roaring Trumpet," and medievalism and feudalism are just as definitely rejected in the second tale, "The Mathematics of Magic." Hence, in the first tale a "cockroach derby" devised by Shea to while away time in a Giant dungeon contributes to the already unappetizing portrait of the Eddic worlds; in the second, murderous tribal Celts, the DaDerga (who speak a comical Scottish brogue), are satirized as irrational religion-mongers who naively profess that their practice of human sacrifice is good for the victim.

As the series developed, in fact, more and more emphasis was put on Shea's modern qualities as his prime virtues, and more and more the original heroes and gods recede into the background. But even when the latter are pointed up in the story, they seem brutal, violent, and sexually repulsive in comparison to Shea, who is able to solve his problems with something besides physical prowess.

However, there are a few hints at cultural relativism since Shea often succeeds, too, by adapting himself to the demands of the Eddic universe where magic works, but science doesn't. Biology, chemistry, and physics have not yet been discovered, so they don't exist, as Shea learns to his chagrin when his matches, revolver, and even his Boy Scout Handbook will not function at critical moments: belief-structures are all-important here. So Shea learns the art and practice of magic (described as "the laws of contagion and similarity" proposed in James George Frazer's *Golden Bough*). Because of his budding control of magical formulas, he shortens a Troll's nose with homeopathic medicine in one case, then he makes a broom fly all the way to Hell in another. In the latter scene, Shea's aerial acrobatics are one of the high points of fantasy adventure in this tale; it is repeated just as effectively in "The Mathematics of Magic," where the aerial broom is used for a wild combat with a villainous wizard aboard a pterodactyl-like Wivern.

The second half of *The Incomplete Enchanter* involves adventures in the universe of Edmund Spenser's *The Faerie Queene,* where Gloriana's knights and ladies are in a sword-and-sorcery face-off with an entire convention of wizards under the archimage, Busyrane. This tale is not so closely modelled on its original as was the previous story, and there are a whole new cast of characters to follow through the plot. This time the elderly and professional Reed Chalmers accompanies Shea on the experimental exploration. He is, of course, much more adept at the "syllogismobile" than his young assistant, but he is also far from heroic. Previously, magic was practiced as an art in the realm of *Faerie,* but Chalmers develops a scheme to put magic on a scientific ("assembly-line") basis until Shea destroys all the wizards' powers. Ultimately there is too much magicking going on in this universe, and the equal-and-opposite reaction which results hurls Shea and Belphebe back into the modern world together, while Chalmers is isolated in *Faerie Queene* at the end of the tale, a situation which, of course, demands a further episode for the series.

The villains of this second tale, the wizards of Busyrane's alliance, are the converse of the stupid Giants met earlier: the wizards suggest a satire against effete intellectuals. Their conclave is a funny burlesque of a college professors' academic convention, complete with dull lectures on obscure topics which put Shea to sleep.[29]

Two other main characters are women, though both are pretty much derived from stereotypes (a type-casting at once sexual and literary). Britomart is a mannish warrior knight in the service of Queen Gloriana who finds true love with the fellow knight of her choice. A more important female figure is Belphebe, an archeress of the deep wood where she pursues the goblinesque Losels who serve Busyrane. She becomes the object of Shea's affection and his ideal mate in this tale whom he either pursues or rescues in melodramatic fashion through the rest of the series. Probably it is in this area of romance that many of today's readers would find the Shea stories dated by their attitude toward women. For their own time, however, they are intelligent and enlightened and do not condescend too much to the heroines. The two heroines are certainly regarded as being as able as any of the male protagonists, and what satire and humor there is in their portraiture is due to the fact that they are female counterparts of Shea, a figure partly satirized, partly idealized.

The overall melodramatic plot structure, however, does become less interesting with so much repetition by the later episodes of the series. At the least, we can appreciate the sly sexual irreverance when, for example, Shea outwits the Blatant Beast by reciting low-class doggerel (explicit obscene parts are, of course, not recited). When the story was written, innuendo rather than explicitness was in vogue, and Pratt and de Camp are masters of the former.

The series, like its wrong-way Corrigan hero, was doomed to be incomplete. A third tale, *The Castle of Iron,* was also published in *Unknown* (April 1941), and, since it is as long as *The Incomplete Enchanter,* it has been re-issued as a separate novel often enough. Trying to get back to *Faerie Queene,* Shea instead reaches the Xanadu of Samuel Taylor Coleridge's poem, "Kubla Kahn," and from there Shea, Chalmers, and Belphebe wind up in the pseudo-Mohammedan universe of Ariosto's Renaissance epic, *Orlando Furioso.* Again the plot is a series of comic encounters with sorcerers and their spells on the one hand and a sequence of melodramatic rescues by Shea of his Belphebe on the other. The very choice of a work like *Orlando,* a fabulatory classic akin to Ovid's *Metamorphoses* and the *Arabian Nights,* like the choice of *Faerie Queene* for the earlier tale, is a strong indication that a new literary goal was aimed at beyond the Conanesque model for sword-and-sorcery.

The last two stories, "The Wall of Serpents" and "The Green Magician," appeared first in ephemeral fantasy magazines (respectively, *Fantasy Fiction* for June 1953 and *Beyond Fantastic Fiction* for October 1954) and have sadly been republished only in obscure or ephemeral books and anthologies.[30] The first of these takes Shea and his expanded cast of modern heroes to the mythical world of the Finnish national epic, *Kalevala;* the second, to the world of Irish mythology—the place Shea had originally set out for in the very first

In Defense of Heroic Fantasy

tale. By now, the engaging Polish-American cop, Pete Brodsky, is more interesting than our original hero, and the authors' interest in the series itself seems to have dwindled. Both the Finnish hero Lemminkainen and his Irish counterpart Cuchulainn are oversexed rogues, and both myth-worlds are more anti-heroic than ever: the brute Kalevalans speak in a sing-song verse that mocks the poetic original, while "The Green Magician" presents "a world where the hysteric type is the norm," and the moderns have to use psychoanalysis and post-hypnotic suggestions to best the Irish. Both works do make a nice introduction to mythologies more exotic than the Greek, Biblical, or Norse.

In his personal correspondence, de Camp indicated he might continue the series with more adventures in mythical worlds like the Iranian, but Pratt was turning his attention to one of his strongest interests, the Civil War and died soon after, in 1956. The Shea stories are, like the other work of this duo, a unique blend of historical realism, fantasy and satire, of high didacticism and low American humor. At the most fundamental level, this series is clearly in the tradition of sword-and-sorcery—it just happens to be much more than that.

In two later works written in tandem, *The Carnelian Cube* (New York: Gnome, 1948) and *Land of Unreason* (*Unknown,* October 1941) the authors again explored the alchemy of multiple universes, but these stories, for all their imaginative brilliance, suggest different literary relationships. Singly, too, they went their own diverse ways in the s&s genre. Pratt created *The Well of the Unicorn* (New York: William Sloane, 1948), whose location is an imaginary world in a Heroic Age that resembles Viking Scandinavia in its geography and sociology though the names are often ancient Greek in sound and construction. De Camp, on the other hand, turned to his knowledge of the ancient Greek and Roman classics and from these constructed the imaginary Lost World of Pusad,[31] which was the object of a series of sword-and-sorcery adventures, the most important being the full-length novel, *The Tritonian Ring* (Twayne, 1953), in which the quest-hero Vakar sets forth across the sinking continent of Pusad (or "Poseidonis") to save his fatherland from the Gorgons by locating the "thing the gods fear most." This turns out to be an iron ring, which renders even the most powerful spells of the ancient gods harmless, so the age of lazy priests and treacherous wizards is doomed to disappear along with the gods they serve when Vakar locates his prize; the era of craven religiosity is ended and that of secular creativity is begun. Again, de Camp takes the side of modernity and civilization over primitivism and barbarity.

Many readers will be amused at a more recent novel of de Camp's, *The Fallible Fiend* (New York: Signet, 1973), which makes nice comparison with Gardner's *Grendel*, though it is a much lighter, less serious work. This comic s&s tale is told in first-person narration from the viewpoint of a Demon of the Twelfth Plane who has the unfortunate habit of taking orders literally. Zdin is, in fact, just too rational compared to us human Prime Planers, though this does not stop him from acts of murder and cannibalism on our own species. The view of humanity definitely compares well with Grendel's:

> During my captivity and flight, I had been inclined to agree with the taverner Hadrubar's unfavorable view of the Zaperazh. As I walked down the trail in the rosy light of dawn, taking a bite now and then from the slab of horsemeat, I achieved a more rational view. The Zaperazh had merely acted in the normal manner of Prime Planers, who instinctively divide up into mutually hostile groups. Each member of such a group regards all other groups as not fully human and therefore as fair game or legitimate prey. These divisions can be formed on any pretext—race, nation, tribe, class, belief, or any other difference that will serve. [p. 96]

Yet again a double picaresque irony is apparent at the conclusion of the tale when Zdin expresses his desire to settle down here someday with his wife now that the kids are grown. *Fiend* thus suggests a broad, humane acceptance of our fallible real world and the necessity of *some* evil in human civilization.

Writers like L. Sprague de Camp and Fritz Leiber are sophisticated, emotionally complex people, multitalented as writers, with accomplishments in a number of literary forms, SF proper included, besides s&s. It is unfair to reduce them in Procrustean fashion to the purported limits of Howard and then pronounce them fascists and proponents of barbarism and decadence when a careful, sympathetic reading would reveal the opposite. Both writers eschew decadence, but with wry humor and a self-confident rationality that leaves room for an individualistic ethic which is not inimical to the best interests of civilization and society. A sense of humor is essential in approaching either writer, as with the whole of s&s.

However, to be fair to critics of this genre, it is important to look closely at the work of a writer who isn't satirical or humorous; who isn't providing a parodic, ironic, or picaresque variation on s&s; whose heroic age, though archaic and violent, is to be taken in some serious way. In the work of Poul Anderson the violence is an essential part of the reality-system of an alien world, one that exists no longer in time, and this is a good thing in some respects, bad in others. The reader is required to enter Anderson's neo-sagas in the same spirit in which he would enter the violent archaic worlds of the original epics and sagas. It is especially germane to discuss the work of this writer because he has done so much to popularize Scandinavian myth and saga (even some of the obscurer elements) in both his heroic fantasy and his science fantasy. Yet even this extensive effort in mythifiction is only a small part of his output, and he is also a prolific and award-winning author of "science fiction" proper.

The Broken Sword (1954)[32] is set in the England of Alfred the Great during the Viking Heroic Age. Orm of Jutland, a free-booting warrior, acquires an estate and a Christian wife, but brings a fatal curse upon himself and his entire clan when he burns his Anglo-Saxon foes in their own house. The Icelandic sagas give several examples of this theme—known as the *brenna inni*, "burning the enemy in his own house"[33]—and in Anderson's novel, which is so obviously inspired by these sagas, the burning leads with tragic inevitability to the death of the hero and his relatives.

In the doom-haunted atmosphere of this brilliant and brutal hero-tale Anderson succeeds in recreating the world of saga. Orm's son becomes the Elf changeling, Skafloc, while the Elf foster-father, Imric, sires a replacement for the human child by means of a Troll woman held in his prison. This truculent and soulless creature, Valgard, reaches maturity only to slay Orm and his two "brothers" in a moment of rage, thus fulfilling part of the curse.

Yet Valgard acquires knowledge of his true origins, and joins the Troll forces for their all-out war on the Elves of England, intending at the same time to destroy Skafloc. From the beginning it is clear that the two changelings are doomed to slay one another, for their every act makes absolutely certain that their blood-feud must continue till the end. Valgard's motivation, indeed, is due to his awareness that he is a mere phantom copy of Skafloc, a mere *Doppelgänger*:[34]

> *Why* am I so? Because Imric made me thus. He moulded me into the image of Orm's son. I am alive for no other reason, and my strength and looks and brain are—Skafloc's. . . . *What am I but the shadow of Skafloc?* [p. 182]

The *Doppelgänger* theme is carefully worked out in detail throughout the novel, not only in the final scene of the book where the doubles complete their tragic destinies in mutual slaughter but also, for example, in the correspondence between Valgard's murdering Freda's first betrothed in the early part of the book and Skafloc's murdering her second betrothed late in the second part. Valgard is a berserker in the first half of the novel before he realizes his Troll nature; Skafloc becomes a berserker in the last section of the novel when he wields the reforged sword.

The *consequences* of war and violence are constantly kept before the reader's eyes, and with each act of violence the consequences reach further and further. When Valgard leaves the world of men, Anderson's narrative moves into the world of Faerie to describe the genocidal racial war between the Trolls and the Elves. Always in the background there appear greater forces: the Aesir, or gods, of Norse mythology, who favor the Elves, and the Giants of Utgard, who second the cause of the Trolls. There are even greater issues at stake, because Ragnarok, the apocalyptic end of the world, may well be brought on if the Trolls and Elves force the Giants and Gods to ultimate combat. And still further on the horizon is the Coming of the White Christ. Ragnarok is therefore viewed ambivalently, for it may be only the prelude to Christianity. The end of the Heroic Age, the end of Faerie and of the greater Pagan beings—Gods and Giants—may just be the beginning of the gentler reign of Christ. In a fascinating passage (p. 14) Skafloc meets a Faun who is a refugee from the South where the White Christ and his priests have already ended the ancient age of the Greek myths. Indeed, I should add that the idea of Christianity ending a mythical heroic age is a theme in Scandinavian and Celtic mythology,[35] and it also appears in the last

In Defense of Heroic Fantasy

canto (50) of the Finnish *Kalevala* where Vainamoinen leaves Kalevala and the age of Finnish heroes comes to a close.

During the war, Skafloc brings disaster upon himself in still another way: he rescues Freda, a human maiden, from Troll captors and mates with her, not realizing she is his own full sister. They live together in the woods while the war goes against the Elves and Valgard becomes earl of Imric's stronghold. Skafloc then remembers his name-gift from the Aesir, the Broken Sword, a powerful weapon which only a human can wield because it is made of iron, a substance inimical to all Faerie-folk. Yet its forger was the blind enthralled Giant, Bolverk, and only he can reforge it. Skafloc retrieves it from Imric's captured fortress and performs a ritual of necromancy in order to learn the road to the Giant's forge in Hell; the unfortunate side effect is that his own dead relatives also inform him of his incestuous relationship with Freda. Though pregnant with his child, as a Christian she refuses further company with him and she returns to humankind. With Freda, as with Valgard, the greatest sufferings come from those closest to the hero and most like him (and ultimately, of course, from *himself*).

As a prelude to his trek to Giant Land, Skafloc journeys to the realms of Irish mythology where the Sidhe dwell in a peaceful, idyllic atmosphere (ch. 21). The Sidhe are themselves described as "half-gods," for their power and influence has been much reduced by the coming of Christianity. Accompanied and aided by the Irish deity, Mananaan (or Lir), Skafloc does perform his quest successfully: Giant Land is mastered, the descent to Hell is survived, and the Sword is made whole by the Giant.

The Sword renders the hero a berserk and fey warrior.[36] This is the price that must be paid for its use and for the Elves regaining their own kingdom. Thus Skafloc's doom is effected by his own Sword, and the novel ends with the mutual slaughter of Valgard and Skafloc, though Freda's newborn son by Skafloc is carried off by Odin to become still another changeling. A Siegfried figure, his destiny is to use the Sword and fight with the Aesir when Ragnarok will come.

Imric's final words place the story very clearly in its tradition of Heroic Age literature when he pronounces an epitaph over his adoptive son:

> Happier are all men than the dwellers in Faerie—or the gods, for that matter. Better a life like a falling star, bright across the dark, than a deathlessness which can see naught above or beyond itself. . . . I feel that the day draws nigh when Faerie shall fade, the Erlking himself shrink to a woodland sprite and then to nothing, and the gods go under. And the worst of it is, I cannot believe it wrong that the immortals will not live forever. [p. 206]

The Trolls and Elves are equally elemental preternatural beings whose emotions and motives do not take into account merely human instruments in the tale (the Gods and Giants are even vaguer and more manipulative). Hence, the Elf women, though hauntingly beautiful and immortal, are cold and dreadful. One should compare Anderson's Elvish mythology to its closest counterpart in Tolkien's *Silmarillion*: in the work of fantasists Elves are pure, vital embodiments of passions (anger, lust, pride, vengeance) and are a mythical and fantasy analogue of the "alien" in normative SF; in fantasy *emotional* alienness, not cognitive alienness, is emphasized. In both, the contrast between these nonhuman preternatural orders of being (something distinct from the Judeo-Christian angelic and demonic orders) and our merely human kind is all-important. In both, too, half-human "changelings" suffer the tragic consequences of their impossible dual nature: too weird for normal human society, too mortal for the timeless universe of Faerie. *The Broken Sword* is a neat synthesis of pre-existent mythological lore—the Viking Heroic Age, Celtic and Scandinavian deities and demigods, and typical mythological motifs—to create a modern heroic fantasy that is *sui generis*. Though it is a violent narrative, it can in no way be called immoral or decadent, and, indeed, rather looks at human violence as the ancient Greek dramatists did: frankly, as a potential in man which will certainly come out with evil consequence if it is not seen and understood for what it is.

Anderson's most recent long work in fantasy literature is dependent on a pre-existent model from Icelandic saga, although the final literary product is truly a fantasy, not a quasi-historical romance like Eddison's *Styrbiorn*. And whereas the original Icelandic prose saga, *Hrolfs Kraka Saga*, is only some 37,000 words in Stella Mills's English translation,[37] Anderson's saga-fantasy is fully three times as long.

Hrolf Kraki's Saga (Ballantine Books, 1973) is a boldly creative reconstruction of the Germanic Heroic Age which is, in the author's own words, "not a hypothetical historical reality, but a myth," taking place "during the *Völkerwanderung* period, when Rome had gone under and the Germanic tribes were on the move, as wild a time as the world has ever seen," when "slaughter, slavery, robbery, rape, torture, heathen rites bloody or obscene, were parts of daily life."[38] It seems the author's aim is not to tell of the life and times of one heroic individual so much as to reproduce a vital portrait of an entire age. It does describe men of gigantic stature, but it is even more concerned to show the violent temper of the times which made them great.

To achieve the right temporal perspective Anderson has a noblewoman of tenth-century England relate the story, complete with the elements of cultural anachronism, romance, pathos, magic, and the supernatural that the medieval narrators disclosed in their own tellings of the sagas. And like the original *Hrolf Kraki* as well as the monumental *Njal Saga* of the thirteenth century, the story ranges over several generations in one family, the Skjoldungs' royal house, and over most of Northern Europe, including Norway, Sweden, Denmark, Finland, and Saxony. It is obvious that the work is deliberately episodic in character, and this also allows the author narrative freedoms. Parts Four and Five, for example, the tales of Svipdag and Bjarki, are excursuses on two of Hrolf's most loyal henchmen.

The overall theme of the work, as in *The Broken Sword*, is the doom that hangs over each and every generation of this family; in fact, the family is in most instances the agency of its own disasters: it is brother against brother and parent against child that ruins the house. Indeed the central figure, the generous and noble Hrolf Kraki, and all his band of heroes are ruined by the treachery of the king's own sister, Skuld, a half-Elvish changeling. The family line is exterminated at the same time as Hrolf's kingdom, although the victory of the forces of Faerie who support Skuld is merely a harbinger of their own eventual demise (see pp. 232–33; the theme is the same one that appeared earlier in *The Broken Sword*).

Hrolf Kraki is a prodigious work of scholarship that goes beyond the original Icelandic saga to include other literary and mythological variants from both the vernacular and Latin languages (the testimony of Saxo Grammaticus, for example); yet Anderson manages to control his novel's dual nature of heroic saga and literary fantasy. In mythological and fantastic vein, Elves, Mermen, Gods, Giants, and Trolls enter the story occasionally, even at critical moments, as in the final battle between Hrolf's heroes and Skuld's conjurings which forms the climax of the book. But unlike *The Broken Sword*, *Hrolf Kraki* never departs from a strictly human universe to describe the worlds of Faerie or Gods; it remains a saga in narrative atmosphere.

Anderson's contribution to Heroic Age fiction has not yet received proper recognition—unlike, say, Tolkien's—but his treatments of the Northern myths are at once substantive and creative and deserve some attention. Over a twenty-year span, his numerous stories have extended the imaginative possibilities of fiction on heroic themes and have achieved the status of being something beyond the limiting category sword-and-sorcery. I should at least mention his translations of heroic poetry for the s&s fanzine, *Amra*. Then, his most important SF stories would include *The High Crusade*, a novel serialized in *Analog Astounding Science Fact and Fiction* (July-September 1960), a story of knights and nobles of fourteenth-century England who defeat all the sophisticated technology of an alien galactic empire; Anderson revises Mark Twain's *Connecticut Yankee in King Arthur's Court* by demonstrating the basic competence of feudal man. In "The Longest Voyage" (*Analog*, December 1960), a novelette which won a Hugo Award in 1961 and has been reprinted often, Anderson depicts a quasi-Viking culture on another planet which destroys a stranded Terran starship in order to protect the integrity of its own future. *Three Hearts and Three Lions* (*F&SF*, September 1953) has many similarities to the Harold Shea tales: a modern Freedom Fighter against the Nazis, who is a reincarnation of Ogier the Dane, is projected into a fantastic medieval magic world where he recovers his original heroic identity and fights for Charlemagne and the Law against the evil Morgana Le Fey and the forces of Chaos. *The Merman's Children* (1973)[39] describes the era of Christianity's victory over paganism and its successful exorcism of the Faerie races. The underwater culture of the Mermen is destroyed by a Christian prelate, and the story concerns the adventures of three half-human, half-merman changelings who are trying to secure enough treasure so that their sister, a fully human Christian, can live out her own life free from the entanglements of the Church. The culmination of the fantasy is the mermen's battle with a Kraken over its treasure hoard.

This story, like *The Broken Sword* and *Hrolf Kraki*, identifies paganness with various alien beings (Trolls, Elves, Mermen, changelings) while Christianity means a more fully *human* world. The end of the pagan deities and mythfolk is also the end of the Heroic Age: a certain kind of raw creative power goes out of the world when Christianity achieves victory over men's minds, but at the same time savagery and violence are diminished, making a civilized world possible (one where murderous vengeance, curse-bringing incest, parricide, and fratricide are aberrational, not the reality-norm). Because of the unleashing of primitive energies and the consummation of desperate passions, Heroic Ages must end, literally burned out by their own violence and warfare. From the vantage point of modern man, therefore, the Heroic Age is typically a Lost Age (though Eddison experimented in the *Worm* with an unusual cyclical view).

It is fairest to say that Poul Anderson favors neither the Heroic Age nor modern civilization completely in his fantastic reconstruction of the Ages of Man myth: the epitaph in Imric's words from *The Broken Sword* expresses a highly disillusioned evaluation of the Heroic Age and concludes on a double-negative which says that modernity cannot be worse than the violent ages of heroes; *The High Crusade*, on the other hand, insists that modern man cannot just blithely assume he's superior. All men are involved in history, and for Anderson modern civilization must remain in constant dialogue with other ages, to determine which is "better," in which ways and under which conditions and criteria. Though his Viking universes are pre-civilized, Anderson is only selectively a primitivist; he certainly isn't preaching barbarity: he always has too much of a sense of history for that; and in our reading of "The Faun" (in chapter 1) we saw him propounding a benign attitude toward modern creative science and its technology to a youthful audience; and it is only fair to say Anderson has thought as much about the future as the past in his fictions.

As with all the other writers of heroic fantasy and sword-and-sorcery encountered in this chapter, Anderson fails to meet the requirements for literary fascism. Like de Camp and Leiber, he is a modernist sensitive to the anti-heroical intellectual climate in which we have lived so long. I cannot pretend that writers in the heroical genre are considered major literary figures (with the exception of Tolkien); but Gardner, Ballard, and Spinrad may yet prove to be just that. Yet I cannot really accept, either, that the causes of a socialist reformer like Alpers are served by misreading of literary narratives deliberately in order to set up a polemical opposition straw-man. The whole of their literary opus as well as their personal lives show that Anderson, Leiber, and de Camp are allies, not enemies, of a modern scientific civilization. A New Wave writer like Norman Spinrad has, of course, strong literary polemical reasons for his attacks on writers of s&s: he and other New Wavers are deliberately trying to mark out a new kind of literature; they want to transcend the old formulas and genres and go beyond the earlier writers' views of science and civilization.

The heroic fantasists are too easy a target: at its worst, s&s and the rest of the heroic subgenre is only harmless fun; at its best, it is a subtle and thought-provoking tonic for a late twentieth-century world already overburdened by intellectual depression and consciousness of individual powerlessness. If heroism is unrealistic, the anti-heroic has proven itself undesirable and unproductive and—it has to be admitted—no more realistic: the antihero, too, is merely a fiction. The polemical animus against heroic fantasy by writers and critics is misplaced zealotry.

A fair assessment of this odd hybrid subgenre of popular F&SF reveals heroic fantasy as a *fictive* response to an all-pervasive anti-heroic literature and consciousness. Sword-and-sorcery writers and other heroic fantasists feel stifled by a pervasive anti-heroic intellectual environment, and in the ancient heroic literature of myths, sagas, and epics they find a source of liberating, nonconformist, often playful, counter-structures. Nor does it seem that this subgenre explicitly promotes any specific political creed, as Alpers charges, but rather it offers highly personal philosophies and individualistic points of view and tries to make its readers more exuberant, more intense about life in our real world of the present. Sword-and-sorcery in particular is not only "this-worldly" but sometimes downright worldly. Its various fans (who are proud that their taste for it is peculiar) claim it even makes them feel good about life.

5) Men like Gods

The superman is no longer merely a fictional hypothesis, no mere speculation. As critic Leslie Fiedler has written in his essay entitled "The New Mutants,"[1] the superman is among us in our own children, for it has been one of the most recurrent themes of the twentieth century that each generation finds its own offspring a kind of "mutant" being whose goals, ideals, values, and behavior seem radical, completely different, and, commonly, frightening. On the other hand, a number of modern cultural phenomena point to our marked tendency to apotheosize youth and live out of our myths and our own desire for godhead in our children: our American youth cult, the cult of childhood initiated in the Victorian period, the American cult of innocence observed by Leslie Fiedler and David Ketterer, and even the Jungian attention to an archetypal myth of the Divine Child.[2]

More and more our century is showing us that what we once thought was a solid conception of "human nature" is just simply no longer adequate from any point of view: the women's rights movement, gay liberation, the transsexual, the clone (almost a reality), authentic bionics, birth control, the recent genetic breakthroughs—all of these indicate that the superman concept involves a very real problem which will become even more difficult in our immediate future. From an ethical point of view, SF has an important educative and critical task in this area.

The term "superman" does not refer, strictly speaking, to the comic book hero (though he is a pop culture example of the idea).[3] Historians of philosophy variously give credit to either Goethe or Thomas Carlyle for the concept in its most nascent form, then to Friedrich Nietzsche in *Also Sprach Zarathustra* for the explicit term, *Übermensch*, which we translate as "superman" or "overman."[4] Extrapolating from the Romantic cult of the creative individual personality, the nineteenth-century superman proponents assumed that metamorphosis was humanity's destiny. There would come — variously, depending on the individual thinker — a better, more heroic race of man, a more satisfying social order, greater aesthetic potential, and in general a possibility for the pursuit of "higher" values. Nietzsche's announcement, in one of his most influential works, *The Birth of Tragedy*, that Homer's *Iliad* is an ideal source for knowledge of heroic existence and heroic values, is just one evidence that the superman was a displacement of older mythical heroic models onto the future history of man. The concept was inherently futuristic and speculative and made to order for imaginative association with the new theory of evolution, which itself suggested the possibility of a greater race of mankind to a writer like Bulwer-Lytton in *The Coming Race* (1871). Ever since, the concept of the superman has remained central to speculative fiction. The works of H.G. Wells, Olaf Stapledon (especially *Odd John*), Philip Wylie (*Gladiator*), Stanley Weinbaum, A. E. van Vogt, and — among more contemporary writers — Theodore Sturgeon (*Venus Plus X*, *More Than Human*) have made the greatest impact.[5]

In strictly science-fictional conceptions of the superman, the theory of evolution has played the most important role from the outset. It has thus been possible to displace the historical imagination onto the future on a scale previously unrealized and speculate that man would be able to transcend his own current limitations. As our own century matured, however, the more naive convictions about evolution had to be cast aside. It was clear that any natural biological evolution would involve a time-scale of a very high order of magnitude, and critical thought soon recognized that human society does not operate in terms of physical laws: the "evolution" of social structures is something far different from the evolution of a biological species. Hence, by the thirties, in writers of such standing as Stapledon, Weinbaum, and van Vogt, credibility was most often achieved by a new quasi-scientific rationale—genetic mutation—which allowed for the appearance of a superior race in the more immediate future. Indeed, our own era would find reasonable some "quantum leap" into the future made possible by just such an artificial (even accidental, but man-created) transformation in the species.

The more recent history of the theme in science-fiction literature is much more complex because the superman can easily be associated with so many other speculative ideas. Thus the superman's origin has variously been ascribed to the work of aliens, as in Sturgeon's *The Synthetic Man*, to a new, "perfect" educational system, as in van Vogt's Null-A stories, or to artificial biological and eugenic techniques like cloning, as in the case of van Vogt's Gosseyn, his Null-A detective. ESP capabilities are introduced as an attribute of the superman by almost all the writers.

Underlying the speculative and futuristic issue, the theme is concerned with transformations in ethical and moral consciousness. This is a constant which seems to have much to do with the generic significance of the superman and does not appear to be just an accident of literary history. It commonly occurs through the juxtaposition of the superman and his transcendent powers, knowledge, and values with normal, limited humanity. From Wells to Sturgeon, the writers have used the contrast between two orders of humanity for speculation as to what values in contemporary man are merely arbitrary (hence, *obsolete* from the perspective of the superman) and which are permanent (hence *not* obsolete and to be learned—or relearned—by the superman from our inferior form of humanity). The SF writers therefore pose critical and cautionary questions to contemporary humanity as now constituted, and the theme should not be viewed as a form of simple-minded prophecy about what the human species necessarily *will* become. The critical purpose of writing about a superman is to think about what present Everyman *might* become, as when Theodore Sturgeon in so many elegant fictions tells us that man—as he is now or as he ought to be—constantly requires a maturation in emotional sensitivity and moral consciousness. This is the most important reason why theological critics like the Roses who believe that human nature is a static God-fashioned, "eternal" entity incapable of historical development (perhaps, too, because they believe in "original sin") are revolted by the science-fiction superman.[6] They simply have not achieved the science-fiction conviction that change and adaptation are essential to anything which might remotely be dubbed "human nature."

Nor is it fair to think of American SF as preaching some master-race mythology. If anything, classic SF, as the next few examples demonstrate, validates normal contemporary humanity. Yet there isn't any issue in these works over the mutability of human nature: all three American writers (Stanley Weinbaum, A.E. van Vogt, Henry Kuttner) view the human species as the product of evolution and history, of processes and forces which are by no means complete with today's version of *Homo sapiens*. But all also assert that man as he is now constituted is real and, all things considered, good. This acceptance of present-day humanity comes only after the superman concept raises questions of *both* a speculative *and* ethical nature: when is it "human" to transcend presently conceived limits and norms (in Darko Suvin's terms, when does such transcendence conduce to further hominization of the species?) and when is a superman a demonic and destructive (anti-social) agent? Though the need for intelligence and intelligent behavior is always important, these writers also say something else is needed for true transcendence: altruism, a concern for something—and someone—beyond narrow self-interest.

The Adamic myth is central to Stanley Weinbaum's superman novel, *The New Adam* (Chicago: Ziff-Davis, 1939),[7] which tells of Edmund Hall, the first member (hence, an "Adam" by analogy) of a post-human race which is no longer *Homo sapiens*, though derived from it and engendered in its midst. Though the hero has the opportunity to share in the future of his new species which seems destined to render normal mankind an obsolescent and dying breed because of the supermen's superior intellectual faculties, this "New Adam" chooses a passionate love for a normal human woman and rejects the call of the future. Like his mythological prototype, he has chosen a fruit at once forbidden and strangely normal ("human") in his passion for beauty and sex, and it finally leads to his death. His love of an "alien" woman, Vanny, drives her mad and saps his own strength, and although she stimulates his imagination to decadent brilliance, Hall fails to become the New Adam of his own kind even as normal men look upon him as a Satan whose presence signals the end of man. Only in his Fall does the superman fulfill the deeper promise of the prefigurative mythical title.

The New Adam never gained much popularity even though it is a very sophisticated book in its technique and ranks on a par with American mainstream writing of the Depression era. Like its parallel, "A Martian Odyssey" (see the analysis in chapter 1), the mythical title comes to be more than a loose metaphor: it identifies a whole set of underlying correspondences.

On the other hand, this story involves an inversion of conventional expectations about the superman: neither the overintellectual, hypercerebral advanced race nor contemporary men's social mores are idealized. The emotion of Vanny, shared by the New Adam, is, however, something real and undeniable, and mortality remains an inescapable limit on the human condition.

Weinbaum's fictive world is here very close to the "zero world" of normal experience, and his mutant version of the Biblical Adam myth recapitulates the original's view of mortality. But it is important to single out two works, van Vogt's *Book of Ptath* and Kuttner's *Mask of Circe,* that are related to more archaic, pagan world-views rather than to the Judeo-Christian; where immortality, however ambivalent its import, is made a part of the reality-system: the main hero is an amnesiac who recovers his memory and identity; and some maturation in consciousness goes hand in hand with this psychic "death-rebirth" ritual.

This kind of story, classified as "science fantasy" and endemic to later sf, depicts the heroic development of a modern protagonist within the conventional monomythic initiatory pattern, but with the result that the modern man rediscovers and recovers an older identity in himself which is that of some superhuman being. The "hero" or "god" is not acquiring his unique personality and asserting it in the world for the first time, but regaining and reasserting his own older, preformed superhuman identity. For all of the initiatory character of the trials, quests, or adventures, these narratives exhibit a fundamental psychiatric quality and presuppose popular psychoanalytical themes like identity crisis, multiple personality, recovery from amnesia, or therapeutic abreaction. Sometimes the original personality lurking in the modern psyche seems like a "second self."[8] It seems in these stories that the quest is mostly a function of the perception-consciousness system of the hero, as if it all happens "in his own mind" and is involved with his personal dreams, memories, and visions. Sometimes, too, a very pseudo-scientific version of the modern science of genetics is used to explain the mechanics of the presence of an atavistic second self in a modern man.[9]

A.E. van Vogt is reknowned for some of the most exciting and dreamlike adventures of the superman, especially *Slan* and the Null-A books.[10] *The Book of Ptath* (1943)[11] is barely, if ever, mentioned, yet it has some claim to be judged a remarkable and seminal work in the history of the mythical SF narrative. Van Vogt extrapolates beyond the typical conception of a superior race descended from normal humans to assert that the religious consciousness contains a powerful divine seed. In 200,000,000 A.D. three beings of normal human origin can function as immortal gods, their incredible powers increased by the prayers addressed to them by their human subjects. These are gods, who, once men themselves, were created by men: "And, somewhere, long ago, a king named Ptath had been lifted up to the status of genuine godhood that had been potential from the first moment that a primitive vassal prostrated himself abjectly at the broad, naked feet of the first chieftain-priest" (p. 106). "Man's terrible penchant to render homage to heroes, kings and non-existent gods had at last created divinity" (p. 90). The language of these passages connotes a sinister, demonic message: normal human beings become no more than slaves of the united power of religion and science.

I will at least offer the conjecture that in these passages the unspecified king was an Egyptian pharaoh, and that "Ptath" is a transmogrified Egyptian deity, *Ptah.* In the ancient Egyptian theology developed by the priests at Memphis, Ptah was the creator god who generated the nine deities of the royal pantheon, the Ennead, out of the power of his own creative utterance. He was therefore the ultimate divine ancestor of the pharaoh, who was himself conceived of as god incarnate and youngest member of the divine family. Is van Vogt consciously telescoping the divine stemma and thinking of Ptath as a pharaoh in origin? Or is the name totally subconscious in origin? (In *Science-Fiction Studies* 1 [1973–74]:220, Damon Knight speaks of van Vogt's writing technique of "dreaming about his stories and waking up every ninety minutes to take notes.")

This seems to be one more clue that van Vogt is, like Edgar Rice Burroughs and Phil Farmer, closer to the "dreaming" pole of science fiction. In such "science fantasy," man's scientific and technological extensions—man's own creations, fashioned from his own ever-increasing scientific knowledge—provide him with powers and capacities equivalent to his primitive deities. It is obvious that all of *Ptath* operates in a mode of hyperbole where the distinction between science and the supernatural is blurred (e.g., a temporal scale of 10^8 years where, except for the handful of deities, normal humans haven't changed at all!; the magnitude of human populations is similarly hyperbolic).

It is true that van Vogt appeals at a high level of wish-fulfillment, where strict scientific credibility or plausibility is not the main goal, yet his many fictions on the themes of man-become-god and science-become-religion are important to demonstrate the ambivalence of twentieth-century man's dreams of his future, which can carry both terrifying and desirable aspects. Especially the merging of science and religion can be demonic enough to call into question the happy endings the author chose for his popular romances. Behind the Odyssean mythos expressed in 800-word scientific idea-as-action scenes lies a Frankensteinian cautionary message.

The story, as pure story, is classic van Vogt, fast-paced and action-packed. Consciousness dawns on the god, and Ptath is perplexed to find himself an amnesiac. His recovery is further complicated by the presence of a personality from an earlier reincarnation, Holroyd, a normal twentieth-century man. The latter soon learns that Ptath's evil first wife, Ineznia, has fabricated a plot to destroy her divine consort forever and rule over a tyrannized, god-ridden humanity in his stead. The god is aided only by his second wife, L'onee, a gentle, loving soul (but completely stereotypic and uninteresting) who is the third, and final, deity in this futuristic temple culture. Most important, the complete restoration of Ptath's original divine self is dependent on Holroyd's series of experiences inside the Ptath body.

However, it is really Ptath who learns, more than Holroyd, because it is the god, originally a man himself, who is re-initiated into the consciousness of normal humanity. This SF version of the Incarnation is psychically a retrograde evolution for the god, but all along it had been his purpose to re-experience the feelings of the race whose beliefs and worship had fathered him, even though his divine memory had to be erased momentarily. In L'onee's view:

> This is what Ptath feared in the old days; it was what he saw growing within himself: A remorseless impatience with human weakness, a ruthless disregard of the race from which we, all three of us, were originally sprung. It was to prevent that beast god from appearing that he merged himself with the race. (p. 133)

This altruistic view contrasts strongly with the will-to-power immorality of the bitch-goddess Ineznia, who pursues only the carnal side of Incarnation. She uses her divine power of mind-transferral for sexual purposes, going among mankind, philandering all the while, inside different bodies. Hence, conventional and stereotypical sexual attitudes of the Depression era are used as the norm by which the inhuman and demonic are defined (to be sure, nothing even remotely indelicate, let alone "obscene," comes up in Ineznia's story). But the idea of taboo-breaking promiscuity is raised only to be let drop at the conventional, status-quo conclusion. Her evil personality and aggressiveness once again stir up old, deep-rooted fears in her human subjects, with the natural result that they pray to Ptath for salvation; ironically, this leads to the god regaining enough of his powers so that he can displace his wife and once again set human history upon a "human" track. Nietzsche's grim visions of the superman and Eternal Recurrence are turned into a popular Depression-era romance where heroes and villains alike are armed with wild super-gadgets and ride pell-mell through a series of frenetic adventures. At its conclusion, the author rejects master-race myths and thus—to be as fair to van Vogt as possible—he comes out as intelligent, critical, and liberal enough for his times. He is certainly strong in storytelling, if one at all likes science-as-adventure fables.

Much the same uneasiness about the godlike superman and the despotism which could result from science-become-religion is expressed in a classic work of mythological science fantasy from the forties, Henry Kuttner's *The Mask of Circe* (*Startling Stories,* January

1948). Like his wife, C.L. Moore, Kuttner is well known as a literary innovator and experimenter in relating myth to SF.[12]

Told in first-person narrative by a man from our world (who is also a psychiatrist), *The Mask of Circe* is a fable about man's creative potential which imagines an alternate dimension of time-space that once belonged to the Olympian gods of Greek myth. The dimension "once belonged" because this superhuman race of scientifically gifted mutants almost extinguished themselves by experiments on life-forms. The catastrophe was specifically caused by their most perfect creation, Apollo, an artificial, inorganic, yet immortal and intelligent *machine* who used solar power to destroy his creators. Apollo is a particularly apt choice for superscientific deity in light of Nietzsche's *Birth of Tragedy* where Apollo serves as a cultural archetype of the principles of individuation, specification, and limit that are fundamental to Western science and philosophy. Analogously, it is important that the one Olympian who survives to oppose Apollo is Hecate, symbolic of the chthonic and intuitive side of human nature that nurtures the human psyche through remembrance of its own rich symbolic and archetypal past. Hecate represents continuity in human nature, Apollo the radical, hyperrational revision of man accomplished by science, which might just destroy him. In this fantasia which combines mythical and psychoanalytical themes, the underworld of man's myths, religions, and old gods—as well as his own subconscious—are his allies against the upperworld of excessive scientific creativity. The further suggestions are that Hecate is feminine, receptive, and intuitive, while Apollo is harshly masculine, manipulative, and analytical.

Kuttner's hero, Seward, is a psychiatric researcher who has experimented with hypnosis and narcosynthesis, with the unfortunate side-effect of having revived a latent other self, Jason of the ancient Greek myth, whose genes he seems to have inherited. Inspired by the characterizations in Euripides' drama, *Medea,* and Apollonius of Rhodes' Hellenistic epic, *The Voyage of the Argo (Argonautica)*,[13] Kuttner's Jason is at best ruthless and treacherous, and Seward has great difficulties controlling this Hyde within his Jekyll.

But in this modern transformation of the original myth, Jason's last love is not Medea, but another witch, encountered by Odysseus in Homer's epic, Circe, who is the daughter of Hecate in Kuttner's account. Seward is soon enchanted by her mysterious call right out of our world, and he finds himself conveyed by a ghostly Argo which eternally tacks back and forth between two polarized dimensions of time-space under the rhythm of the hero Orpheus' mysterious song until it reaches Circe's island, Aeaea, which is not the original world of ancient Greek mythology but the descendant of that world, just as our own is. For in three thousand years what was once one world ruled by a race of mutants with superhuman powers—we remember them from their heyday as the Olympian gods—has split into two polarized universes, ours a rational and empirical world, theirs retaining a disposition to magical forces and mutant beings, though the movements of the Argo indicate that the two dimensions still have some mutual attraction and can exchange objects and energies.

The history of the parallel world reveals that the superhuman mutants had one major limitation—mortality—so they experimented to create a race that could live forever. One result is the hybrids who crowd Aeaea: Centaurs, Fauns, and others unnamed in the ancient myths who are immortal, but they are flawed Frankensteinian creatures because their natures have the taint of the beast. Still a later Faustian experiment on artificial intelligence brought complete catastrophe when the Olympians finally created a perfect immortal being whose aspect was radiant heat and light from the sun itself. This was Apollo, an unliving *machine* of inhuman beauty and power who waged war against the race of his makers and utterly destroyed them and their celestial city. Only Hecate, mother of Circe, survived (inexplicably, she seems to be immortal) to carry on the war against Apollo.

Seward discovers that Circe, like the original Jason, was a mortal who died millennia ago, but her facial features and her psyche live on in a mask designed by Hecate and worn by countless generations of priestesses, for the ancient prophecies insist that Jason will someday return to fulfill an unfinished quest he promised to Hecate and Circe, and the enchantress must herself be present to reward the hero with her love. Seward's heroic destiny in this other dimension is to satisfy Hecate's claim upon the Jason in him. In contrast to the monstrous Apollo, the "Mask of Circe" represents the benign, enchanting side of science—a sort of feminine *anima*-figure that makes us look on the future, and the unknown, with desire instead of dread. But this haunting image of the man-machine encounter remains unresolved in the tale: Seward doesn't get the girl, but is still following the call when last we see him.

Seward's lesson in heroism is precisely the opposite of an identification with his ancestor and prototype, Jason, for the captain of the Argo was a coward and traitor who turned and fled from Apollo in their first encounter. As narcosynthesis had made Seward realize the Jason in him, so the original Jason had also been a double personality and it was his stronger, more heroic side that had appealed to Hecate and Circe in the first place. This turns out to be nothing other than the "Seward" part of Jason-Seward, so in the parallel world it is by still a second psychic catharsis—in the face of Apollo's awesome solar energy—that Seward cuts through the cowardly, treacherous Jason in himself and discovers authentic herohood by realizing the equivalent of his original self, *the modern Seward!* Armed with the Golden Fleece that was his by right of genetic predestination—the Fleece is another superscientific machine, constructed by Hephaestus—Seward so enfolds Apollo in its fabric that the god's solar power is forced inward to his own destruction.

In retrospect, every reader can recognize that the hero's initiation is psychological in character, constituting the acquisition of self-knowledge and the integration of his own multiple personality; that Seward's experiences on Aeaea are adventures of memories regained; and that the perception-consciousness of Seward the narrator is the center focus of the story. Yet the narrative is left open-ended: Kuttner restores Seward to his own world momentarily, but in the final scene of the novel—no longer in first-person narration—he is called away again in mysterious fashion to the interdimensional Argo.

Both van Vogt and Kuttner reaffirm that normal contemporary humanity is real, is a product of past history, and has a future of change and development ahead. And yet, after the sojourn in the estranged realms of godhead, which is delineated in terms of immortality and freedom from current sexual norms, the power and freedom of the superman conjure up a demonic atmosphere, an uneasiness in the face of potentially so radical a transformation of the human species. Both *Ptath* and *Circe* seem to ambivalently straddle the confident Odyssean and cautionary Frankensteinian attitudes toward the future and leave the tension unresolved.

It is revealing that this same ambivalence toward an immortal and sexually demonic superman prevails in more recent SF. How these two basic concerns inform four contrasting examples of important contemporary SF is the subject of the rest of this chapter: in turn, we will consider a TV show, a Hollywood film, and the works of two leading writers in American SF today. All have the advantage of being explicitly mythical, and all offer contrasting parallels and affinities with the classic works already discussed.

In an episode of the TV series *Star Trek* with the suggestive title of "Who Mourns for Adonais?" (vol. 7 in *Star Trek* book series by James Blish),[14] the starship Enterprise visits an unexplored region of space and there encounters a planet inhabited by the god Apollo. He is the last surviving Olympian, a race of superscientific beings who had lived long ago on our planet earth. It was in the Heroic Age of Greece—Apollo specifically remembers the heroes of the Homeric epics—that our human ancestors rebelled and refused to serve the gods and worship them. The Olympians could not endure rejection by mankind and so retired to this obscure corner of the universe and then passed away into the cosmos one by one since they could no longer survive without the love and worship of an inferior but fully intelligent species. This allegory is repeated when the human beings of the Enterprise rebel against the authority of the god into whose power they have blundered, until they weaken and destroy him by refusing to worship or love him (cf. the power of worship in *Ptath*).

Hence, the title based on the ancient Near Eastern myth of Adonais, a Dying God whose annual resurrection from the dead was closely connected with a ritual performed by his female worshippers. While it was the ancient believers' weeping for their deceased god that revived him to relive his annual myth, it is crewwoman Carolyn's rejection of Apollo as her lover that is the last straw—the god in effect commits suicide because he has already been rejected by the rest of the Enterprise's crew. Kirk remarks to the god as he disappears forever, "we have outgrown you." Mankind belongs in the future, not in the past—this is true even of historian and archaeologist Carolyn who comes closest to worshipping the ancient deity as we might expect of any scholar who should confront a fantastic relic from the distant past. Yet the "god" lives on in some sense, for Carolyn becomes pregnant by him, and as the Enterprise sails off until its next episode, Kirk and McCoy half comically wonder what will happen when this "son of god" is born.

This tale cannot be put down as a strictly conservative one in its message: it opts for human rationality, science, and independence of thought over passive religiosity or static inflexibility in the face of trans-human powers. Yet, somehow, this episode comes off as defending the social status quo of the American mid-60s: it makes us feel good about staying the way we are rather than urging us to grow and change. Perhaps this is best typified in the choice of actress Leslie Parrish to play the role of would-be academic Carolyn: so sensual and beautiful a woman is highlighted, so sexual and romantic a situation is imagined, that any more cogitative message gets lost. But it is not at all unusual in the history of television programming for there to be a strong conflict between the visual and intellectual content of a show, with the former—imagery—dominating.

In the seventies, a significant Hollywood film on the subject of the superman was made, but it never achieved a following even remotely as large as that of the popular TV series. The film is much more discomforting than *Star Trek*, often shocking and violent, and it provides the kind of critical and speculative disturbance in our intellects we associate with the best controversy-provoking SF in its written forms (e.g., Ellison, Moorcock, Delany).

John Boorman's *Zardoz* is an excellent science-fiction movie (20th Century-Fox, 1974) as well as a novel of some stylistic elegance (Signet Books, 1974)—although the book gives away its primarily cinematic inspiration by being cast in the form of discrete gorgeous scenes rather than continuous, coherent narrative. In the film version, the special effects are modest, but convincing, and the cinematography is beautiful.

Zardoz (inspired by L. Frank Baum's *Wizard of Oz*) is an artificial god, used in the Dark Age of earth's future to keep the benighted serflike and mutant peasants in line. The worshipful servants of the god, the Exterminators, periodically run amok, killing and raping at will among the Brutals (peasants treated as subhuman), according to the god's will, to prevent the earth from ever again becoming as overpopulated as it was in our era. At the other end of the human scale are the manipulators of this pseudo-religious spectacle, the Eternals, a race of immortals, equipped with all that human scientific knowledge could save from the atomic cataclysm. For all of their perfections and superhuman powers, however, the Eternals are a race sterile in every way: they have become sexually impotent with the passing of the centuries, and the number of those who are sane and competent is daily dwindling. Some Eternals become Renegades from their order and are punished with permanent aging, then locked away in a surreal penitentiary, the Starlight Hotel, where there is a perpetual ballroom dance and it is still impossible for them to die, no matter how senile or psychotic they become. Still others become Apathetics, subsisting in a permanent death-like state of catatonia, unable to *really* die. Other images of stasis are interspersed throughout; an especially powerful one is the archaeological storeroom, where the remains of the artistic treasures of our civilization lie in a state of suspended animation. Boorman constantly reinforces his theme: immortality is only the permanent fixing of death, not an escape from it.

Into the protected enclosure of the Eternals known as the Vortex, which is depicted as a static paradise, at once frivolous and effete, comes Zed the Liberator (played effectively by Sean Connery).[15] He is a *mutant* Exterminator (created, as we discover, by the same Eternal who created Zardoz), and the heroic boon he brings as Redeemer is death. His is a genetically programmed task of disrupting life in the Vortex and annihilating the source of its power—the "Tabernacle," a diamond crystal capable of infinite light refraction, in which is stored all the Eternals' scientific knowledge. Zed himself, in the climactic confrontation with this godlike machine, must refuse the temptation to join the immortals in order for his mission to succeed, but the revival of the forces of life, change, and history is symbolized even more strikingly in two other scenes. One is a sexual orgy—Zed mates with many of the female Eternals bringing them back to sexual life, impregnating them so they can leave the Vortex and begin a new human society. The other is a scene of madness in which the Eternals destroy the museum and its contents—thus making human history start to work again.

At the end, the Eternals are reduced once more to normal humanity, all but the women impregnated by Zed being annihilated by the Exterminators. It is thus Boorman's theme, not merely that sex is a function of death (the first being impossible without the second), but the more universal one that life and death are parts of one process and the two are mutually interdependent.

Is it possible to recognize in *Zardoz* an inversion of the Christian mythos? Zed, whose name is in British English the name of the final letter of the alphabet, is the "Omega and Alpha" (in that order) of this future decadent universe: the salvation he brings mankind is *from* immortality; as inverted Redeemer, he brings death, not life eternal.

We now turn back from these visualizations of the superman to narrative fiction; to two major figures of contemporary SF, both rightly characterized as popular, accessible, "readable" authors. Yet their works are unmistakably more than just readable. Roger Zelazny possesses studied literary erudition, and Philip José Farmer makes convincing application of psychoanalytical researches. Neither likes his readers to figure him out completely, and both seem to have something of the elusive, half-satirical Trickster about them, but they also show an androgynous mentality in their writings. Inasmuch as they are both still at the peak of their output as of this writing, I have chosen for detailed consideration their mythological novels produced in the late sixties: these works are unconventional in many respects, but still seem closer in spirit and attitude to traditional SF as distinct from contemporary New Wave.

Roger Zelazny has been consistently popular for a decade and a half now, with several Nebula and Hugo awards already to his credit. He must now be recognized, too, as the most important single writer of the mythical science-fiction narrative to date, both for the quality and quantity of his opus. In Zelazny's rewritings of Greek, Hindu, and Egyptian mythology, science comes to serve as modern man's religion, and technology creates inhuman deities prefigured by van Vogt (*This Immortal, Lord of Light, Creatures of Light and Darkness*).

Zelazny's fictions seem to fall into two broad classes, those of the Amber series, which correlate the superman fiction with sword-and-sorcery conceptions, and another based heavily on a knowledge of mythology. The latter class can itself be divided into two kinds of narratives. In one, Zelazny uses a complete mythological basis, original names, events, and conceptions (though purposeful distortions are equally in evidence); in the other, he uses quasi-mythical structures, themes, and patterns without explicit use of, or even allusion to, specific myths. The first, or explicit, type could be characterized by *Lord of Light* and *Creatures of Light and Darkness*, the second or "displaced" type by *Isle of the Dead* and *Jack of Shadows*; "A Rose for

Ecclesiastes" and *This Immortal* seem to fit somewhere between the two categories.[16] But in all his narratives this writer manages to isolate the essential forms of archaic myths and shows like Farmer that ancient dreams of transcendence and modern dreams of transcendence are basically the same, very human experience.

These narratives also all come off as half-comic parodies of conventional SF tale-types, and Zelazny is never far from satire, though he is sly, elusive, and ironic: the intelligent allusions to classics of world literature are clearly there but an attitude of humor is also ever present.

The themes traditionally associated with the superman (immortality, demonic sexuality) are also central. The main distinctive thing about Zelazny's supermen is that we aren't returned to normalcy as in the classic tales: his heroes remain free, successful, and immortal and they get away with their free sexuality (sixties style). His heroes are also "lone wolf" types, suggesting that loneliness is part of the cost of the freedom his immortal supermen enjoy.

This Immortal (1966),[17] which won a Hugo Award, combines explicit allusions to ancient Greek mythology and modern Greek folklore with the superman theme. At some unspecified time in the future, after Earth has devastated itself in an atomic war and much of mankind has consequently evolved into a mutant species, our planet is only a museum. Most humans, in fact, no longer live on Earth; they have migrated to distant planets where they live indolently under the tutelage of an extraterrestrial race, the Vegans, who are now the absentee landlords of Earth and who use it only for a resort.

This Immortal is therefore a study of our human birthright, for a Greek-born hero, Conrad Nomikos, is at once the guardian of our past and guarantor of our future. Officially, he is Commissioner of Arts, Monuments, and Archives on Earth and his assignment is to conduct a guided tour for the Vegan, Cort Myshtigo, whose clan owns the planet. On the other hand, he is really a Greek folklore hero, Kallikanzaros,[18] once the leader of the revolutionary forces known as Radpol, an invincible fighter, a mutant who seemingly will never age or die, and an avatar of the ancient Greek heroes.

The tour on which Conrad takes Myshtigo is supposed to retrace human history up to the moment when the Three Day War brought

Men like Gods

a cataclysmic end. There is a visit to Egypt, though the entire second half of the novel deals only with Greece, a land that the hero calls "lousy with myth" (p. 156). Hence, Conrad must recapitulate the trials of the ancient Greek heroes and regain Earth for its own species, for atomic war has plunged the remnant of mankind back into a time when heroism of the ancient Greek type is both possible and necessary.

Mutations in particular provide a revival of the heroic landscape: there are satyrs, cannibalistic brigands known as Kouretes, their villainous chief, Procustes, and an albino idiot vampire called the Great Dead Man. Conrad's words also suggest that it is this mutant landscape that contains the revival of the ancient mythology:

> Centaurs, too, have been seen here—and there are vampire flowers, and horses with vestigial wings. There are sea serpents in every sea. Imported spider-bats plow our skies. There are even sworn statements by persons who have seen the Black Beast of Thessaly, an eater of men, bones and all—and all sorts of other legends are coming alive. . . . The age of strange beasts *is* come upon us again. Also, the age of heroes, demigods. [pp. 94, 98]

Zelazny is often cavalier with Greek mythology and the names of his science-fiction characters are poorly assimilated (if at all) to their prototypes, but this seems deliberate on the author's part: mythology, too, bears the character of a mutation, as it does in Delany's *Einstein Intersection* (see chapter 2). Zelazny is a true comparativist: whereas the phenomenon "myth" per se is very significant, he sees as less essential this or that particular culture's formulation or specification; myth transcends single specific cultures and is a human universal, geographically and temporally.

As a revolutionary hero who would assert the independence of human destiny on Earth as opposed to acquiescence of the human extraterrestrials before their Vegan masters, Conrad is based on the age of the Greek war for independence against the Turks in the nineteenth century; as a slayer of mutant beasts and monsters, Conrad harks back to the ancient Greek heroes, Heracles in particular (to whom he is likened in two specific passages, pp. 65 and 164). It was Heracles whose famous labors were regarded by the ancient Greeks as mythical analogues of the civilizing act, of bringing human culture to raw, chaotic, brute nature. Like Heracles, Conrad does achieve success with the help of his son, Jason, and his bride, Cassandra, who had been feared lost; for upon the death of Myshtigo, Conrad as heroic civilizer inherits the earth because his slaying of a series of monsters is a prelude to re-pacifying Earth for its human population.

No doubt at a mythic level, the novel is concerned with heroic redemption of an Earth become a "waste land." But Conrad is a delightful "pop" figure of the sixties, who brazenly identifies himself in dialogue with the reader via first-person narration.[19] Conrad is an early example of the Trickster figure who is Zelazny's trademark; too, this is in keeping with the personality of Kallikanzaros. He is also optimistic about the survival capacity for man in a world where the worst happens (nuclear catastrophe—as it does in Zelazny's later work of heroic redemption, *Damnation Alley*[20]). This attitude, highly individualistic, makes Zelazny seem different from the mostly Frankensteinian New Wavers; but in literary sophistication and experimental fiction-making, he is their equal.

Zelazny uses other indirect techniques in his narration like literary allusions, symbols, and metaphors—several kinds of stylistic techniques which had earlier been associated with poetry, but which from the time of James Joyce on have become more and more the preserve of prose writers as well. To take one very representative example, the first likening of Conrad to Heracles on p. 65, the hero is facing a mechanical opponent (a Robot-Golem or "Rolem") dispatched to assassinate him. Conrad throws all of his powers into the combat, then hurls his opponent to the ground: "But he sprang up immediately, and I knew then that he was no mortal wrestler, but one of those creatures born not of woman; rather I knew, he had been torn Antaeus-like from the womb of the Earth itself" (p. 65—in Conrad's words). If his opponent is like the giant Antaeus, of course Conrad must be Heracles; but at the same time, given science-fiction technology, it is reasonable that the mechanical killer is "not born of woman." Without muting action and adventure—traditional *story* values in SF—Zelazny can cleverly use his skill at literary allusion to extend the sophistication of the genre and create a richly textured mythological novel.

Lord of Light (1967)[21] received a Hugo Award, and one of its novel features is the satirical and parodical connection made between ancient Hindu mythology (and the revolution of the Buddha) and a futuristic SF universe. The superhuman hero is known as Sam, short for Mahasamatman, alias Siddhartha, Kalkin, Lord of Light, Binder of the Demons. He is also one of the First, that is, one of the original crewmembers of the starship from earth who colonized this new world unspecified ages ago. Once upon a time he locked up the Rakashi Demons, the alien high-energy beings who were this planet's original inhabitants; but now he has long been a lone wolf and nonconformist going his own way and ignoring the history of the planet he helped found.

Normal mankind, however, has regressed after several generations, for a combination of genetic mutations, advanced technology, and developed psychic powers has promoted the First, the original crew, to superhuman godhead while the general mass of humanity—their own descendants—live in subjection as the lowest caste, with all science, political freedoms, and, above all, immortality (as a technological achievement) withheld from them by the gods.

This is a static cosmos in which even the gods are bored with their own perfection, tired even of the unlimited sensuality available in their Celestial City. A representative passage portrays Brahma, the chief deity of the pantheon:

> *Ili*, the fifth note of the harp, buzzed within the Garden of the Purple Lotus.
>
> Brahma loafed upon the edge of the heated pool, where he bathed with his harem. His eyes appeared closed, as he leaned there upon his elbows, his feet dangling in the water.
>
> But he stared out from beneath his long lashes, watching the dozen girls at sport in the pool, hoping to see one or more cast an appreciative glance upon the dark, heavily muscled length of his body. Black upon brown, his mustaches glistened in moist disarray and his hair was a black wing upon his back. He smiled a bright smile in the filtered sunlight.
>
> But none of them appeared to notice, so he refolded his smile and put it away. (pp. 71–2)

Sexual excess and decadence, the artificial atmosphere surrounding the pool, and the artificiality portrayed in the god ("he refolded his smile and put it away") poetically represent the problem of this god-ridden universe of the future: it is a world which has nowhere to go. For Sam to exist here at leaves him with only one response: revolution. Thus he becomes the "Enlightened One," a second Buddha who leads men away from the crude and blood-thirsty Hindu religion which worships horrible "deities" like Kali, goddess of death, Agni, god of fire, Yama, death personified, and Shiva, god of destruction. There is sixties-style political revolution, too, for Sam is determined to wreck the rigid caste system that preserves the karma machines for the gods and their favorites. Hence, the insurgency movement known as "Accelerationism."

In addition, *Lord of Light* can be recognized as an experiment in narrative technique. Its plot is by no means a one-dimensional sci-fi "yarn": rather than unfolding his story in a direct chronological scheme, Zelazny "spatializes" (to use Sharon Spencer's term) his narrative by juxtaposing and intercutting three distinct time schemes.

The first of these is always described in the past tense, from the point of view of either of the other two schemes, both of which use the vivid present tense. It was the days of the Firstlings, when Sam was a great power in the world and used his control of electro-direction to lock the Demons up in Hellwell. Seemingly, many, if not all, the First possessed such superhuman powers, later identified as their divine "aspect," by way of genetic mutation.

The second era (comprising sections ii through vi in the novel) is generations later when even the name of Earth is but dimly remembered as "vanished Urath" (pp. 31 and 55), when the Masters of Karma suppress their fellow men, so Sam founds Buddhism as a religious foil, frees the Demons and uses them and other old and new powers in the world, including many heretic gods, to bring down the Celestial City. Sam fails at this first attempt, and the gods capture him and transmit his *atman* electronically into the great magnetic cloud that encircles the globe.

Yet a half century later (sections i and vii of the book), in the third temporal scheme, which frames the second, Sam's allies recall him from "Nirvana" to break the powers of the divine Masters once and for all; now humanity can progress as it was supposed to when this world was first colonized.

And yet, for all the sophisticated narrative techniques which it shares with New Wave SF and avant-garde mainstream literature,

Lord of Light is a "great read," a dazzling, spectacular story told on a lavish scale. Only John Brunner's finely wrought short story, "The Vitanuls,"[22] is as intelligent in its presentation of Indian thought. On the other hand, Zelazny is no Zen Master, as dissertation writer John Rothfork has maintained; rather, there is a Western consciousness of the necessity of intellectual pluralism behind Zelazny's choice of Hindu mythology to prefigure a speculative, futuristic "Eternal Return" of man to a static, god-ridden existence: the Hindu religion led to a crushing and inhumane social order, the caste system. In the name of the religious consciousness, this system banished the problem of death, of being-in-the world, and rendered creative thought and individual self-assertion impossible. Indeed Sam, the democratic, open-minded, and free-wheeling hero in the sixties mold, is really the only true individual personality in the story. The others, i.e., the deities, are merely a function of their divine aspect—and other human beings can, and are, easily drawn on to play divine roles when vacancies occur. Sam is a special person, but then—to Zelazny—a hero is.

Zelazny chose Egyptian mythology for one of his less popular novels—*Creatures of Light and Darkness* (New York: Doubleday, 1969)[23]—which also depicts godlike beings, variously termed "Immortals" or "Angels." Some fans who didn't like the book thought the entire thing was a parody of his own earlier myth narratives, *Lord of Light* in particular. Perhaps "demonic parody" or "hellish parody" might be more accurate.

The futuristic cosmos of Zelazny's novel is god-ridden, flawed, perhaps even "fallen." A group of "Middle Worlds" inhabited by six intelligent but mortal races is the seething battleground for a polarized combat between two groups of gods: the House of the Dead, led by the dog-headed Anubis, and the House of Life, led by the bird-headed Osiris and his son, Horus, the god of vengeance. It is the cosmological function of these two Mafia-like Houses (or "Stations" as they are sometimes termed) to regulate and balance the forces of life and death in the Middle Worlds, regardless of the horrible consequences that the mortal races often must suffer (this theme is annunciated in Anubis' speech, p. 24).

In accordance with their traditional roles in ancient Egyptian mythology, Osiris and Anubis hold the positions of god of life and god of the underworld, respectively, but far from being examples of an opposition, they resemble each other closely. Zelazny's Osiris and Anubis are in constant communication with each other and share their power over the Middle Worlds for the sake of keeping that usurped power away from others. They both consider Thoth (the Prince That Was a Thousand) as their enemy. Both Orisis and Anubis send assassins out into the Middle Worlds to find and kill Thoth (Osiris sends Horus and Anubis sends Wakim.) The both oppress their subjects sadistically.

In the opening scene of this book, Anubis has the dead raised up to participate in a grotesque feast:

> "You who are dead . . . tonight you will disport yourselves for my pleasure. Food and wine will pass between your dead lips, though you will not taste it. Your dead stomach will hold it within you while your dead feet take the measure of a dance. Your dead mouths will speak words that have no meaning to you, and you will embrace one another without pleasure. You will sing for me if I wish it, you will lie down again when I will it. . . . Let the revelry begin." [p. 13]

Anubis, the god of death, makes his subjects imitate life. The reader is given a similar impression of Osiris' ghastly nature. Osiris keeps all his old enemies alive in the House of Life in transformed shapes for his sadistic pleasure. Osiris says:

> "True, the Angel of the Nineteenth House attempted to slay me, and true, others of my enemies exist in elementary forms at various points within My House such as fireplaces, icelockers, and ashtrays." [p. 119]

The underworld creatures experience life in death while Osiris' subjects experience death in life; little difference exists between these two states. Despite their different Stations (Life and Death), the behavior of the two gods is very similar; if they are representatives of the oppositional forces of Light and Dark, they obscure (even satirize) rather than define these oppositions.

On Thousandth Year Eve, Anubis forces Wakim to go through an ordeal calling into question the difference between being alive or dead and man or machine. Various parts of Wakim's body are cut off and finally his entire body is replaced with machinery. Anubis then questions Wakim as to how he knows whether he originated as a man or machine (all memories previous to the thousand years have been erased.) As a machine that does not breathe and has a nervous sytem of wire, Wakim is asked if he is alive or dead. Anubis turns off all the sensory mechanisms of Wakim's new body for a moment, and then asks him again whether he is alive or dead. Anubis sees little distinction between life and death, as can be seen from this dialogue:

> "What is at the same time the greatest blessing and the greatest curse in the universe?"
> "I do not know."
> "Life" says Anubis "and Death."
> "I do not understand," says Wakim. "You use the superlative. You called for one answer. You named two things, however."
> "Did I?" asks Anubis. "Really? Just because I used two words, does it mean that I have named two separate and distinct things?" [p. 21]

A large portion of *Creatures of Light and Darkness* seems to set up a series of anomalies that confuse the traditionally accepted oppositions. The problem of the distinction between men and machine pervades the book. The Steel General is an immortal who at various times in his life has been metal, wearing a ring of human skin to remind himself of his humanity. At other times he has been in a humanoid body with a metal ring. Megra is another example of the man-machine anomaly. She is joined by the angry Isis to a computer that gives predictions when the inquirer has sex with the human torso.

Another problem explored by *Creatures of Light and Darkness* is the distinction between god and man. Isis maligns Megra because she is disgusted that Megra, a mere human, has made love with the great god of destruction, Set. Humans are not isolated from gods in the book: Horus "marries" Megra. Set himself is a strange example of a god; when Anubis takes away his memory, he is merely Anubis' slave. Marduk (one of the 283 immortals) is a religious man; though constantly in the company of Thoth, Anubis, and Set he prays to some unknown universal God.

The art of temporal fugue makes the past and future difficult to distinguish. By achieving the power to travel back and forth through time, cause and effect are confused. Set is the father of Thoth by Isis, but Thoth is also the father of Set by Nephythia because of Thoth's time traveling.

Isis, the traditional Egyptian Mother Goddess, seems to be a very strong focus of the anomalies. She is described in conflicting terms as lustful, cruel, wise, and motherly. The Prince That Was a Thousand describes her as the ultimate love that is ultimate destruction. It is said of Isis that she had traded life and death for oblivion. She is a personality of conflicting traits, or rather a personality who transcends conflicts and oppositions; she snubs Megra for being a mere human, but flirts with Vramin who is also a human. She is "married" to Osiris of the House of Life, but has an affair with Set the Destroyer. She has two sons by Set: Thoth, who embodies a totally creative life-force, and Typhon, a dark form from the abyss.

There is also a mythical ("Once Upon a Time") past tense that often appears in the narration. Thoth, the Prince That Was a Thousand, once had regulated the various energies and forces of this universe in a more tranquil fashion and all the Immortals and Stations followed his benign and orderly decrees. But a monstrous and alien power (Set describes it as "an old god," p. 177), called "the Nameless," arose and disrupted the cosmic organization. Since the time of that lost cosmic paradise, Thoth has had to use all his own powers to coerce this Thing (to create meaning out of nonmeaning); and he also lost his two warrior sons, Set the Destroyer and Typhon,[24] in the process, while the Angels revolted and abandoned their proper Stations, so the rebel Houses of Life and Death shared the mastery of the universe and only their Stations maintained their regulatory functions (pp. 95–102). Now in the present tense of the novel, both rebel Houses are trying to preserve this status quo and to liquidate Thoth. Yet Thoth's original cosmic order is restored when Typhon returns unexpectedly from Chaos and Set the Destroyer is reborn from the House of the Dead as Wakim, the victim of amnesia and the would-be agent of Anubis. One major narrative frame of *Creatures*, consequently, lies in Set's re-acquisition of his original name, identity, and powers, his successful conquest of the Nameless, the defeat of the rebel Houses by Thoth and Typhon, and the temporary restoration of the more benign—yet unstable and dynamic—cosmos under the rule of the Prince That Was a Thousand.

In this novel, it is primarily the names themselves that act as prefigurations of the Immortals in the science-fiction story, for many of the themes and motifs are definitely not Egyptian: Thoth's visit to the Norns (pp. 129-133) conflates a Greek motif (Perseus and the Graiae) with a Norse one (how one-eyed Odin acquired his wisdom); Cerberus, the three-headed dog of the Greek underworld, is overpowered by the Immortal champions, Madrak and Typhon (pp. 121-23). The distinctively cosmological emphasis of *Creatures* is a feature it shares with ancient Egyptian mythology; however, the book discloses an inversion of the static cosmos portrayed in the ancient mythology. *Darkness* deals with an entire universe, and the forces of chaos and order which are eternally locked in combat within it, for the cosmic war will never cease. It has all the dynamic mutability of Leiber's Change War in *The Big Time* (see chapter 2). Restless, seething conflict is the mode of creativity, whether we speak of normal man, the superman, or even the superman-as-god. Without such conflict there is no history, only stasis.

Yet this is a parodic cosmology, of *meaning and language* rather than of nature per se. *Creatures of Light and Darkness* seems to define the basic divisions between nature and culture, god and man, dark and light, but also gives us impressions of the erratic interaction between these opposites and undermines the duality. The anomalous figure Isis summarizes these multiple interactions:

> "The creatures of Light and Darkness don and discard the garments of man, machine, and god; and Isis loves the dance. The creatures of light and darkness are born in great numbers, die in an instant, may rise again, may not rise again; and Isis approves of the garments." [p. 185]

It is possible, in retrospect, to see that these three major novels form a series which has some overall direction. We move from the nonconformist superman as redemptive hero in *This Immortal*; to supermen as gods who are so aloof from human concerns in *Lord of Light* as to leave normal humanity in caste subservience (though here too there is a nonconformist redeemer); to the monstrous, inhuman, and alien gods of *Creatures of Light and Darkness*. This progressive demonization of Zelazny's supermen-gods continues in *Jack of Shadows* (Signet, 1971) whose hero is a perverted god and a destructive Trickster-figure, combining in a Jungian "coincidence of opposites" the qualities of both Prometheus and Satan. The "shadow" in this novel combines what in the earlier work remained more polarized as "light and dark."[25]

There is no opportunity to do justice here to the Amber novels.[26] At a surface level, they are a popular sword-and-sorcery series, though the clever use of tarot symbols, images, and game techniques forbids a simplistic reading. The central figures are a family of immortal supermen, siblings contending for power against one another and especially their own father, an ogrish destroyer of his own offspring. Amber suggests a futuristic version of Freud's "primal horde"[27] and brings to life a modern psychoanalytical myth, and Zelazny's series thus bears comparison with a similar series by Philip José Farmer. In addition to the primal horde idea, the two writers share an interest in Tricksters, multiple universes, and demonic sexuality; in both series, too, the supermen have the ability to manipulate whole realities and whole universes.

In Farmer's "World of Tiers" series, now in its fifth volume, the supermen called Lords are cruel, vindictive superscientists.[28] These beings create entire artificial universes and people them with altered life-forms of their own devising: it even turns out that our own Earth is one of them.[29]

Ancient myths are central to this series. In typical fashion, the fifth volume, *The Lavalite World* (Ace, 1977), opens with the following sentence: "Kickaha was a quicksilver Proteus." Kickaha is the Trickster hero of the later books of the series, a character adaptable to every situation of the hostile Lords' worlds, but the Lord-created "Lavalite world" is equally Protean: it is a planet constantly undergoing metamorphosis on a grand scale, involving changes in landforms, mountains, oceans, and gravity. The myth of Proteus, a Greek water-god who could assume myriad shapes, prefigures, not only the hero, but his demanding mercurial environment. Thus, in the series as a whole, the supermen, led by the evil parent-figure Red Orc, suggest a Frankensteinian view of scientific creation while the adaptable Trickster is a complementary Odyssean figure.

The first novel, highly indebted to Henry Kuttner, is *The Maker of Universes* (Ace, 1965). Farmer depicts a parallel universe, which was artificially created by a superhuman science and modeled on the Sumero-Babylonian ziggurat, the most famous example of which is called the Tower of Babel in the Old Testament Book of Genesis (11.1–9). Farmer's alternate world revives the Biblical image of demonic pagan power: his world consists of five layers arranged one on top of the other with a majestic monolith separating each layer. Beyond the overall mythological inspiration for this zany cosmos, many of the individual layers and the creatures who inhabit them are mythological or inspired by myth.

Through the agency of a mysterious horn created by superscience, Robert Wolff—a man whose origins are obscured by a case of amnesia—leaves our world and finds himself in an unknown landscape at the bottommost level of this parallel universe. Thereafter the novel is centered on Wolff's ascent of the many levels of this cosmos, encountering heroic adventures and finally reacquiring his original identity: he ultimately realizes that he is none other than the original creator of this world, its Lord, and had been exiled by a rival superman, Arwoor, who usurped his place and caused the erasure of his memory. Yet Wolff's journey really amounts to a symbolic, heroic initiation, and after his personality is healed, he is no longer the cruel and capricious "god" he once was but a provident benefactor. Again, as in so many of the narratives encountered in this chapter, amnesia sets up a death-rebirth ritual for the superman with the result that he achieves an ethical awareness ("a memory") of normal human proportions.

The bottommost level in the tiered universe is the Garden, an Edenic world of pastoral innocence, peopled three thousand years ago by captives from Homer's Troy, including Wolff's lover Chryseis (in the original Homer, she was Agamemnon's prize and the cause of his quarrel with Achilles). In its decadence and artificiality, however, the Garden is a Satanic Eden; the role of desirable sexual objects like Chryseis is equally demonic, and even Wolff's human name intimates the Lords' wolflike manipulation of normal humanity. Other artificial creatures, like the unfortunate harpy Podarge, also confirm the Lords' evil Frankensteinian powers to remodel normal humans.

The next level is Amerindia, the American Indians' Happy Hunting Ground which is identified with the North America of ten thousand years ago and is a hunter's paradise. One wild scene describes the tribes of Indians fighting Centaurs of Greek myth, and Wolff gets involved because of his friendship with Kickaha, once a normal human being from Bloomington, Indiana, who made his way to Amerindia by one of the Lords' devices for moving between the dimensions. Now a picaresque adventurer, Kickaha moves at will through the many levels where he has a separate identity on each. On one his is an avatar of the Trickster God of the American Indians, on another, Edgar Rice Burroughs's Tarzan, a figure who is practically an obsession of Farmer's anyway.[30] His original Hoosier name, Paul Janus Finnegan, also points to his Trickster identity: Janus was the ancient Roman god of doorways: he had two faces pointing in opposite directions and embraced both sides of a duality.[31]

Dracheland is next highest, a quasi-medieval world whose name connotes Dragon ("Draco"); then Atlantis, a world in deluge by the time Wolff arrives there because its king, Rhadamanthus, has tried to construct his own Tower of Babel in order to assail the Lord's palace at the topmost level.

Wolff and Kickaha survive the final climb, and with the help of Podarge, the harpy and enemy of the Lord, Wolff regains mastery of the superhuman science and has plans to make this universe an authentic paradise for its inhabitants instead of his private playground. Of course, none of this happens, and instead we readers pursue one or another of these heroes and their girlfriends through four more novels; in Burroughsian fashion, the villainous Lords never quite succeed, but neither do the heroes.

Much more remains to be said in the next chapter about Phil Farmer, about his interest in androgyny, his treatment of regression fantasy, his respect for the primitive, and his literary erudition. But for the immediate issue of the superman, it is fair to say that Farmer, like Zelazny, is ambivalent: his supermen, even Kickaha, are always involved in violence as part of their freedom. Thus, for both these contemporary writers, the superman is by no means completely desirable, yet for both he seems more real, i.e., more inevitable, than for the writers of the classic years.

6 The Return to the Primitive

Ouroboros-like, we keep circling back to the same issue raised in every preceding chapter. Namely, how is it that so much modern SF purposely and continually reproduces a large number of outmoded, archaic, and anachronistic hypotheses and world-images, while at the same time it contains modern, pertinent, critical and intellectual messages? This question leads us to consider just what kind of "modern consciousness" it is that is inculcated by SF. Whether the world is getting better or worse, what makes one group of human beings seem "better" or "worse" than another, what constitutes progress vs. degeneration—these questions admit of no absolute resolution, as historians of ideas A. O. Lovejoy and George Boas remark in their famous study, *Primitivism and Related Ideas in Antiquity:*

> As the generations pass, does the condition of mankind grow better, or grow worse, or remain, except in external and relatively unimportant ways, the same; has the advance of civilization been a gain or a loss for the species responsible for it; is it a manifestation of man's superiority among the creatures, a legitimate ground for racial pride, or is it an evidence of his folly or depravity; are those peoples the most fortunate among whom it never began, or was speedily halted?[1]

One of modern SF's major tasks lies in responding to this complex, challenging question which must be asked of every civilization. Modern SF and fantasy uses its techniques of estrangement and distortion to investigate how our modern "scientific" civilization matches up against those in other times with which it cannot have ever had direct contact: the match-up can occur via an imaginary device, like time-travel; or by depicting a far future where archaeological pieces of our civilization turn up as clues for imaginary peoples; or by imagining a future world which, in its collapse and ruin (new Dark Age), shows the failures and excesses of our own civilization. A post-holocaustal New Earth, commonly involved with some version of the Adam and Eve myth, is encountered from the early ninteenth century on and has been met often enough in the previous chapters.

We have to look very widely in modern SF and fantasy if we are to understand the literature's strong tendency to hark back to archaic worlds and states. Not only is the history of what constitutes primitivism rich and varied in its fictional themes and devices, but mythic resonances abound from the beginning.

It is significant that Wells's fictive transformation of the far vistas of the future in *The Time Machine* was contemporary with an altered, highly expanded sense of the distant past, which was produced by coordinated developments in the sciences of geology, biology (especially, the theory of evolution), and astronomy. The interest evinced by SF writers after Wells in the sciences of the past like archaeology, paleontology, and paleobiology is indicative of the interdependence between an educated sense of the past and an intelligent, articulate sense of the future.

In the nineteenth century, retrograde evolution constituted an important theme with mythic consequences. Everyone knows one or another version of the "Dr. Jekyll & Mr. Hyde" fable written by Robert Louis Stevenson in 1886:[2] under the influence of radical experiments on the self, supposedly to better and "purify" the self of its evil parts, an intelligent, enlightened human being degenerates into a subhuman, simianlike creature. In Stevenson's original, Hyde's utter indecency and immorality are emphasized, and the being's unbridled sensuality threatens an enlightened "Christian" (i.e., Victorian) moral code. On the other hand, society and Christianity are just as threatened by the excessive rationality and perfection-seeking represented in Jekyll, the scientist. Basically, "Jekyll & Hyde" is an important adaptation of the Frankensteinian critique of the myth of uncontrolled scientific progress: a monster is created, but both Creator (scientist-as-god) and Creature (Monster) are complementary aspects of the same self. Because it views the passionate, demonic, and destructive side of human nature as ineradicable and irrepressible, the "Jekyll and Hyde" mythos conforms well to a major tenet of Freud's psychology.

Arthur Machen's intricately plotted tale of supernatural Gothic horror, "The Great God Pan" (1894),[3] also involves retrograde evolution (degeneration) to subhuman violence and pre-Christian anti-morality. A Frankensteinian scientist cruelly experiments on a young woman's intellect, unleashing her capacity to experience the evil pagan deity Pan. The demonic epiphany leaves her in a completely demented condition and she soon dies, but not before a half-human daughter is born: the fact that the mother's name is Mary and her daughter's is Helen (after the Greek Helen of Troy) is still another intimation of the pagan reversal of Christian norms and history. Around this horrific woman there always circulate rumors of perverse sexuality and secret lusts and vices, but nothing is ever very specific.

For Machen in this and other tales, the world of evil spirits is, really, the past: the mythical, ghostly, demonic past of race memory and dream that constantly haunts all modern, "civilized" humans. It is a reasonable generalization that the twentieth-century horror story, too, is largely and closely connected to this fantastic hypothesis of an evolution-in-reverse. Typical is the make-believe mythology of H. P. Lovecraft, rightly regarded as the chief writer of the horror story in this century.

The horror stories in the Cthulhu-series raise the possibility of retrogressive cosmology where the universe reverts to the control of violent, chaotic deities known as the Elder Gods and Great Old Ones; the degenerate New England family met in the Dunwitch horror tales crosses several generations also. In the culminating tale of this group, "The Rats in the Walls," a late scion of the clan degenerates completely into subhuman idiocy: drawn by an irresistible urge to investigate the lower recesses of his ancestral castle, the hero Delapore lapses into dementia, passing in reverse evolutionary order through several cultural stages—Roman, prehistoric pagan Briton, protohuman (the language of the text mirrors each change, perhaps in imitation of T. S. Eliot's practice in "The Waste Land").[4]

Closely allied to horror literature in the narrow sense are the lost-world fantasies, from the countless "rediscovery of Atlantis" tales to H. Rider Haggard's *She* and Arthur Conan Doyle's *The Lost World*, and tales of encounters with prehistoric protohumans (e.g., Edgar Rice Burroughs's Tarzan,[5] or his Pellucidar series). Here again there is a paradoxical combination of attraction and repulsion with either fantastic hypothesis. The lost-world fantasies of the highly popular Abraham Merritt (*The Ship of Ishtar, Face in the Abyss, The Moon Pool*) introduce preternaturally beautiful women, dangerously seductive temptresses who would plunge the male hero and his Western-style society into a pagan sensuality (again the Victorian dread of excessive sexual expression causing a social evolution-in-reverse). L. Sprague de Camp and Philip José Farmer have also made considerable application of these hypotheses in many later fables.[6]

So far we have considered fictions which are close to the "dreaming pole" of fantastic literature, but classic American magazine SF of the thirties and forties produced a new formula, closer to "hard" SF, but still probably best classified as "science fantasy." The return to the primitive is characterized by the lapse of science into magic and religion.

An exemplary formulation of a New Dark Age resulting from just such a collapse is Fritz Leiber's *Gather, Darkness!* (originally published in *Astounding Science Fiction* in May, June, and July 1943).[7] In the twenty-fourth century, a cast of technocratic "priests" have perverted the use of science for their own ends, erecting a static and repressive society modeled on the medieval church. Superscientific gadgets are used to control dissidents: halos and robes project forcefields to protect priests and keep them inviolate; laserlike rods of wrath provide powerful weapons not available to the nonprofessional classes; "Angels" are highly armed hovercraft that patrol the skies and maintain strict curfews.

Instead of liberating the intellect, science serves the narrow interests of a closed group of rulers called the Hierarchy. Vague superstition and fears replace understanding of the workings of technology. A new witchcraft arises, which purportedly increases allegiance to the Lord of evil, Sathanas, but which really turns out to be a revolutionary program based on a nonsuperstitious understanding of science and human history.

However, there remains an underlying ambiguity in the attitude toward *magic* which makes this story highly representative of all science fantasy. False beliefs and superstitions are rejected by the critical side of the SF intellect, but on the other side SF writers and fans are attracted to magic because it presupposes *as yet unknown and unpredictable changes* in our reality system. Science fiction rejects narrow, confining orthodoxies, including science when it becomes deterministic and behavioristic; magic appeals to a freedom of thought among imaginative writers. Our science is not the last word—there's still another way of understanding the world if only we are responsive enough to learn it; there are new sensitivities still to be born in us.

The age of the Hierarchy looked back on the era of free scientific enquiry and creativity as a Golden Age. It ended in atomic holocaust, another popular SF theme, and one of a number of ways in which writers of imaginative literature envision the future as a new Dark Age: atomic warfare, germ warfare, political repression (e.g., Ayn Rand's *Anthem*) or repressive religious elites all can account for the transition to the simpler, more primitive state for the world (small population, loss of art, literature, music, science, or material deprivations suggest a "harder" life for future human beings). Above all, though, it is the loss of intelligence and the lowering of consciousness which render the postholocaustal primitive worlds Dark Ages of the Mind (e.g., Orwell's *1984*, Aldous Huxley's *Ape and Essence*). In dystopian SF, a dominant perception of our future since World War II, the primitive state is associated with the imagery of hell and the Greek underworld.

However, in several classical types of primitivism, simplicity is understood as a positive virtue, and a desire is expressed to withdraw from the paralyzing complexity and stifling conformity of technological civilization.[8] The natural world is often idealized or sentimentalized and is imagined as a counterfoil to a strictly human universe. But writers like André Norton and the late Thomas Burnett Swann do raise a valid point: why destroy the nonhuman world (of insects, birds, flowers, and free mammals) before we even understand it?

Especially illuminating is G. McDonald Wallis's *Legend of Lost Earth* (Ace Double, 1963): it is old-fashioned in style and content and organization for 1963, yet this very quality reinforces the explicitly avowed primitivism. On the other hand, in its announcement of environmentalist ideas and themes this novel anticipated many concerns and ways of thinking that are now very widespread. In other words, it is not so out-of-date.

Wallis's world of "Niflhel" is an allusion to one of the several hells of Scandinavian mythlore. This is actually the name of the future Earth, but this revelation is withheld from us until far into the narrative—we think it is another planet. It is an ecological dystopia where only a high technology keeps humans alive in an incredibly polluted environment. At the climax of this story a group of escapees from the ecological underworld of Niflhel flee to a renewed, purified Earth—and it is the latter which offers a few humans the possibilities of a "primitive," non-technological life-style close to nature.

The treatment of the romantic love-interest is conventional—the hero chooses between two women, one representing evil, the other good (Wallis, does, however, reverse the imagery of the traditional romances—the light Nordic woman is the fatal temptress, the dark earthy woman is the true heroine). There is also extramarital sex in Niflhel, with a definite demonic connotation.

Ironically, its most progressive notion is one that is politically charged today: its central idea of an ecologically ruined earth, where society's scientific hardware is only a last-ditch, inadequate defense against our own self-destruction, certainly anticipates contemporary concern about the future of the natural world on this planet. Wallis's story shows that as early as the fifties he could "see" what was happening to our cities (air and water pollution, elimination of contact with the natural world—or with anything which wasn't produced through human artifice).

At least one major anthropologist, Victor Turner,[9] has suggested that cultural "progress" is not to be evaluated as a simple, straight vector, for cultures too pass through death-rebirth rituals. They return to earlier, outmoded forms of sensibility and living habits. Turner calls such states "liminal"—periods of latency that terminate an earlier state of society whose institutions and ideas had grown stale with time (as in the case of our high-speed and high-technology urban societies) and as prelude to an as yet unknown future state. In such a dynamic as this—and Turner and Wallis have it in common—periods of return to basic or primitive modes would be part of any concept of progress. Wallis's story as literary art may be simple, conventional, and somewhat old-fashioned as, sadly, were too many of the narratives whose form was derived solely from the specialty SF magazines, but his overall ecological message is well-considered.

But it is true that the resolution of the narrative—rescue from Niflhel, the Earth that is Hell, to a new Eden on Earth—is explicitly primitive and a return to an archaic mythical idea: the World's Body, the planet we live on perceived as a living, sentient being who is able to be resurrected (Earth is female and a Mother). As man's technological civilizations "ruined" her, her retaliation was to create Niflhel around mankind, until her real self (the totality of the natural environment) was restored to a pristine state and ready to receive mankind once more (though one does wonder from the preceding account why Earth takes man back.)

Most ecologists would say that once ruined to the degree intimated in Niflhel, Earth could never return to the state it was in, say, two million years ago when the first humans were evolving, but would ultimately become some new "eco-system" whose characteristics we cannot predict. Wallis's idea is a wish-fulfillment and not a scientific possibility. On the other hand, "progress" to many today would indeed involve some "return to the land" movement (though this might cover a large range of life-styles from subsistence farming to middle-class small town life) as well as some rise in ecological consciousness—the latter constituting the futuristic or science-fictional dimension.

We are never able to get away from the fact that SF and fantasy literature shares the twentieth century's ever growing quest for the primitive, for the instinctual, whose roots lie in the unconscious mind, whether collective (Jung) or personal (Freud).

Of the authors discussed so far, Philip José Farmer best represents the interests of a primitivistic world-view in contemporary American fiction. Like the heroes of Edgar Rice Burroughs, Farmer's heroes (Kickaha, his many "Tarzans") show the value of the versatile nonspecialist. As a writer, Farmer is himself the best exemplar of this philosophy. To be fair to him, he is a masterful, sly ironist, and many of his best tales take up different attitudes toward regression. In particular, four tales from Farmer's popular anthology, *Strange Rela-*

tions (Ballantine, 1960) involve distinct, often conflicting postures toward this mode of fantasy.

Though it was first published in 1953, very little in the story of "Mother" seems dated, except perhaps for the obvious and deliberate portrayal of the central characters, human and alien alike, in terms of stereotypes of the 1950s. Paula, the human mother, is a domineering female scientist, cold, competent, and calculating. Her son is the classic overprotected child, recently divorced from his wife because his mother-fixation broke up the marriage. Eddie is dependent, infantile, and his deepest wish-fulfillment is to be (s)mothered.

Trying to escape their problems on a scientific expedition, Paula and Eddie crashland on the planet Baudelaire and find themselves among a race of intelligent vegetables who have only the female sex and are completely sedentary in their adult phase. Their males are any "mobile" life-forms captured in the vicinity by their powerful and manifold tentacles. This is what happens to Eddie and Paula, each captured by a different Mother.

The deftness with which Farmer characterizes Mother Polyphema's maternal psychology and sexuality are masterful: Eddie lives inside the stomach/womb of his Mother, is fed like her own sluglike babies on her own stew, becomes her mate and lover (the sex act suggests rape and violence—to "impregnate" her Eddie has only to tear apart the tissues in the womb-spot in the wall), and sucks at will on the "nipples" on the wall for drugs and chemicals. Because she is so elementally maternal, Eddie comes to identify her as his real mother. Progressively, Eddie adapts himself to his uterine environment (since he cannot escape anyway) and transfers his allegiance from his human mother who is captured and killed by the giant plant to get rid of the competition. Polyphema comes to regard Eddie as the perfect lover. He becomes progressively more infantilized, more foetalized, and by the end of the story has been altered by his dependent existence into a baby physically as well as psychologically. Yet, for Eddie with his mother-fixation, this retrogression to the womb is the perfect happy ending: Eddie has everything he wants for his body and psyche, so does Mother, and the fable ends on a deeply ironic awareness that it has all been a sly satire on a love story.

According to a legend circulated popularly among the fans, the sequel to "Mother" was eagerly awaited, only for Farmer to play the trickster on his readers as he has done so often in his career. Though an honest sequel, too, "Daughter" is mainly a literary joke: the tale is a thinly disguised re-telling of the story of "The Three Little Pigs" with a number of puns in Pig Latin to reinforce the humorous message. The alien carnivore who kills and devours Mother is called "the olfway"; Father Eddie communicates with his Daughters by Mother via a language called "Orsemay;" and the last line of the story is "The Wolf and the Three Little Pigs" rendered in Pig Latin.

As in the previous story, the description of Mother's biology, as well as the "olfway's," is fascinating and shows off Farmer's skill in portraying the interaction of life-forms that have never existed and never will, but whose elemental relations—eating, procreating (these are so often identical for Farmer)—strike some subconscious, archetypal resonance in his readers. Whereas two sisters perish because they are thoughtless, vegetative "bubbleheads" (again the satire on 1950s types), Daughter is a highly adaptable organism who adds to her Mother powers the *scientific* principles of biology and chemistry she learned from her human father: she alters her body structure to better protect her brain from the enemy; she destroys the olfway in an acid of her own devising. Daughter has also learned to think imaginatively from Father's "not-so" stories, that is, from make-believe tales, one of which is specified as "The Three Little Pigs"! Thus, the tale circles back, paradoxically and self-consciously, on its own fictional origins (another narrative Möbius strip), and it comments on the necessity for the creative interaction of science and imagination in a manner at once serious and flippant.

"Son" is in many ways the converse of "Mother." It is set during an imaginary "hot" flare-up of the Cold War. A Russian submarine torpedoes an American ocean-liner in the Pacific and captures one survivor, Jones. Like Eddie in the earlier tale, this male hero is again mother-dependent and has failed in his marriage. However, Jones's brief encounter turns out differently. Though equipped with sophisticated artificial intelligence and able to project a domineering Mother personality to keep her victim under control, the submarine is involved with the human only in a psychological drama, strictly at the level of personality conflict, and no biological or sexual dimensions are considered. Ultimately the hero breaks out from under her influence, sabotages her machinery, and becomes "reborn" after his sojourn in her belly (images of the inner space of the sub as both womb and tomb abound). Jones has become a mature adult able to cope with the problems of life and marital love. Unlike Eddie's submergence and regression into the elemental and instinctual, the fable about Jones is a male maturation myth, and the hero emerges both literally (the hero finds himself on the ocean's surface after he defeats her) and figuratively (he is no longer a mama's boy).

"Father" is an outstanding psychoreligious fable based on a common theme of science fiction, "encounter with an alien god." On another planet in the same fictive universe as "Mother" lives an alien being with the godlike powers to turn his world into a perfect paradise for all living creatures. Father arrived from another world 10,000 years ago and this world has not changed since; nothing has been born, because nothing dies without being reborn, for Father controls resurrection as a superscientific biological process still beyond mankind's control. Although nothing is born nor really dies, it is an interesting Freudian touch that all the animal forms are now female; Father is the only male until He causes some Earthmen to crashland there; Father needs a replacement caretaker for this world so he can travel to another. Father is, in fact, an evil deity because he feeds off his all-powerful capacity to play god, to make reality perfect and undying for inferior species. And like some cosmic vampire, he needs new worlds to feed on.

With the convincing portrayal of Bishop André, Father's intended replacement, a special psychological dimension is added to the story. In many works, Farmer has analyzed the psychosexual problems caused by an overzealous religious upbringing (the hero of *The Lovers*, Sarvant in *Flesh*). Bishop André was beaten by his overly strict father, forced to be the perfect young Catholic, so he now has impossible standards of moral perfection, purity, and self-control, especially since he is so powerful and important a churchman. There are many similarities between the Bishop's and Father's obsessions with perfection and control.

However, not every Christian is a neurotic-become-suicide like the Bishop. "Father" has a third major character, Father John Carmody, a sort of Friar Tuck figure who is the likeable and *very* human hero

The Return to the Primitive

of several other tales by Farmer. One is always aware that Carmody lucks out because he is superlatively human, not because he is a priest. There is always a danger the Bishop will abandon his fellow humans to take on the powers and responsibility of the alien Father because of his traumatic psychic and family history: André needs to be perfect, to be god in fact, to satisfy the demands made by his real father that he be perfect and never sin. With John, there is never any such danger; it is only a matter of time and energy before the wily priest figures out the truly deceitful nature of the alien superbeing. In some ways, Farmer has merely worked out a Freudian formula that says our first gods are our parents: indeed, the alien god's powers are so great on his world that he is as far above his subjects, the stranded humans included, as a parent is above a small child. No wonder that the conflict with such a powerful authoritative figure leaves André no way out except suicide, to make sure he will not be manipulated psychologically to do the god's bidding. Yet even here John Carmody generously defends his friend's motives and prefers to judge him a heroic martyr for humanity.

Finally, there is one novel-length work by Farmer which may summarize this primitivist streak in modern SF and which may act as the concluding vision in this critical study of mythology and SF.

Flesh (1968) was inspired by the mythological system that Robert Graves formulated over his long career as poet, novelist, and critic, and which culminated in *The White Goddess* — a nonfictional statement of his mythological credo.[10] Subtitled "A Historical Grammar of Poetic Myth," Graves's book is a massive, grotesque compilation of pseudo-scholarship, brimming with random bits of folklore, imaginary natural history, arcane religious rituals, and esoteric mythological erudition, ranging variably from the Mediterranean to Northern European cultures, and from the Paleolithic through the Middle Ages. This is, in fact, the recording of a poet's private vision, on the order of Yeats's *A Vision* or Pound's *Guide to Kultur*, and central to it as an imaginative construct is Graves's "theme" of the triune Goddess who is an archetype of woman in her three life-phases of Virgin, Matron, and Hag (or as bride, mother, and layer-out respectively). Her male counterpart, representing the poet himself, is a Dying God,[11] merely an adjunct to the Mistress who is both all-powerful Goddess and poetic Muse. All of this may be read as another of Graves's many sorties against modern culture, which are only half-serious and which often read like academic "put-ons."[12] The author vacillates between deliberate mysteriousness and barely comprehensible irony in his tone, yet his overall intention is to advise us to restore vitality and interest to daily modern living by substituting a purposefully avowed primitivism, symbolized by female dominance and matriarchal codes, for the sterility and boredom of scientism and technocracy, thus making way for a rebirth of true poetry and free imaginative creativity. The reign of the Mother will also mean the victory of sexual expression, of the unconscious, and of instinct and intuition. To deny Her, by rejecting the mythic, primitive, and ritualistic, is to abandon our own animality, an intrinsic part of our make-up, hence to profane and desensitize our human potential. To Graves's mind, there is just as much a human capacity for growth in emotional sensitivity as in scientific understanding.

Although Graves's conception of the White Goddess is the fictional hypothesis for *Flesh*, Farmer uses it as a point of departure for a different kind of speculation. Farmer eschews the entire allegory of poetry and the poetic imagination so essential to Graves and, instead, is concerned to portray an *entire* futuristic world, alternative to our own, that worships the Goddess and preserves her fertility religion. The critical dimension in this book, as in so much of Farmer's other work, lies in its juxtaposition of another kind of sexual code and erotic sensibility with that native to our own time and place, leading to the reader's new understanding of the relativity of our own preconceptions about human love. Insofar as Farmer identifies the sex drive as *the* foundation of human culture, being latent in so many of our social rites and institutions, he is more explicitly Freudian than Graves is.

After eight centuries of exploring the stars, an American spaceship, the *Terra*, returns to Earth. The planet has, in the interval, suffered an ecological disaster so complete as to have ended our world altogether and ushered in a new era of agricultural primitivism. The dominant religion is that of the Great Mother Goddess under her three aspects of maiden (Virginia), matron (Columbia), and hag (Alba). This system of archaic religious practices, taboos, and credos in many ways recalls the primeval world of Frazer's *Golden Bough*, but the world of the Goddess is a naturalistic one like our own, not a

The Return to the Primitive

supernatural one: we never see the Mother, only her human representatives and the effect of her cult on the lives of human beings. Nor is this a magical universe: events that may now be impossible, like the biological reconstituting of the hero Stagg, are predicated upon future developments in technology and are thus potentially natural.

Into this world of mother-right and female dominance the *Terra* brings Peter Stagg, starship captain, who is captured and biologically altered. Antlers are grafted onto his head, and he becomes the Great Stag, the Sunhero, the living embodiment of power and virility for the entire nation of Deecee. In reality, the strange antlers are specially adapted organs; though Stagg develops a tremendous appetite for food and drink, he is rewarded with a correspondingly tremendous satyriasis which makes him capable of inseminating all the women of the nation. His sexual career in Deecee also traces the path of a solar myth, as he moves North from Washington, D.C., in the direction of Albany, New York, beginning on the winter solstice, December 21, in the South where he impregnates Virginia, and ending at the summer solstice of June 21 in the North where Alba, the toothless hag, will cut his throat and bury his remains to insure the fertility of soil and crops. And in the next year the seasonal pattern will recur all over again with a new Sunhero.

Stagg is really two people. His "normal" self, deriving from our world, dreads individual death when the end of the Dying God will mean real, permanent death for him, but an even greater source of horror is his loss of rationality, of control over his own actions, and even of the entire conscious mind when the antlers assert their overpowering needs for food, sex, and violence.

Five of the eight occurrences of the word "flesh" do, in fact, refer to Sunhero's loss of individual ego in the blind, esctatic, Dionysian frenzy generated by the rule of appetite and emotion. On p. 18, Stagg is "surrounded by flesh" in the mob scene at his investiture as Dying God; on p. 90, the god goes berserk and rides a giant stag into a crowd of priestesses—a "trap of lace and flesh"—dismembering and decapitating the women; on p. 96, Mary Casey refers to the Stagg body as a "cage of flesh"; on p. 99, Stagg refers to his nightly orgies as "visions of screaming white flesh"; on p. 119, his powerful hunger becomes a "fire raging within him, flesh devouring flesh."

The other three references are no less significant and related to the title of the book: on p. 38, the female biological surgeons of the Mother are described as "artists in flesh"; on p. 122, the Pants-Elfs give as the rationale for repressive treatment of women in their society that "the flesh was weak"; and on p. 160, Mary Casey expresses the same sentiment from the Caseyland perspective, declaring that it is obvious that men and women who spend time alone "must succumb to the flesh."

Ultimately, Stagg can reassert control over his own body only by starving himself, thereby inhibiting his sex drive. Only by self-inhibition, too, can the masculine, control-oriented, "rational" values of our civilization reassert their dominance. Stagg is thus a representative of the kind of Western civilization that is depicted in the pages of Freud's *Civilization and Its Discontents*, Herbert Marcuse's *Eros and Civilization*, and N. O. Brown's *Love's Body*: in simplest outlines, this libidinal theory supposes that a progressive human culture is made possible only by a process of sublimation—what is sacrificed in individual sexual expression and free erotic activity is regained, in displaced form, in the permanent, stable institutions of society. In such a theory, civilization is regarded as the by-product of inhibited eroticism. And for their part, Stagg, his crew, and the starship itself are the most perfect representatives of the male-dominated, assertive, power-oriented, and technology-based society which produced them.

On the one hand, we are told explicitly that the mission of the starship was to locate "virgin planets" (p. 21). On the other, there were no women on the *Terra*, and despite being helped through the 800-year ordeal by suspended animation, Stagg is fairly screaming his sexual repression when he returns to Earth: "Eight hundred years without seeing a single, solitary, lone forlorn woman! . . . I feel like Walt Whitman when he boasted he jetted the stuff of future republics. I've a dozen republics in me!" (p. 22). The restraints placed on the starmen in order to succeed in the highest enterprise of our masculine civilization to date—space travel—correspond in their intensity, but in a reverse direction, to the demands for libidinal release required by the Goddess's world.

It is most accurate not to characterize New Earth as either utopia or dystopia, but as a fictional universe that stands in an ambivalent relationship to our own "real" one. Simultaneously it offers opportunities for greater creativity and more violent destruction. Correspondingly, the Mother herself is a Jungian "coincidence of opposites," being a figure both good and evil, sexual temptress and castrating ogress, at once benign and destructive. And so, too, Stagg's career is at once a sexual wish-fulfillment and the ultimate demonization and dehumanization of the total man, who is reduced to being a function only of his nonrational faculties and his gonads. He is thus an ambivalent answer to the speculative question, "what if a male did have unlimited sexual capacity?" Stagg himself recognizes the ambiguity: "last night I enjoyed what I was doing. I had no inhibitions. I was living the secret dream of every man—unlimited opportunity and inexhaustible ability. I was a *god!*" (p. 59; cf. p. 86). Farmer himself, whose tone modulates between the serious and the outright satiric throughout the novel, seems ambivalent about New Earth's relationship to the present world. I mean by this the reader is not sure whether he is supposed to sympathize with the characters and identify with their problem or to distance himself from them, particularly through satiric laughter.

First, New Earth's advantages. The rites of the Mother promote human fertility and environmental improvement in a world devastated by ecological cataclysm, a world nearly sterilized, and still severely underpopulated. Perhaps this best explains why its only technology deals with biology and human sexuality, for it was our own civilization's continued assaults on nature in an attempt to exploit its resources to the full that brought about the collapse. Like Frankenstein on a macrocosmic scale, Western man experimented to tap new power sources in the very core of the Earth but exceeded the physical limits of the planet (pp. 27-28 and cf. p. 67). Even from outer space the planet looks totally different from the one the starmen left (pp. 19-20).

The world of the Mother is also superior psychologically insofar as its regular calendar of rituals and ceremonies allows for release of inhibitions as an accepted part of social life: periodic sexual orgies, wild drunkenness, blood sports, temple prostitution, and sadistic violence are the norm in this culture. It is a world controlled by feeling, rather than thought, a world where the heights of both pleasure and pain may, and should, be experienced. Thus here again we seem to be dealing with that "oral" phase of Farmer's literary persona mentioned by Leslie Fiedler in his popular essay,[13] for the mythical dimensions of the world of the Goddess are based in large part on the Gargantuan "appetites" (for food, drink, sex, violence) of its denizens. This world values the intensity of experience above all, and this attitude in turn invests every fundamental act like eating or sexual intercourse with deeper emotional satisfaction.

Fiedler and Franz Rottensteiner, Farmer's two most prestigious critics, have both said that all his books are about sex, religion, and violence.[14] They are correct, yet the very fact that the three come clustered together in a trinity presupposes some larger principle at work. Rollo May suggests the term "daemonic" for this same triad and means by it to identify man's inner, unconscious drive to transcend his current limitations—whether imposed on him from within or without—and to achieve a new, larger "self."[15] The "daemonic" thus would not only characterize Stagg as a savage god, often rendered subhuman by his own abnormal powers, but it would go far to explain the violent character of all of Farmer's supermen (as in the World of Tiers series), particularly his Tarzan, who is his most perfect representative of daemonic passion and power. This same daemonic triad might also lead us to second Fiedler's view that Farmer's essential contribution to science fiction is located in the field of depth psychology. Beneath the exciting and racy adventure yarns that owe so much to Burroughs, there is an awareness, based on a thorough understanding of psychoanalytical literature, that man must always be searching for new, creative confrontations with the world. Hence, sex, religion, and violence as man's three basic, elemental drives to achieve ever more intense, ever more creative experience.[16]

From the satiric perspective, too, New Earth appears superior to our own, for *our* social rites and institutions seem to pale beside the undiluted myths and rituals in the realm of the Mother: thus, in Deecee, the Washington Monument has been re-erected explicitly as a giant phallic symbol, and the U.S. Capitol now sports *two* domes to symbolize the twin breasts of the Mother; the White House Honor Guards are bow-brandishing amazons, while Georgetown University now houses the castrated musician-priests of the Goddess; social fraternities like Moose, Elk, and Lions are now full-fledged totem clans, the Speaker of the House in Congress goes by the name of John Barleycorn,[17] and baseball is a sadistic rite, played with a spiked ball which is hurled about in order to spill as much blood as possible.

Sometimes, in fact, this kind of satire is purely verbal, and Deecee and the other nations and institutions of New Earth often come down to being nothing more than a series of word-plays. There can be a fairly gratuitous travesty — like "Deecee" for "Washington, D.C." — to more complex sequences of associations, like the nation "Caseyland," named after the "K. of C." (Knights of Columbus), which gives away its Roman Catholic inspiration and all of whose citizens are named "Casey;" most telling of all, its national sport is baseball, and the captain of its team always bears the name "Mighty Casey!" In another briefer sequence like this, Alba, the woman-as-crone whose name means "White," is cleverly tied to the partly homonymous city of "Albany."

Sometimes, too, figurative statements from our world become literally true in the future: "kill the ump" means just that in Farmer's version of the game, and George Washington's honorific title, "father of his country," becomes a mythical fable about the sexiest procreator of them all. The fact that the word-plays form complete systems of reference, plus their sheer quantity, is a striking feature of *Flesh*. This kind of wit is recurrent enough to call to mind the exuberant Joycean punning in Farmer's "Riders of the Purple Wage."

Perhaps, though, Freud is as much an inspiration as Joyce. In particular, the name of still another nation of New Earth, the "Pants-Elfs," comes close to Freud's discussion in *Jokes and Their Relation to the Unconscious*. The first part of the name is a shortened homonym of "pansies"; the second is a synonym for "fairies." Thus "Pants-Elfs" is a facetious and barely disguised slur against a nation of homosexuals who are regarded as fierce warriors, worshippers of the Goddess who yet cloister their wives, with a culture somewhere between that of Amerindian tribal castes and that of ancient Sparta. A second pun shares both a Freudian and Joycean dimension: "Horneycums" (p. 119; repeated on p. 125). One of the Pants-Elfs, a would-be lover, calls Stagg this as a term of endearment in baby-talk, but "cums" is also a well-known obscene verb and "Horneycums" is a barely disguised reference to the Stagg's impressive appetite for orgasms.

Still other contrasts between old and New Earth show the latter to advantage. In particular, two other starmen represent sexual codes that many would find arbitrary and archaic by the 1980s. Sarvant, the ship's chaplain, is a religious fundamentalist whose outmoded spiritual fervor is conducive to masochism, and he has much of both the would-be martyr and the sexual invert in his makeup. Finding himself in a world of constant sexual overstimulation puts his archaic beliefs under too much pressure. Finally, he falls in love with a woman who happens to be barren. When he discovers that she is a participant in promiscuous rites at a certain temple to cure her infertility, he is overwhelmed by conflicting emotions and, finally, he rapes her. For profaning the worship of the Mother, Sarvant is hauled off and hanged by a mob, though to his own narrow religious sensibility the woman was never anything more than a cheap whore. Churchill, the first mate, fares better, falling in love with the daughter of a wealthy merchant sailor; the love is reciprocated and all is well, until it is revealed that the bride-to-be is pregnant by Sunhero. This is cause for rejoicing in the girl's family, but a rather severe blow to Churchill's ego—it had always been his male fantasy, primitive in its own way, to marry a virgin (p. 110).

However, it is important to remember that the world of the Mother, as an alternative to our own, is limited and relative. For in addition to the nation of Deecee which maintains the worship of the Goddess in its "orthodox" (that is, Gravesian) form, New Earth contains other viable cultures which stand in contrast to both Deecee and our Earth in regard to both sex and religion. In addition to the Pants-Elfs and Caseylanders, one should also mention the only nation that is anything like a world power, the Karelians, Finnish pirates whose empire is scattered over three continents.

Even in the central issue of sexual mores, the religion of the Mother is not always superior. One evidence is still another love relationship in the novel: between Stagg when he is in his right mind and a young captive virgin from Caseyland. Whereas Stagg acquired his first wife, Virginia, simply by taking her as Sunhero, he has to win Mary Casey under her nation's code, by allowing her to remain a virgin, proving that his rational self has disciplined control over the Stagg appetites (even here we might suspect a half-serious parody of American boy-girl courtship behavior typical of the 'fifties).

The Return to the Primitive [167]

An even better clue to the non-absoluteness of the Goddess's world is evident in Stagg's fate. Ultimately, to be sure, the captain cannot escape his preordained mythical doom. Though he escapes the Deecee for a time, Alba finally does recapture and sacrifice him; the entire myth of the Dying God is completed. However, the sophisticated technology of the *Terra* is able to resurrect Stagg, though the brain damage incurred while dead leaves him without any memory of his days as Sunhero. Yet his death-rebirth pattern—with the rebirth deriving from the male-generated technology of our civilization—undercuts the power of the Mother-system as depicted by Graves, where the Mother herself is the final and sole repository of all capacity for death or rebirth. In fact, it is highly significant that the end of the novel dissociates into two distinct perspectives which leave open the question of the relative superiority of "male" and "female" cultures.

On the male side, Stagg and his crew steal women from Earth and again leave for the stars with the intention of reestablishing society as they had known it in another world. More than once this act of starting a new civilization is likened to rape, and the kidnapping of wives is compared to the Roman historian Livy's story of the rape of the Sabine women, a tale associated with the founding of Rome by Romulus and Remus:

> "Violence, abduction, rape," Churchill said. "What a way to start a brave new world!."
> "Is there any other way?" Wang said.
> "Don't forget the Sabine women," Steinborg said. . . .
> Churchill frowned. There seemed no way to get away from violence. But then it had always been so throughout man's history. (p. 146)

N. O. Brown was soon to express this same notion of the origin of higher (scientific, technological) culture in male violence, best symptomized by the violent power-oriented act of rape (and Brown also analyzes the rape of the Sabines as a mythical statement of the origin of culture).[18] Yet even here there are ironies: Stagg has two wives, the Caseyland maid and his pregnant Virginia—a *ménage à trois* sure to be explosive—and Churchill is well aware that he has just begun a life-long challenge from his new wife to keep "taming the shrew."

The very last word, in the Epilogue, is reserved for the Goddess and the feminine viewpoint after all. Three priestesses representing the three (Gravesian) phases of Woman meet to assess events and plan future strategy, for they have by no means been defeated by the starmen out of the masculine past. The Mother still rules Earth and may someday gain sway over all of mankind, even out among the stars; after all, the Dying God really did die and Virginia is still his bride.

This epilogue is a deliberately vague and mysterious passage, unlike any other in the book, and makes one think of Todorov's term, "fantastic," referring to fictional worlds which are ambivalently structured in order to conceal the difference between natural and supernatural laws.

In particular, the enigmatic last three sentences of the epilogue, being a reminiscence of the opening scene of Shakespeare's *Macbeth*, heighten the mysterious atmosphere:

The maiden says, When shall we three meet again?
The matron replies, When man is born and dies and is born.
The hag replies, When the battle is lost and won.

The matron's reply seems to refer to the Dying God, who is born and dies and is born (that is, "reborn") in the cyclical vegetative myth, but we should also remember that in the Goddess's religion the god is the mythical prototype for every *man*. Thus one other meaning for the riddling answer of the matron is that every time a man is born there shall be a woman present—his mother, of course.

The hag's reply, however, refers to that most famous and eternal battle of the sexes, and one specific interpretation of her riddling answer is that woman is the matrix out of which all change and human history must emerge; that wherever time and mankind intersect, there too must woman be (the alternations of time are suggested by the word, "battle," by the rhythm of "lost and won," as well as by the matron's "born and dies and is born," the latter being reinterpreted anew in light of the hag's response).

Thus, this very last sentence of *Flesh* leaves the work open-ended in the sense that the conflict between male and female can never be resolved totally in favor of either sex so long as human history remains a creative interplay between conscious and unconscious, reason and instinct, the erotic and inhibitory, the emotional and the

The Return to the Primitive

contemplative, science and religion, technology and ritual. Farmer leaves his fictional universe in a state of dynamic incertitude as to its future, with *both* male and femal societies in full flower. Insofar as human history requires both male and female components for Farmer, his vision is androgynous.

So one of contemporary science fiction's greatest visionaries leaves open the question of primitivism: we might well return to a more archaic state, cyclically, but we might just find it superior (a death/rebirth). By any standards, one of the greatest problems of consciousness for our time is androgyny, understanding not only the other sex but also the "other sex" latent inside each of us, male or female. More than ever, women writers are adding new alternatives constantly, from the violent and satirical feminism of Joanna Russ (*The Female Man*) to the balanced Taoist androgyny in the work of Ursula K. Le Guin (*The Left-Hand of Darkness*). The images of women in SF are becoming far more complex and subtle; no longer do female characters merely serve as symbols of the sexually demonic and the emotionally primitive.

However, understanding the "sexual other" is something I still understand only intuitively and obscurely, so as a male critic I am as yet unable to go beyond the male androgyny of writers like Farmer and Graves. Instead of plunging further into the future of SF mythopoesis—and undoubtedly it will be a prosperous and creative future—it is time to turn back full circle and draw some conclusions from the vantage point of these six chapters.

7 The Future of Eternity

A Vision of SF Myth-Making

These chapters have tried to describe a whole era of modern science fiction and fantasy literature where speculative science and myth-making interact; the concepts, world-views, and images of these narratives are located at various points along a myth-science interface. It is an extensive and important group of fictions. I cannot say that *all* science fiction is mythical in exactly the terms I have observed so far, but I can say from my own personal experience in reading SF that there are countless stories where myths come up in ways which are clear and explicit. There is definitely a kind of science fiction much closer to our mundane and empirical reality of today (many works by Jules Verne or John Brunner, for example), where the estrangement effects and/or the scale of the vision don't suggest affinities with myths. However, the authors of such tales are found to have other works where myths are important; or even in apparently nonmythical works there are images, allusions, and prefigurative titles giving away the typical fascination with myths.

More specifically, the results of this investigation into archaic models may be schematized as follows. Ancient Greek and Biblical myths (from both Old and New Testament) are the two most popular systems, with the myths of northern Europe a distant but solid third. Throughout the two-century history of modern SF unusual

Conclusion: The Future of Eternity

myths have appeared sporadically, but in the last two decades of Anglo-American science fiction, New Wave in particular, exotic mythologies turn up much more commonly. There has increasingly been a tendency in modern SF to deal with the myths eclectically and comparatively (even in the original *Frankenstein* we find both Greek and Biblical myths integrated); the writers show an awareness of the relativity of the world's myths and the multiplicity of myth theories. Today the New Wavers show that myths are being used extensively in narrative and stylistic experimentation, but nonetheless all modern science fiction has been interested in myths as intriguing speculations: thus throughout the genre there has definitely been an "experimental" cast to myths.

Greek myths appear in modern science fiction in a number of different lights, but with none of them is there any issue of "belief." One side of ancient Greek mythology suggests fantastic and enchanting wish-fulfillments, often of an erotic nature; but another equally suggests humor and an easy whimsy. (Even the ancient Greeks were famous for not always taking their gods seriously. Besides, much of science fiction and fantasy hovers close to satire, so we musn't be surprised that the majority of mythical narratives, not just those incorporating Greek mythology, treat the subject of myth in ways satirical, humorous, parodic, and/or critical.) However, this is still too simple a view to do for the profound influence of ancient Greek myth-making on science fiction. Certainly, the informing archetypes of Odysseus and Prometheus (Frankenstein) are one demonstration. Another is the observation that much of ancient Greek literature and philosophy constituted a kind of proto-SF (e.g., pre-Socratic philosophy, Aristophanes, Lucian, Plato, and the utopian romancers) and often overlapped in content with the traditional myths, so, again, we might expect fabulous hypotheses like Atlantis and pre-Socratic cosmologies to keep cropping up in the modern form.

Because for so long the Bible has been the central belief-code of our culture, its legends and heroes often seem to be not myth but history (today scholars of many persuasions don't allow the Bible so much literal historicity), yet even here for modern science fiction there is only rarely the propounding of any specific religious doctrine. Indeed, by far the most popular of all the Biblical myths in modern SF is Genesis, but the Old Testament version of creation is taken in as much a fantastic vein as anything in the Greek or other myths. What Genesis does offer is best regarded as two interrelated archetypes of creation for modern science fiction: (1) the creation of the universe, from the beginning to the end of all time: the concepts and speculations of modern science now project our vision onto so grand a scale in both macrocosmic and microcosmic dimensions that the limits of the Judeo-Christian view of creation are shattered altogether and any literal-minded interpretation of Genesis is impossible; (2) the creation of humans, an "origin of species" played out on a temporal continuum from the first man to the last; this creation metaphor has long been reinterpreted in terms of the theory of evolution so that a naturalistic rather than supernatural understanding of our creation story has emerged. The Judeo-Christian deity is commonly a satirical figure, the New Wave writers especially seem irreverent and satirical though they allude often and accurately to the Bible and recent scholarship on it.

But when you get right down to it, no one figure or myth is special for modern science fiction: Biblical myths like all others are valued relatively and critically. It may be said in favor of science fiction, too, that it has been equally skeptical of "the myth of science" and, decades before New Wave, satirized and debunked science when it could be understood as a belief-code or authority-system—science taken in any "religious" or absolutist sense. Science fiction prizes freedom of thought; it does not let *any* interpretation of reality, no matter how prestigious, whether religious or scientific, become rigid orthodoxy. In SF our understanding of the world is open-ended; there is always more to know, and in the future things will be different, unpredictable, mutant.

The myths of northern Europe are most often associated with a heroic view of life and appear in conventional SF as well as several kinds of fantasy, especially sword-and-sorcery (see chapter 4). The outlook on life may be described as tragic and existential, though again humor and self-parody turn up in some forms. But at whatever level of seriousness, heroic myths remain as popular as ever because the anti-heroical consciousness fails to satisfy: it is too depersonalized and depressing a prospect. If people have to turn to the psyche for the heroic quest, we will (Joseph Campbell also says this in *The Hero With A Thousand Faces*).

Conclusion: The Future of Eternity

Science fiction's application of myth theories has also become progressively more diverse and eclectic. In the genre's first century, the most prevalent theory was Euhemerism. An original theory of the ancient Greeks, Euhemerism is a quasi-scientific conviction held about myths that they are somehow a dim and confused memory of actual "historical" events. Commonly Euhemerism was brought in to explain the existence of lost worlds, of which our myths are but an obscure remembrance; the "rediscovery of lost Atlantis" tale especially comes to mind here. This Euhemeristic type of narrative has endured well into recent American SF of the more conventional sort—as when writers posit that the Greek or Norse or other gods actually existed and were aliens or superhumans or superscientists; some sort of superbeings, the grounds of whose superiority over normal humans is *not* supernatural, but, hypothetically, naturalistic/scientific. There are countless variations on this and other Euhemeristic notions in modern SF and fantasy, but this seems the weakest and least challenging theory of myth because it has become a cliché. Taking myths as literally true—that they really happened—is the least interesting way of reading them. Roger Zelazny has been successful with an ironical and satirical/parodic Euhemerism (*Lord of Light, This Immortal*).

In SF's second century, writers have expressed a greater interest in psychological and psychoanalytical researches into myth (from the outset, myths have been an important object of theory and speculation across the field of psychology, recent social psychology included). Terms like "archetype," "collective unconscious," "race memory," "anamnesis," and "abreaction" seem ever more appropriate. Sigmund Freud and Carl Jung are, of course, the most important contributors, but typically the SF writers show a broad and general awareness of psychological theories, and don't feel obliged to follow any narrow model. It is only fair to say that the psychological theory (e.g., in Arthur Clarke or, later, in Samuel Delany) has enriched and matured SF myth-making far beyond the possibilities of Euhemerism.

Anthropological and sociological approaches to myth have penetrated SF mostly in the last three decades, with Frazerian themes or ritualistic death-rebirth patterns or concepts of the so-called "primitive" a regular part of the genre by now. Science fiction's understanding of systems and the interconnectedness of systems allies it loosely with the recent intellectual movement and methodology known as structuralism (Robert Silverberg's "Breckenridge and the Continuum" and Anthony Burgess's *M/F* make explicit and formal application of structuralism). Works like Samuel Delany's *Einstein Intersection* go one step further and indicate that now SF can make its own genuine and insightful contributions to myth-theory.

Ours is the century of psychology and psychiatry, and during it humanity's Odyssean quest-adventure into the "inner space" of the psyche has been as significant as technological culture's Frankensteinian conquest of the physical world and outer space. This psychic journey is shared by all the voyagers on spaceship earth, not just the handful of astronauts who have managed the physical journey to outer space. Whether it carries us even further into the inner depths of our human minds, even closer to the instinctual roots that lie at the heart of consciousness (a Dionysian image), or outward to understand ourselves as a unity with our whole environment in a planetary consciousness which includes more species than humans, SF expands the possibilities and range of our world-view.

Signs are that myth-making is flourishing in our culture as never before, and SF is only one of a number of forces shaping its resurgence. Science itself, for example, has contributed a great deal to the mythical cast of our age; fantastic images of creative science's accomplishments and potential accomplishments take the place of conventional religions in some cases and reinforce existing cults and religions in others. One should list the popularity of *Star Wars* and *Battlestar Galactica*, and of the recent spate of horror films; the rise of pseudo-scientific cults and religions on an unprecedented scale: Dianetics, the Moonies, Loch Ness, Bigfoot, the search for Noah's Ark, the resurgence of Atlantis, the theories of Von Daniken and Velikovsky; the domination of our perceptions as never before by the glittering, fantastic, irrational imagery of television, and a continued obsession with alternate states of consciousness. These and many other phenomena only reinforce the conclusion that ours is an age of myth and dream where we act out in belief and ritual the shapes of our imagination. Certainly the German novelist, Hermann Broch, was correct when he characterized the twentieth century as "the mythical age," meaning specifically by that, "return to myth in

Conclusion: The Future of Eternity

its ancient forms." The mythic is viewed as a mode of thinking about the world which is at once fantastic and unrealistic, but also wonderfully stimulating, refreshing, free, and life-enhancing.

Whether this obsession with myth will turn out to have positive or evil effects is a relative issue. If one could identify a clear-cut case of a modern mythology that contrasts with SF mythology, it is Nazism. This political mythology is alive and well on the international scene today, with loyal adherents in many nations; though it is no longer the expressed political creed in any contemporary nations, the ideologies of many are kindredly "fascist." But its enemies equally signal that Nazism is a mythology. It has fascinated film-makers and their viewers for over forty years; now TV too lavishes some of its most extravagant productions on Nazism (*Holocaust* had an incredibly large TV audience). Norman Spinrad's *The Iron Dream* (ch. 4) showed the typical combination of fascination plus repulsion.

Thus at one end of the spectrum there are the actual party members who participate actively and willingly in the cult and who actively try to live out this would-be heroic myth. At the other end, the fear and loathing of its enemies and victims make Nazism a demonic and Satanic mythology: its opponents, and even everybody else, take Nazism seriously and are fully cognizant of its mythic, if evil, power. Just because Adolf Hitler lost World War II doesn't mean the mythology he created isn't a living force. Unfortunately, too, Nazism has to be considered a "scientific" mythology, however perverted we judge that use of science.

I have tried to describe modern Anglo-American SF and fantasy in terms quite different from Nazism or any other cults. I have emphasized features which are humorous, satirical, critical, skeptical, and antiauthoritarian: that side of SF which tries to wake the mind up and alert it to new possibilities, not to lull it to sleep with a pseudo-scientific spell.

The myth-making of science fiction contrasts strongly with pseudo-scientific cults which seem much closer to conventional religions because of the high demands for investment in rituals and belief-codes. It must be admitted, though, that for a large segment of SF fandom, certain books, films, or authors achieve celebrity status and even receive "worship": a harmless, if decadent, cult practice. The authentic SF attitude is to ask us to live out our own myths—to stay in control of our own minds and powers—whereas the cultic posture promotes being under the power of others (namely the authorities of the given cult).

In modern SF mythology, humanity is a self-creator. The future remains in our own hands, to fail or succeed at: the Odyssean mythos points to our self-confidence to ride with change and succeed in the great adventure of the future; the Frankensteinian, dystopian vision urges us to make the necessary changes in ourselves and in the world to prevent the terrifying visions from coming true. We are ultimately responsible for our own beliefs and opinions.

Science fiction mythology proper concentrates on what humanity might make of itself in the future, whereas the religious/cultic posture is to accept whatever the transhuman authority has in store for us. Intellect, personal decision-making, criticism are all important to the mythopoesis of SF, as are increased moral and social consciousness. Ideologically, Anglo-American SF is pluralistic and relativistic.

Cults and religions substantialize their visions (i.e., declare that their eschatologies and prophecies are actual empirical models of reality), whereas the sense of SF myth-making is always one of a make-believe alternative to the normal empirical world. In cultic or religious myths, the estrangement-effects are masked and mystified, while for SF the whole notion of the "wonder effect" resides in presenting both a radical and a recognizable change on the known world. Science-fiction narratives all exhibit and advertise clearly enough that they are "not-so" stories.

However, this train of thought is developing a critical and analytical view of SF myth-making that overlooks its integration of consciousness and the unification of many intellectual dissociations. Basically, modern SF transcends—hence, rejects—the breach between fantasy and cognition, or between myth and reason, or between intuitive imagination and rational intellect. It further denies a distinction between inward and outward forms of imagination: SF is a literature which looks simultaneously in two directions, inward toward the mind and its creative products, outward toward unknown reality, the still unexplored universe. Thus SF mythopoesis succeeds in wedding the analytical/critical mode of thought usually associated with science to the mystical/visionary, which is an inclusive and synthetic mode of thought evident in myth, cult, and religion.

Conclusion: The Future of Eternity

More particularly, SF heals the apparent split between science and literature—unifying the "two cultures" envisioned decades ago by C. P. Snow, Aldous Huxley, I. A. Richards, and others. One of the things we have to remember is that all along, from Graeco-Roman antiquity to modern times, literature has affected our sensibilities every bit as much as scientific discovery. For centuries most people have registered the great changes achieved basically by science through the intervening medium of literature, prose and poetry alike. Science fiction is, of course, a kind of literature that appears in a world where science is so pervasive and important. Traditionally SF which fails to take into account actual scientific researches has been highly suspect, but at least in our part of the twentieth century we have to allow for some sort of time-lag for consciousness to catch up to the demands of science when mediated through SF. In specific areas of both scientific research and artistic, aesthetic literature the SF now being written is more sophisticated and compelling than ever before.

Modern SF, now far along into its second century, has performed well in anticipating by several decades changes in our world that were held by the general population to be impossible until they actually happened. These include the unleashing of nuclear power, space exploration, large-scale population control by artificial means, control of the genetic code, behavior modification, and a broad variety of other specific technological developments.

One might say that up to the New Wave era SF was always bold and original in dealing with scientific speculations and researches and could in some respects be considered as modern and progressive a world-view as there was. It also produced *some* acknowledged literary classics, and most of the older SF that we remember today is better written than it is usually given credit for anyway. New Wave SF is the equal of contemporary mainstream fiction in literary technique, openness to experimentation, and general intellectual sophistication. In a few decades, or even years, it will be difficult to distinguish SF as a special genre at all: it is becoming *the* mainstream so quickly; this is happening because SF is a new mode of consciousness, a new integrated way of viewing ourselves in the context of the universe, as much as it is a body of literature and film and TV.

Science fiction appears to be growing more and more popular on a worldwide scale, itself a positive sign of the growing planetary consciousness. In Europe, Japan, and the Soviet Union, SF is increasingly a more popular genre in both native languages and in translations of Anglo-American writers.

Its habit of creating new syntheses out of long-standing oppositions of the thesis-antithesis mold might explain why SF continues to engage ever greater numbers of intellectuals in Marxist countries. There is nothing which is necessarily antagonistic or inimical to Marxism, though SF is typically pluralistic and relativisitic and in the USSR one might assume a need for close adherence to Marxist dogma. But in the Soviet SF I've sampled so far (admittedly a very minimal amount for so large a literature), it seems like *other* (i.e., Anglo-American) SF—if not actively encouraging intellectual freedom, it is certainly not doctrinaire or monistic.

In any case, SF by Marxist writers is like all other SF I know in stressing the interconnectedness of events and systems, on a global scale. I believe it significant that, though Anglo-American SF is the most important single body of fictions within the genre, what constitutes a "classic" writer or story is not so nation-bound (here one could cite writers like Karel Capek or Stanislaw Lem, the latter probably the most important figure in world SF today; nor should Argentinian fantasist Jorge Luis Borges be ignored in this connection).

The entire genre proposes three speculative myths where creative science and the myth-making faculty are mutually complementary. All three myths offer challenges to self-transcendence and self-knowledge for contemporary humanity. Yet these are not static archetypal images but dynamic encounters with an as yet ambiguous import: the outcome of these three mythic confrontations is so far neither Frankensteinian nor Odyssean for sure. These three SF myths are the superman, the machine, and the alien.

(1) *The man-superman encounter.* This may be the most crucial mythic confrontation of the three: will we be able to cope with future versions of ourselves? Increasingly our altered interpretations of human nature and possibility become a problem for an integrated consciousness; SF tries to unify a still-fragmented perception of the myriad changes registered by recent humanity. In this sense, the metamorphosis of the species is a Frankensteinian theme, dealing with cautionary areas, like genetic engineering, which are now becoming not only possible but even likely (see chapter 5).

If one changes the focus, we come upon the mythic themes of androgyny and sexual transformation, one modality of the superman. In real cases, it means actual biological alteration; though we still aren't able to transform a fertile human adult of one sex into a fertile human adult of the opposite sex, yet this is still a pioneer era in that area (we are still not thirty-five years from Dr. Kinsey's first published scientific researches into human sexuality). But psychic androgyny remains as important as biological androgyny: in our inner lives we wish to achieve female/male wholeness and integration (hence SF shares a basic theme of Jungian depth psychology).

(2) *The man-machine encounter.* This mythic confrontation raises both speculative and cautionary questions concerning the interaction of humans and machines (originally human-created artifacts, often artificial intelligences). The man-machine interface is still largely an unknown; this remains an open-ended speculation which is highly ambiguous in its import today. We haven't even begun to ferret out the possibilities in this one. Since Samuel Butler's "Book of the Machine" in *Erewhon* (1872), it has been possible to think of machines in terms of a new stage of evolution—a posthuman one.

The human-machine encounter usually includes a Frankensteinian caution about so radical a man-created change in the world, and this particularly comes out in the "machine-becomes-God-and-takes over" tale. But there has also been a more confident strain in SF (e.g., Stanislaw Lem's *Cyberiad*, Robert Silverberg's *Tower of Glass*) which is willing to be open-minded and allow full "humanness" (whatever that entails) to future possible machines. Continual dramatic accomplishments in cybernetics and robotics alone, from the large-scale changes they are registering on the world of today and the near future, make this speculative encounter one of mythic consequences.

Its ambiguous import is best signalled in Roger Zelazny and Philip K. Dick's strange collaboration of 1976, *Deus Irae* ("God of Wrath"), which describes a mutant postholocaustal future where the boundaries between animate and inanimate, human and machine, are blurred and indistinct: the Oedipus-like hero is an anomalous combination of man (limbless torso) and machine (prosthetic limbs) who successfully outwits and eludes an anomalous cannibalistic sphinx-like computer. This and other versions of the man/machine myth indicate how much we still have to learn about the two primary concepts of "thinking" and "being alive."

(3) *The human-alien encounter.* This remains the most speculative and otherworldly of the three mythic confrontations. So far the greatest consequences of this myth have turned up in the psychic world—in altering our beliefs, rather than in indisputable, verifiable facts and researches. But its effects on the imagination are indisputable.

For example, twenty years ago it was rare to encounter a person who would admit to a belief in UFOs; but an audience poll on a recent TV game show showed that 53 of the 100 people in the audience actually believed there were such things and they were already here. In our own heads, at least, the alien is present as never before.

Recently Erich Von Daniken (*Chariot of the Gods?*) and a whole host of followers, as well as two very popular television shows (*Ancient Astronauts* and *In Search of Ancient Mysteries*), explain the ancient "gods" as antique astronauts. Even if this theory as "science" is inconsistent and is intellectually trivial, as a modern cultural myth it is extremely important, for it shows that contemporary man is expanding his intellectual vision and his imagination, however naively, to the extraterrestrial mode; if modern man no longer has a mysticism dealing with his God or gods and the perfect, transcendental world of Being that exists somewhere apart from our mutable world of Becoming, yet the new openness of our vision is evident, and man has discovered a new analogue of the "other world" in the extraterrestrial.

But there is a less attractive implication in this myth. In his crazy but intriguing little book, *Flying Saucers*, Carl Jung saw in the Alien a kind of "divine midwifery," meaning modern man feels he has lost control of his own destiny on his own planet and that our "salvation" must lie in more powerful beings from outer space—perhaps *they* will be able to save us from ourselves.

I merely raise the question: will we really be able to experience the alien before we achieve the awareness that we are one human species, interconnectedly inhabiting one limited planet? Or before we understand and appreciate the non-human "aliens"—the plants and animals—of our own planet? Shouldn't these concrete, immediate issues of human population and natural environment take prece-

Conclusion: The Future of Eternity

dence over an as yet unknown Outsider? Or is it possible that the alien is the very image which makes us think out these problems of planet earth from a new perspective and on a large scale? Will this "far-out" speculation bear any empirical fruit, or is it ultimately doomed to go the way of Atlantis and Mu?

The broad genre we've visited in these chapters tells us the future is open-ended, and not yet determined. These and so many other myths, good and bad, are actively with us. We do not yet know the outcome for our species and planet, and "the battle may yet be won or lost." To paraphrase an argument from philosopher of science Karl Popper, we aren't able to predict new knowledge (or we would already know it), but new knowledge will in itself constitute a large part of any new "reality" of the future. So humanity's journey into the future is unpredictable and undetermined—it is a heroic journey inspiring both hope and fear, and the myths will be there to guide and comfort and challenge—and even frighten—us. The myths aren't going home. They're already here, to stay.

SELECTED BIBLIOGRAPHY

This list includes only secondary works of general importance; works that were cited only once or for specific purposes have been relegated to their proper places in the notes.

I. Critical Works on Science Fiction, Fantasy, and Utopian Fiction

A. BIBLIOGRAPHICAL AIDS, CHECKLISTS, AND ENCYCLOPEDIAS

Barron, Neil, ed. *Anatomy of Wonder: Science Fiction*. New York and London: R. R. Bowker Co., 1976.

Bleiler, Everett F. *The Checklist of Fantastic Literature: A Bibliography of Fantasy, Weird, and Science Fiction Books in the English Language*. 2d ed. Naperville, Ill.: FAX Collector's Editions, 1972.

Briney, Robert E. *SF Bibliographies: An Annotated Bibliography of Bibliographical Works on Science Fiction and Fantasy*. Chicago: Advent, 1972.

Clareson, Thomas. *Science Fiction Criticism: An Annotated Checklist*. The Kent State University Press, 1972.

Cole, Walter R., ed. *A Checklist of Science-Fiction Anthologies*. New York: Arno Press, 1975.

Day, Donald. *Index to the Science-Fiction Magazines 1926–1950*. Portland, Oregon: Perri Press, 1952.

Index to the Science Fiction Magazines 1966–1970. New England Science Fiction Association, 1971.

Locke, George. *Voyages in Space: A Bibliography of Interplanetary Fiction 1801–1914*. London: Ferret Fantasy, 1975.

McGhan, Barry. *Science Fiction and Fantasy Pseudonyms*. Misfit Press, 1973, with Supplement. (Available from Howard DeVore, 4705 Weddel St., Dearborn, Mich.)

Metcalf, Norman. *The Index of Science Fiction Magazines, 1951–1965*. El Cerrito, Calif.: J. B. Stark, Publisher, 1968.

Nicholls, Peter, ed. *The Encyclopedia of Science Fiction*. London, New York, etc.: Granada Publishing, 1979.

Pfeiffer, John R. *Fantasy and Science Fiction: A Critical Guide*. Palmer Lake, Colo.: Filter Press, 1971.

Randall, David A., S. C. Fredericks, and Tim Mitchell. *Science Fiction and Fantasy: An Exhibition*. Lilly Library Publications 21. Bloomington, Ind.: Indiana University Publications, 1975.

Schachterle, Lance and Jeanne Welcher. "A Checklist of Secondary Studies

on Imaginary Voyages." *Bulletin of Bibliography* 31, no. 3 (July-September 1974), p. 99.
SFBRI: Science Fiction Book Review Index. Compiled by Hal W. Hall (Beginning with vol. 1 for 1970; subsequent volumes published annually), 3608 Meadow Oaks Lane, Bryan, Texas.
Siemon, Frederick. *Science Fiction Story Index 1950–1968.* Chicago: American Library Association, 1971.
Stella Nova: The Contemporary Science Fiction Authors. Unicorn and Sons, 1970.
Strauss, Erwin S. *The MIT Science Fiction Society's Index to the S-F Magazines, 1951–1965.* Cambridge, Massachusetts, 1966.
Tuck, Donald A. *The Encyclopedia of Science Fiction and Fantasy.* 2 vols. Chicago: Advent. Vol. 1, *Who's Who, A-L*, 1974. Vol. 2, *Who's Who, M-Z*, 1978.
Tymn, Marshall. "A Checklist of American Critical Works on SF: 1972–1973." *Extrapolation* 17 (1975–76): 78–96. Subsequent updatings of this bibliography appear annually.
Versins, Pierre. *Encyclopédie de l'Utopie, des Voyages Extraordinaires, et de la Science Fiction.* L'Age d'Homme, Lausanne, Editions, 1972.

B. CRITICAL BOOKS AND ARTICLES

Aldiss, Brian W. *Billion Year Spree: The True History of Science Fiction.* Garden City, N.Y.: Doubleday & Co., 1973.
Armytage, W. H. G. *Yesterday's Tomorrows: A Historical Survey of Future Societies.* Toronto: University of Toronto Press, 1968.
Bailey, J. O. *Pilgrims Through Space and Time.* Westport, Conn.: Greenwood Press, 1972; reissue of original ed. New York: Argus Books, 1947.
Bernabeu, E. P. "Science Fiction: A New Mythos." *Psychoanalytic Quarterly* 26 (1957): 527–35.
Birkhead, Edith. *The Tale of Terror: A Study of the Gothic Romance.* London: Constable & Co., 1921.
Burgess, Andrew J. "SF in the Classroom: Teaching Religion Through Science Fiction." *Extrapolation* 13 (1971–72): 112–15.
Carter, Lin. *Imaginary Worlds: The Art of Fantasy.* New York: Ballantine Books, 1973.
Clareson, Thomas D., ed. *SF: The Other Side of Realism.* Bowling Green University Popular Press, 1971.
Clareson, Thomas D., ed. *Voices for the Future: Essays on Major Science Fiction Writers.* Bowling Green University Popular Press, 1976.
Clareson, Thomas D., ed. *Many Futures, Many Worlds: Theme and Form in Science Fiction.* Kent State University Press, 1977.
Cohen, John. *Human Robots in Myth and Science.* London: Allen & Unwin, 1966.
Davenport, Basil, *et al. The Science Fiction Novel: Imagination and Social Criticism.* Chicago: Advent, 1964.
De Camp, L. Sprague. *Literary Swordsmen and Sorcerers: The Makers of Heroic Fantasy.* Sauk City, Wis.: Arkham House, 1976.
Delany, Samuel R. *The Jewel-Hinged Jaw: Notes on the Language of Science Fiction.* New York: Berkeley Windhover, 1978.
Franklin, Bruce; Isaac Asimov; Frederik Pohl; and Darko Suvin. "Science

Selected Bibliography

Fiction: The New Mythology. MLA Forum." *Extrapolation* 10 (May, 1969): 69–115.
Fredericks, S. C. "Problems of Fantasy." *Science-Fiction Studies* 5 (1978): 33–44.
Gerber, Richard. *Utopian Fantasy: A Study of English Utopian Fiction Since the End of the Nineteenth Century.* 2d ed. New York: McGraw-Hill, 1973.
Green, Roger Lancelyn. *Into Other Worlds: Space-Flight in Fiction, From Lucian to Lewis.* London and New York: Abelard-Schuman, 1958.
Gunn, James. *Alternate Worlds: The Illustrated History of Science Fiction.* Englewood Cliffs, N.J.: Prentice-Hall, 1975. Introduced by Isaac Asimov.
Hillegas, Mark. *The Future as Nightmare: H. G. Wells and the Anti-utopians.* New York: Oxford University Press, 1967.
Irwin, W. R. *The Game of the Impossible: A Rhetoric of Fantasy.* Urbana: University of Illinois Press, 1976.
Ketterer, David. *New Worlds for Old: The Apocalyptic Imagination, Science Fiction, and American Literature.* New York: Anchor Books, 1974. Published simultaneously in hardback by Indiana University Press, Bloomington, Ind.
Knight, Damon. *In Search of Wonder.* 2d ed. Chicago: Advent, 1967.
Lem, Stanislaw. "On the Structural Analysis of Science Fiction." *Science-Fiction Studies* 1 (1973–74): 26–33.
Lem, Stanislaw. "The Time-Travel Story and Related Matters of SF Structuring." *Science-Fiction Studies* 1 (1973–74): 143–54. rpt. Mark Rose, *Science Fiction*.
Lovecraft, H. P. *Supernatural Horror in Literature.* 2d ed. New York: Dover Publications, 1973; new Intro. E. F. Bleiler; rev. of 1945 ed. which had a Foreword by August Derleth.
Manlove, C. N. *Modern Fantasy: Five Studies.* Cambridge and London: Cambridge University Press, 1975.
Mobley, Jane. *Magic is Alive: A Study of Contemporary Fantasy Fiction.* Doctoral dissertation. University of Kansas, 1974. *Dissertation Abstracts* 36.2: 881A.
Mobley, Jane. "Toward a Definition of Fantasy Fiction."*Extrapolation* 15 (1973–74): 117–28.
Mohs, Mayo. "Science Fiction and the World of Religion." Introduction to *Other Worlds, Other Gods.* New York: Doubleday & Co., 1971. In paperback, New York: Avon Books, 1974.
Moskowitz, Sam. *Seekers of Tomorrow: Masters of Modern Science Fiction.* Cleveland: World Publishing Co., 1961.
Moskowitz, Sam. *Explorers of the Infinite: Shapers of Science Fiction.* Cleveland: World Publishing Co., 1963.
Nicholls, Peter, ed. *Science Fiction at Large.* New York: Harper and Row, 1976.
Philmus, Robert M. *Into the Unknown: The Evolution of Science Fiction from Francis Godwin to H. G. Wells.* Berkeley and Los Angeles: University of California Press, 1970.
Plank, Robert. *The Emotional Significance of Imaginary Beings: A Study of the Interaction Between Psychopathology, Literature, and Reality in the Modern World.* Springfield, Ill.: Thomas, 1968.
Rabkin, Eric S. *The Fantastic in Literature.* Princeton: Princeton University Press, 1976.

Radford, John. "Science Fiction as Myth." *Foundation* 10 (June 1976): 28–33.
Rose, Lois and Stephen. *The Shattered Ring: Science Fiction and the Quest for Meaning.* Richmond, Va.: John Knox Press, 1970.
Rose, Mark, ed. *Science Fiction: A Collection of Critical Essays.* Twentieth Century Views. Englewood Cliffs, N.J.: Prentice-Hall, 1976.
Rothfork, John. *New Wave Science Fiction Considered as a Popular Religious Phenomenon: A Definition and an Example.* Doctoral dissertation. University of New Mexico, 1973. *Dissertation Abstracts* 35.3: 1670–71A.
Rottensteiner, Franz. *The Science Fiction Book: An Illustrated History.* New York: New American Library, 1975.
Russ, Joanna. "Towards an Aesthetic of Science Fiction." *Science-Fiction Studies* 2 (1975): 112–19.
Sanders, Joseph. *Fantasy in the Twentieth Century British Novel.* Doctoral dissertation. Indiana University, 1972. *Dissertation Abstracts* 33.2: 764A.
Scholes, Robert. *Structural Fabulation: An Essay on Fiction of the Future.* Notre Dame and London: University of Notre Dame Press, 1975.
Scholes, Robert, and Eric Rabkin. *Science Fiction: History, Science, Vision.* New York: Oxford University Press, 1977.
Suvin, Darko. *Metamorphoses of Science Fiction: On the Poetics and History of a Literary Genre.* New Haven: Yale University Press, 1979.
Suvin, Darko. "On the Poetics of the Science Fiction Genre." *College English* 34 (1972–73): 372–82. rpt. Darko Suvin, *Metamorphoses of Science Fiction*, and in Mark Rose, *Science Fiction*.
Suvin, Darko. "Science Fiction and the Genological Jungle." *Genre* 6 (1973): 251–73. rpt. Darko Suvin, *Metamorphoses of Science Fiction*.
Todorov, Tzvetan. *The Fantastic: A Structural Approach to a Literary Genre.* Trans. Richard Howard, with new Foreword by Robert Scholes. Ithaca, N.Y.: Cornell University Paperbacks ed., 1975.
Tolkien, J. R. R. "On Fairy Stories." In *Tree and Leaf* (London: George Allen & Unwin, 1964) and *The Tolkien Reader* (New York: Ballantine Books, 1966).
Walsh, Chad. *From Utopia to Nightmare.* New York: Harper, 1962.
Warrick, Patricia; Martin Greenberg; and Joseph Olander, eds. *Science Fiction: Contemporary Mythology (The SFWA-SFRA Anthology).* New York: Harper and Row, 1978.
Wollheim, Donald A. *The Universe Makers: Science Fiction Today.* New York: Harper and Row, 1971.

II. Books on Myth and Related Subjects

Bolle, Kees. *The Freedom of Man in Myth.* Nashville: Vanderbilt University Press, 1968.
Brandon, S. G. F. *Creation Legends of the Ancient Near East.* London: Hodder and Stoughton, 1963.
Brandon, S. G. F., ed. *Dictionary of Comparative Religion.* New York: Scribner, 1970.
Bratton, Fred G. *A History of the Bible.* Boston: Beacon Press, 1967.
Campbell, Joseph. *The Hero With a Thousand Faces.* 2d ed. Princeton: Princeton University Press, 1968.

Selected Bibliography

Campbell, Joseph. *The Masks of God*. 4 vols. New York: Viking Press, 1959–68.
Cassirer, Ernst. *Language and Myth*. Trans. Susanne Langer. New York: Dover Publications, 1946.
Cassirer, Ernst. *Mythical Thought*. Trans. Ralph Manheim. The Philosophy of Symbolic Forms, vol. 2. New Haven: Yale University Press, 1955. Original publication in German, 1925.
Chase, Richard. *Quest for Myth*. Baton Rouge: Louisiana State University Press, 1949.
Cohen, Percy. "Theories of Myth." *Man* N.S. 4 (1969): 337–53.
Eliade, Mircea. *Cosmos and History, or The Myth of the Eternal Return*. Trans. Willard R. Trask. New York: Pantheon Books, 1954.
Eliade, Mircea. *Rites and Symbols of Initiation*. Trans. Willard R. Trask. New York: Harper & Row, 1958. Previously *Birth and Rebirth*. New York: Harper, 1958.
Eliade, Mircea. *Myth and Reality*. Trans. Willard R. Trask. New York: Harper & Row, 1963.
Eliade, Mircea. *Patterns in Comparative Religion*. Trans. Rosemary Sheed. New York: Meridian Books, 1963.
Ellis-Davidson, H. R. *Gods and Myths of Northern Europe*. Baltimore: Penguin Books, 1964.
Evans-Pritchard, E. E. *Theories of Primitive Religion*. Oxford: Clarendon Press, 1965.
Feldman, Burton, and Robert D. Richardson. *The Rise of Modern Mythology 1680–1860*. Bloomington, Ind.: Indiana University Press, 1972.
Frankfort, Henri, and others. *Before Philosophy*. Harmondsworth, Middlesex: Penguin Books, 1949. Short version of *The Intellectual Adventure of Ancient Man*. Chicago: University of Chicago Press, 1946.
Gaster, T. H. *The New Golden Bough: A New Abridgment of the Classic Work by Sir James George Frazer*. Garden City, N.Y.: Anchor Books ed., 1961.
Graves, Robert and Raphael Patai. *Hebrew Myths, The Book of Genesis*. Garden City, N.Y.: Doubleday, 1964.
Gray, L. H., et al., eds. *The Mythology of All Races*. 12 vols. plus index vol. Boston: Marshall Jones, 1916–32.
Hastings, James, et al., eds. *Encyclopedia of Religion and Ethics*. 12 vols. plus index vol. Edinburgh, 1908–26. rpt. New York: C. Scribner, 1961.
Henderson, Joseph. "Ancient Myths and Modern Man." In *Man & His Symbols*. Ed. C. G. Jung. Garden City, N.Y.: Doubleday, 1964.
Herd, Eric W. "Myth Criticism: Limits and Possibilities." *Mosaic* 2 (1969): 69–77.
James, E. O. *Christian Myth and Ritual: A Historical Study*. London: J. Murray, 1933.
James, E. O. *The Concept of Deity: A Comparative and Historical Study*. London and New York: Hutchinson's University Library, 1950.
James, E. O. *Creation and Cosmology*. Leiden: Brill, 1969. *Studies in the History of Religion*, Supplements to *Numen*, 16.
Jung, C. G. *The Archetypes and the Collective Unconscious*. Trans. R. F. C. Hull. 2d ed. Princeton: Princeton University Press, 1968.
Jung, C. G. *Flying Saucers: A Modern Myth of Things Seen in the Sky*. Trans. R. F. C. Hull. London: Routledge & Kegan Paul, 1959.

Jung, C. G. and C. Kerenyi. *Essays on a Science of Mythology.* Trans R. F. C. Hull. Princeton: Princeton University Press, 1969.

Kirk, G. S. *Myth: Its Meaning and Functions in Ancient and Other Cultures.* Sather Classical Lectures, vol. 40. Berkeley: University of California Press, 1970.

Kirk, G. S. *The Nature of Greek Myths.* Harmondsworth, Middlesex: Penguin Books, 1974.

Kramer, Samuel Noah, ed. *Mythologies of the Ancient World.* Garden City, N.Y.: Doubleday, 1961.

Lévi-Strauss, Claude. *The Savage Mind.* Trans. George Weidenfeld and Nicolson Ltd. Chicago: University of Chicago Press, 1966.

Lüthi, Max. *Once Upon a Time: On the Nature of Fairy Tales.* Trans. Lee Chadeayne and Paul Gottwald. Intro. Francis L. Utley. New York: F. Ungar Publishing Co., 1970.

Munz, Peter. *When the Golden Bough Breaks: Structuralism or Typology?* London and Boston: Routledge and Kegan Paul, 1973.

Murray, Henry A., ed. *Myth and Mythmaking.* New York: George Braziller, 1960. Rpt. *Daedalus* 88, no. 2 (1959).

Neumann, Erich. *The Origins and History of Consciousness.* Trans. R. F. C. Hull. Princeton: Princeton University Press, 1954.

Onians, R. B. *The Origins of European Thought.* 2d ed. Cambridge: Cambridge University Press, 1954.

Peradotto, John. *Classical Mythology: An Annotated Bibliographical Survey.* Special Publication of the American Philological Association. Urbana, Ill., 1973.

Pritchard, James B., ed. *Ancient Near Eastern Texts Relating to the Old Testament.* 3d ed., with supplement. Princeton: Princeton University Press, 1969.

Rose, H. J. *A Handbook of Greek Mythology.* London: Methuen & Co., 1928.

Seligmann, Kurt. *Magic, Supernaturalism and Religion.* New York: Pantheon Books, 1948. Also published as *The History of Magic.*

Seznec, Jean. *The Survival of the Pagan Gods: The Mythological Tradition and Its Place in Renaissance Humanism and Art.* Trans. Barbara Sessions. New York: Pantheon Books, 1953.

Stanford, W. B. *The Ulysses Theme: A Study in the Adaptability of a Traditional Hero.* 2d ed. Oxford: Blackwell, 1963.

Stevens, Gregory I. *Literature, Myth, and Folklore.* Revised form, Oct. 12, 1973. A bibliography acquired from the University of Michigan's Center for the Coordination of Ancient and Modern Studies, Ann Arbor, Mich.

Thompson, Stith. *The Folktale.* New York: Holt, Rinehart and Winston, 1946.

Thompson, Stith. *Motif-Index of Folk-Literature.* 6 vols. Rev. ed. Bloomington, Ind.: Indiana University Press, 1955–58.

Vickery, John B., ed. *Myth and Literature: Contemporary Theory and Practice.* Lincoln, Nebr.: University of Nebraska Press, 1966.

Vivas, Eliseo. "Myth: Some Philosophical Problems." *Southern Review* 6 (1970): 89–103.

Vries, Jan de. *Heroic Song and Heroic Legend.* Trans. B. J. Timmer. London: Oxford University Press, 1963.

Vries, Jan de. *Forschungsgeschichte der Mythologie.* Freiburg: K. Alber, 1961.

Watts, Alan W. *Myth and Ritual in Christianity.* Boston: Beacon Press, 1968.

Weisinger, Herbert. *The Agony and the Triumph: Papers on the Use and Abuse of Myth*. East Lansing, Mich.: Michigan State University Press, 1964.
Wilson, Colin. *The Occult: A History*. New York: Random House, 1971.

III. Works on Theory of Fiction and the Literary Narrative

Altieri, Charles. "Ovid and the New Mythologists." *Novel* 7 (1973-74): 31-40.
Booth, Wayne C. *The Rhetoric of Fiction*. Chicago: University of Chicago Press, 1961.
Burke, Kenneth. *The Philosophy of Literary Form*. 3d ed. Berkeley: University of California Press, 1973.
Frye, Northrop. *Anatomy of Criticism*. Princeton: Princeton University Press, 1957.
Frye, Northrop. *The Educated Imagination*. Bloomington, Ind.: Indiana University Press, 1964.
Jameson, Frederic. *The Prison-House of Language: A Critical Account of Structuralism and Russian Formalism*. Princeton: Princeton University Press, 1972.
Kermode, Frank. *The Sense of an Ending: Studies in the Theory of Fiction*. New York: Oxford University Press, 1967.
Lewis, C. S. *An Experiment in Criticism*. Cambridge: Cambridge University Press, 1961.
Rabkin, Eric S. *Narrative Suspense*. Ann Arbor, Mich.: University of Michigan Press, 1973.
Scholes, Robert, and Robert Kellogg. *The Nature of Narrative*. New York: Oxford University Press, 1966.
Scholes, Robert. *The Fabulators*. New York: Oxford University Press, 1967.
Scholes, Robert. *Structuralism in Literature: An Introduction*. New Haven and London: Yale University Press, 1974.
Scholes, Robert. "Stillborn Literature." *Bulletin of the Midwest Modern Language Association* 7 (1974): 1-12.
Schorer, Mark. "Technique as Discovery." *Hudson Review* 1 (1948): 67-87.
Slochower, Harry. *Mythopoesis: Mythic Patterns in the Literary Classics*. Detroit: Wayne State University Press, 1970.
Spencer, Sharon, *Space, Time, and Structure in the Modern Novel*. New York: New York University Press, 1971.
Steiner, George. *Language and Silence: Essays on Language, Literature and the Inhuman*. New York: Atheneum, 1967.
Walsh, Dorothy. *Literature and Knowledge*. Middletown, Conn.: Wesleyan University Press, 1969.
Wellek, René and Austin Warren. *Theory of Literature*. 3d ed. New York: Harcourt, Brace & World, 1956.
Wheelwright, Philip. *Metaphor and Reality*. Bloomington, Ind.: Indiana University Press, 1962.
White, John J. *Mythology in the Modern Novel*. Princeton: Princeton University Press, 1971.
Wilson, Colin. *The Strength to Dream: Literature and the Imagination*. Boston: Houghton Mifflin, 1962.

IV. Works on History and Philosophy of Science and on History of Ideas

Asimov, Isaac. *The Intelligent Man's Guide to Science.* Vol. 1, *The Physical Sciences.* Vol. 2, *The Biological Sciences.* New York: Basic Books, 1960.

Bachelard, Gaston. *The Philosophy of No: A Philosophy of the New Scientific Mind.* Trans G. C. Waterson. New York: Orion Press, 1968. Original French ed. Paris, 1940.

Barrett, William. *Irrational Man: A Study in Existential Philosophy.* Garden City, N.Y.: Doubleday, 1962.

Becker, Ernest. *The Birth and Death of Meaning: An Interdisciplinary Perspective on the Problem of Man.* 2d ed. New York: Free Press, 1971.

Bentley, Eric. *A Century of Hero-Worship: A Study of the Idea of Heroism in Carlyle and Nietzsche, with Notes on Wagner, Spengler, Stefan George, and D. H. Lawrence.* 2d ed. Boston: Beacon Press, 1957. 1st ed. also published in London, 1947, as *The Cult of the Superman.*

Bronowski, J. *The Common Sense of Science.* Cambridge, Mass.: Harvard University Press, 1953.

Bronowski, J. *The Identity of Man.* Garden City, N.Y.: Natural History Press, 1965.

Bury, J. B. *The Idea of Progress: An Inquiry into its Origin and Growth.* London: Macmillan & Co., 1920.

Cassirer, Ernst. *An Essay on Man.* New Haven: Yale University Press, 1944.

Cassirer, Ernst. *The Myth of the State.* New Haven: Yale University Press, 1946.

Cohn, Norman. *The Pursuit of the Millennium: Revolutionary Messianism in Medieval and Reformation Europe and Its Bearing on Modern Totalitarian Movements.* 2d ed. New York: Harper & Row, 1961.

Collingwood, R. G. *The Idea of Nature.* Oxford: Clarendon Press, 1945.

Collingwood, R. G. *The Idea of History.* Oxford: Clarendon Press, 1946.

De Camp, L. Sprague. *Lost Continents: The Atlantis Theme in History, Science, and Literature.* 2d ed. New York: Dover Publications, 1970.

Gardner, Martin. *Fads and Fallacies in the Name of Science.* Rev. ed. New York: Dover Publications, 1957.

Holton, Gerald, ed. *Science and the Modern World View.* Daedalus, 87.1 (Winter 1958).

Hook, Sidney. *The Hero in History: A Study in Limitation and Possibility.* New York: The John Day Co., 1943.

Huxley, Aldous. *Literature and Science.* New York: Harper & Row, 1963.

Koestler, Arthur. *The Act of Creation: A Study of the Conscious and Unconscious in Science and Art.* New York: Macmillan, 1964.

Kuhn, Thomas S. *The Structure of Scientific Revolutions.* 2d ed. Chicago: University of Chicago Press, 1970.

Langer, Susanne K. *Philosophy in a New Key.* Cambridge, Mass.: Harvard University Press, 1951.

Langer, Susanne K. *Feeling and Form.* New York: Scribner's, 1953.

Lovejoy, A. O. and George Boas. *A Documentary History of Primitivism and Related Ideas in Antiquity.* Baltimore: John Hopkins University Press, 1935.

Peckham, Morse. *Man's Rage for Chaos: Biology, Behavior, and the Arts.* Philadelphia: Chilton Books, 1965.

Selected Bibliography

Piaget, Jean. *Structuralism*. Trans. Chaninah Maschler. New York: Basic Books, 1970.
Priestley, J. B. *Man and Time*. Garden City, N.Y.: Doubleday, 1964.
Russell, Bertrand. *The ABC of Relativity*. 3d ed. London: Allen & Unwin, 1969.
Ryle, Gilbert. *The Concept of Mind*. London: Hutchinson's University Library, 1949.
Slater, Philip. *The Wayward Gate: Science and the Supernatural*. Boston: Beacon Press, 1977.
Toffler, Alvin. *Future Shock*. New York: Random House, 1970.
Vaihinger, Hans. *The Philosophy of "As If": A System of the Theoretical, Practical, and Religious Fictions of Mankind*. Trans. C. K. Ogden. 2d ed. London: K. Paul, Trench, Trübner, 1935. Based on the 6th German ed.
Whitehead, Alfred North. *Science and the Modern World*. New York: The Macmillan Company, 1925.
Whitehead, Alfred North. *Adventures of Ideas*. New York: The Macmillan Company, 1933.
Zweig, Paul. *The Adventurer: The Fate of Adventure in the Western World*. New York: Basic Books, 1974.

NOTES

1. Old and New Myths in Science Fiction

1. The story originally appeared in *The Magazine of Fantasy and Science Fiction* (henceforth, *F&SF*) for November 1969; it was reprinted in Donald Wollheim and Terry Carr's *The World's Best Science Fiction 1970* (New York: Ace Books, 1970), pp. 36–45.

For a bibliography of Silverberg's writings by Donald Tuck, see *F&SF*, April 1974, an all-Silverberg issue that includes appreciative essays by Thomas Clareson and Barry Malzberg.

In addition, for all the authors met in this study, see Donald M. Tuck, *The Encyclopedia of Science Fiction and Fantasy*, 2 vols. (Chicago: Advent. Vol. 1, A-L [through 1968 only], 1974. Vol. 2, M-Z, 1978). It is best to check both the biographical and bibliographical entries against other resources since reviewers have found many errors; yet reference librarians will find this a most valuable addition to their collections.

2. For neo-Kantian theory, see Ernst Cassirer in *Language and Myth*, trans. Susanne Langer (New York: Dover, 1946) and *Mythical Thought*, trans. Ralph Manheim, *The Philosophy of Symbolic Forms*, Vol. 2 (New Haven: Yale University Press, 1955). Jungian theory is discussed often in my later chapters, and Frazer is taken up in detail in chapter 6.

On Jung's concept of archetypes, see Arthur Koestler, *The Act of Creation* (New York: Dell Laurel ed., 1967), p. 353: "Jung described archetypes as 'the psychic residua of numberless experiences of the same type' encountered by our ancestors, and stamped into the memory of the race—that is, into the deep layers of the 'collective unconscious' below the level of personal memories. Hence, whenever some archetypal motif is sounded, the response is much stronger than warranted by its face value—the mind responds like a tuning fork to a pure tone." For a comparable explanation see Maud Bodkin, *Archetypal Patterns in Poetry* (Oxford Paperbacks ed., 1963), p. 4.

3. *Angels and Spaceships* (London: Four Square, 1962), p. 8; cited by Sam J. Lundwall, *Science Fiction: What It's All About* (Ace Books, 1971), p. 23.

4. I took up this question earlier in "Lucian's *True History* as SF," *Science-Fiction Studies* (henceforth *SFS*) 3 (1976): 49–60.

For an even stronger assertion that Lucian is SF, from a closely structuralist point of view, see Roy Arthur Swanson, "The True, the False, and the Truly False: Lucian's Philosophical Science Fiction," *SFS* 3 (1976): 228–39; I believe the latter article is the most perceptive and intelligent essay on Lucian I have encountered in the critical literature.

5. For a detailed list of the myths, see S.C. Fredericks, "Plato's Atlantis: A Mythologist Looks at the Myth," in E.S. Ramage (ed.), *Atlantis: Fact or Fiction?* (Bloomington: Indiana University Press, 1978). The references mentioned earlier in the text are James Gunn, *Alternate Worlds* (Englewood Cliffs, N.J.: Prentice-Hall, 1975), p. 32; L. Sprague de Camp, *3,000 Years of Fantasy and Science Fiction* (New York: Lothrop, Lee, and Shepard, 1972).

6. Brian Aldiss, *Billion Year Spree* (New York: Doubleday, 1973), pp. 18–25; Robert Scholes and Eric Rabkin, *Science Fiction: History, Science, Vision* (New York: Oxford University Press, 1977), pp. 6 and 191–96.

7. I have used the edition by M. K. Joseph, *Mary W. Shelley: Frankenstein, or the Modern Prometheus* (London: Oxford University Press, 1969; based on the edition of 1831). For a brief account of Shelley's writings, I follow Edith Birkhead, *The Tale of Terror: A Study of the Gothic Romance* (London: E.P. Dutton, 1921), pp. 158–69. For *Frankenstein* specifically, I also refer the reader to Robert M. Philmus, *Into the Unknown: The Evolution of Science Fiction from Francis Godwin to H. G. Wells* (Berkeley: University of California Press, 1970), pp. 82–90; and a chapter in Muriel Spark, *Child of Light: A Reassessment of Mary Wollstonecraft Shelley* (Hadleigh, Essex: Tower Bridge, 1951), pp. 128–49. Also germane to our discussion is Aija Ozolins, "Dreams and Doctrines in *Frankenstein*," *SFS* 2 (1975): 103–12; and the same author's valuable review-article, "Recent Work on Mary Shelley and *Frankenstein*," *SFS* 3 (1976): 187–202.

8. Spark (note 7 above), p. 134.

9. Scholes and Rabkin (note 6 above), pp. 191–96.

10. Philmus, *Into the Unknown* (note 7 above), pp. 79–107; H. Bruce Franklin, *Future Perfect: American Science Fiction of the Nineteenth Century* (Oxford University Press, 1966), pp. ix–92; Eric Rabkin, *The Fantastic in Literature* (Princeton University Press, 1976), p. 186; Aldiss, *Billion Year Spree*, p. 26.

11. On this novel, also see Richard Mathews, *Aldiss Unbound: The Science Fiction of Brian W. Aldiss*, The Milford Series, *Popular Writers of Today*, vol. 9 (San Bernardino, Calif.: The Borgo Press, 1977), pp. 49–52; Aija Ozolins, "Recent Work on *Frankenstein*" (note 7 above), pp. 198–99.

12. New York: Avon Books, 1974; often reprinted. The story also appears in Bond's anthology, *No Time Like the Future* (New York: Avon, 1954). There is a valuable entry on this author in Tuck's *Encyclopedia*. I have been unable to locate a reference to the original "1942" publication in any SF index, encyclopedia, or bibliography.

13. David Ketterer, *New Worlds for Old: The Apocalyptic Imagination, Science Fiction, and American Literature* (Bloomington: Indiana University Press [hardcover]; Doubleday Anchor [paperback]; simultaneous publication 1974).

14. The story first appeared in *Thrilling Wonder Stories* (December 1950), and was reprinted in the Berkeley Medallion edition of Harness's *The Rose* (1969). Though a *minor* master who wrote little, Harness is widely prized for his technical polish and stylistic elegance. For his career, see Tuck's *Encyclopedia*.

15. The story was first published in *Fantastic Adventures* (October 1951) and was reprinted in a Belmont Books edition (1968) where it has the less

attractive title, *A Lamp for Medusa*, and is bound with Dave Van Arnam's *The Players of Hell*. For further knowledge of the ancient myth, see J.M. Woodward, *Perseus: A Study in Greek Art and Legend* (Cambridge: The University Press, 1937).

16. These and other details of the ancient Greek version are taken from Apollodorus' *Library* (in the Loeb Classical Library translation by James George Frazer, Cambridge, Mass., 1921), vol. 1, book 2, ch. 4, sections 1–5.

17. For a reliable introduction to this problem, see G. S. Kirk and J. E. Raven, *The Presocratic Philosophers*, corr. ed. (Cambridge: The University Press, 1969), esp. pp. 108–16; cf. Benjamin Farrington, *Science in Antiquity* 2d ed. (Oxford: Oxford University Press, 1969), pp. 21–23.

18. Blish is cited by Alexei Panshin, *Heinlein in Dimension* (Chicago: Advent, 1968), pp. 92–93. For "All You Zombies" and other fictive SF games that play with time-loop paradoxes, see Stanislaw Lem, "The Time-Travel Story and Related Matters of SF Structuring," *SFS* 1 (1974): 143–54. This famous short story appears in many anthologies, including the popular Heinlein anthology, *6XH* (New York: Pyramid, 1961; originally titled *The Unpleasant Profession of Jonathan Hoag*).

The critical literature on Heinlein is quickly becoming extensive. The most perceptive, sympathetic, and intelligent single essay on Heinlein as a whole is by David Samuelson, "The Frontier Worlds of Robert A. Heinlein," in Thomas D. Clareson (ed.), *Voices for the Future* (Bowling Green University Popular Press, 1976), pp. 104–52. In addition to Panshin's popular study cited above, one should also mention two Borgo Press pamphlets by George Edgar Slusser, *Robert A. Heinlein: Stranger in His Own Land* (1976), and *The Classic Years of Robert A. Heinlein* (1977), respectively vol. 1 and vol. 11 of the Milford Series, *Popular Writers of Today* (San Bernardino, Calif.: The Borgo Press).

19. Fredric Jameson, "Generic Discontinuities in SF: Aldiss's *Starship*," *SFS* 1 (1974): 57–68. Jameson specifically treats the "spaceship as universe" genre in Heinlein's *Orphans in the Sky* as well as Brian Aldiss's *Starship*.

20. Also published in *F&SF* issues for July-September in that same year.

21. Originally published in 1949 by the Bollingen Foundation, Inc. (N.Y.). This is one of the single most significant works of myth scholarship for contemporary SF writers. Samuelson (note 18 above), p. 140, mentions "Frazer, Jung, and Joseph Campbell" as the basis for Heinlein's "archetypal trail."

22. For background on Aztec myth, see Miguel Léon-Portilla, *Aztec Thought and Culture*, trans. Jack Emory Davis (Norman: University of Oklahoma Press, 1963), esp. pp. 52–53 and 98 for Coatlicue.

23. Jameson (note 19 above), p. 65. Also cf. *SFS* 2 (1975): 3–67, a special forum on "The Science Fiction of Philip K. Dick," including articles by Fredric Jameson, Stanislaw Lem, Brian Aldiss, Darko Suvin, and Dick himself.

24. Ketterer (note 13 above), p. 13 and passim.

25. Tzvetan Todorov, *The Fantastic: A Structural Approach to a Literary Genre*, trans. Richard Howard, with new foreword by Robert Scholes (Cornell Paperbacks ed., 1975), p. 44. For a highly polemical exchange on Todorov's "theory," see *SFS* 1 (1974): 227–37 (Stanislaw Lem in attack) and 2

(1975): 166–70 (defense of Todorov by Robert Scholes and Richard Astle; another response by Lem).

26. Scholes and Rabkin (note 6 above), p. 88; for a brief but helpful introduction to the "New Wave," also see Gunn (note 5 above), pp. 234–37.

27. All references are to the Avon Books edition of 1970. This story also appeared in *New Worlds S.F.*, September, 1966. Although the specific myth the novel deals with is the life of Christ, Moorcock leans heavily on Carl Jung for the *theory* of myth.

A shorter version of this interpretation appears in "Revivals of Ancient Mythologies in Current Science Fiction and Fantasy," in Thomas D. Clareson (ed.), *Many Futures, Many Worlds: Theme and Form in Science Fiction* (Kent State University Press, 1977), pp. 56–58.

28. Moorcock actually cites Jung (*Modern Man in Search of a Soul*) on the idea that even the identification with Christ as a model might lead to insanity if carried out in absolute terms.

A converse example, where the reenactment of myth is used as a form of psychotherapy, is presented in Roger Zelazny's *The Dream Master* (1966), though here too living out a myth finally leads to insanity at the novel's end.

John White, *Mythology in the Modern Novel* (Princeton: Princeton University Press, 1971), p. 239, discusses several examples in mainstream mythological novels where the reenactment of myth is a form of insanity.

29. New York: Swallow Press, 1974.

30. The story first appeared in *F&SF*, July 1969; it has since been published in two Ellison anthologies, *The Beast That Shouted Love at the Heart of the World* (New York: Avon, 1969) and *Deathbird Stories* (New York: Harper and Row, 1975).

31. On this story, see also George E. Slusser, *Harlan Ellison: Unrepentant Harlequin*, The Milford Series, *Popular Writers of Today*, vol. 6, (San Bernardino, Calif.: The Borgo Press, 1977), pp. 52–53.

32. For a detailed critique of this dystopian posture, see Gérard Klein, "Discontent in American Science Fiction," *SFS* 4 (1977): 3–13.

33. For information concerning Weinbaum's career and influence I am indebted to the chapter, "Dawn of Fame: The Career of Stanley G. Weinbaum," in Sam Moskowitz's *Explorers of the Infinite* (Cleveland: World, 1963), pp. 296–312, and to the introductory essay in Moskowitz's collection, *A Martian Odyssey*, of five of Weinbaum's stories in the Lancer Science Fiction Library (New York, 1962). All the stories by Weinbaum I discuss appear in this collection and also in *The Best of Stanley G. Weinbaum*, (New York: Ballantine, 1974), which has an Introduction by Isaac Asimov on Weinbaum's importance.

34. Robert Oppenheimer, "The Growth of Science and the Structure of Culture," in Gerald Holton (ed.), *Science and the Modern World View* (*Daedalus* 87, no. 1 [Winter 1958]): pp. 67–76; Thomas Kuhn, *The Structure of Scientific Revolutions* 2d ed. (Chicago: University of Chicago Press, 1970).

35. "Science Fiction and the Future," *College English* 37 (1975–76): 345–52. The author specifically aims his remarks at the "Golden Age of SF"—the 30s, 40s, and 50s.

36. Cited in note 34 above.

2. "Estrangement" in Myth and Science Fiction

1. "Myth, Symbolism, and Truth," in Thomas Sebeok (ed.), *Myth: A Symposium* (Bloomington: Indiana University Press, 1958; reprint of *Bibliographical and Special Series of the American Folklore Society*, vol. 5, 1955), pp. 22 and 23 respectively. Bidney's essay was also published in shorter form in John Vickery (ed.), *Myth and Literature* (Lincoln: University of Nebraska Press, 1966), pp. 3–13.

2. *Cosmos and History*, trans. W.R. Trask (Princeton: Princeton University Press, Bollingen Series, 1954) esp. pp. 154–62. The same author's *Patterns in Comparative Religion*, trans. Rosemary Shead (New York: Meridian Books, 1963), esp. pp. 459–65, reconfirms the attack against the fragmentation of modern existence and the need for a revival of a mythico-religious worldview. For Plato's philosophy of Ideas (or Forms) as a prefiguration of Eliade's Archetypes, see *Cosmos and History*, pp. 34–35.

3. *Cosmos and History*, pp. 153–54.

4. Philip Rahv, "The Myth and the Powerhouse," in Vickery (ch. 2, note 1), p. 114. This essay is reprinted from the author's *The Myth and the Powerhouse* (New York: Farrar, Straus, and Giroux, 1965). This kind of attitude is popular in myth criticism. In addition to Bidney, already cited, see Richard Chase, *The Quest for Myth* (Baton Rouge: Louisiana State University Press, 1949), p. 97; Herbert Weisinger, *The Agony and the Triumph: Papers on the Use and Abuse of Myth* (East Lansing: Michigan State University Press, 1964), passim; Eliseo Vivas, "Myth: Some Philosophical Problems," *Southern Review* 6 (1970): 89–103.

5. *Occidental Mythology*, Masks of God, vol. 1 (New York: Viking, 1964), p. 520.

6. My remarks on the history of the term "estrangement" are derived from Darko Suvin, "On the Poetics of the Science Fiction Genre," *College English* 34 (1972–73):374 and note 4 (in Suvin, *Metamorphoses of Science Fiction* [New Haven: Yale University Press, 1979]), p. 6 and note 2). I have also taken into account the important recent discussion of Brecht and Shklovsky in Fredric Jameson, *The Prison-House of Language* (Princeton: Princeton University Press, 1972), pp. 50–59.

The word "defamiliarization" still appears in some critical writing as an alternative rendering of Shklovsky's *ostranenie*. Brecht's term *Verfremdung* is also translated as "alienation"—a term which has the fault of leading us away from its strict cognitive application. In origin the concept has nothing to do with the many other kinds of alienation.

I have used the translation of "Short Organum" which is printed in John Willet (ed. and trans.), *Brecht on Theater* (New York: Hill and Wang, 1964), pp. 179–205.

7. "Short Organum," p. 192; cf. Suvin "On the Poetics . . ." (ch. 2, note 6), p. 374.

8. For this citiation from Brecht, see Willet (ch. 2, note 6), p. 96.

9. See Barry Wadsworth, *Piaget's Theory of Cognitive Development: An Introduction for Students of Psychology and Education* (New York: McKay, 1971), pp. 74–75.

10. The two examples are drawn from Piaget's *Comments on Vygotsky's Criti-

cal Remarks, bound with 1962 edition of L.S. Vygotsky's *Thought and Language* (Cambridge, Mass.: M.I.T. Press), translated by E. Hanfmann and G. Vakar, p. 3. For a series of similar examples from the history of science, see Part Two of Arthur Koestler's *The Act of Creation* (New York: Dell, 1964), pp. 101–267.

11. See Morse Peckham, *Man's Rage for Chaos: Biology, Behavior, and the Arts* (Philadelphia: Chilton Books, 1965), esp. pp. 217–22. Robert Canary, *SFS* 2 (1975): 131, has also recognized a similarity between Shklovsky's "estrangement" and Peckham's "rage for chaos."

12. *Classical World* 67, no. 5 (March, 1974): 283–90.

13. I refer, respectively, to Arthur Koestler, *The Act of Creation* (ch. 2, note 10), and Thomas Kuhn, *The Structure of Scientific Revolutions*, 2d ed. (Chicago: University of Chicago Press, 1970).

14. "On Fairy-Stories," *The Tolkien Reader* (New York: Ballantine Books, 1966; reprinted from *Tree and Leaf* [London, 1964]), p. 57.

15. G.S. Kirk, *Myth: Its Meaning and Functions in Ancient and Other Cultures*, Sather Classical Lectures, vol. 40 (Berkeley and Los Angeles: University of California Press), pp. 268–69. Another recent myth critic, Peter Munz, in *When the Golden Bough Breaks* (London and Boston: Routledge and Kegan Paul, 1973), p. 56, confirms Kirk in practically the same words:

> The significant feature of the stories we are concerned with, whether they be folk-tales or myths proper, legends or dreams, is that the events they consist of always appear in non-normal relations. People are larger than life-size, dwarves fly through the air, heroes are immortal, the dead return to life. In short, the normal position in which events stand to one another is changed. Events, it seems, are re-shuffled like a pack of cards and thus they emerge in relationships in which they do not normally stand to one another.

16. This point is also confirmed explicitly by Munz (ch. 2, note 15), p. 56.

17. I note in passing that the Jungian theory of myth—in particular its three interrelated concepts of "archetypes," the "collective unconscious," and inherited "race memory"—is completely unacceptable to most contemporary myth scholars. For a list of references to views critical of the theory, see John J. White, *Mythology in the Modern Novel* (Princeton: Princeton University Press, 1971), p. 104, note 62.

My remarks on this psychological theory here and elsewhere throughout the book are based on Carl Jung's *The Archetypes and the Collective Unconscious*, trans. R.F.C. Hull, 2d ed. (Princeton: Princeton University Press, Bollingen Series, 1968). For the application of the theory of archetypes to ancient mythology specifically, see C.G. Jung and C. Kerényi, *Essays on a Science of Mythology*, trans. R.F.C. Hull (Princeton: Princeton University Press, Bollingen Series, 1969; based on 1949 ed.). The latter book is also the best introduction to Jungian interpretations of myth.

John Peradotto, *Classical Mythology: An Annotated Bibliographical Survey* (Urbana, Ill.: The American Philological Association, 1973), pp. 29–33, has a useful review of works that illustrate the Jungian analysis of myth. In general, I am indebted to this valuable survey of theoretical literature on myth and to Gregory I. Stevens, *Literature, Myth and Folklore* (a bibliography available from the University of Michigan's Center for the Coordination of Ancient and Modern Studies, Ann Arbor, Mich.; revised form, October 1973).

Percy Cohen, "Theories of Myth," *Man* N.S.4 (1969): 337–53, offers good introductory accounts of the several theories of myth, Jungian and others, which are described throughout various parts of this study. For an additional critique of the Jungian position, see Kirk, *Myth* (ch. 2, note 15), pp. 275–80.

18. See Paul Radin, *The Trickster: A Study in American Indian Mythology* (New York: Philosophical Library, 1956; 1972 ed. with introductory essay by Stanley Diamond and commentaries by Carl Kerényi and C.G. Jung). For a classical Western Trickster, see Kerényi's essay in Radin, and his "The Problem of Evil in Mythology," in *Evil*, edited by the Curatorium of the C.G. Jung Institute, Zürich (English trans., Evanston, Ill.: Northwestern University Press, 1967), pp. 3–17. Roger Zelazny's *Jack of Shadows* (Ace, 1971) is a very significant SF treatment of Trickster. Since I have already analyzed this book in a lengthy study, I will not repeat myself here. Entitled "Roger Zelazny and the Trickster Myth: An Analysis of *Jack of Shadows*," the essay has appeared in vol. 2, no. 2 (October 1979) of the new periodical, *Journal of American Culture*, a special issue on "Myth and the Popular Arts."

19. Radin (ch. 2, note 18), pp. xxiv and xxiii respectively.

20. In his introduction to Radin, pp. xii–xiii.

21. Claude Lévi-Strauss, "The Structural Study of Myth," in *Structural Anthropology*, trans. C. Jacobsen and B.G. Schoepf (New York: Doubleday Anchor Books ed., 1967), pp. 200–204.

22. See Kirk, *Myths* (ch. 2, note 15), pp. 1–41, and esp. p. 7 and note 4, as well as the same author's *The Nature of Greek Myths* (Harmondsworth, Middlesex: Penguin Books, 1974), pp. 13–91, for an extensive critical treatment of the inadequacy of monolithic myth theories and definitions.

23. *Nature of Greek Myths*, p. 29.

24. In *A Grammar of Motives* (New York: Prentice-Hall, 1945), pp. 430–40. The point is also made in the opening pages of Kees Bolle, *The Freedom of Man in Myth* (Nashville, Tennessee: Vanderbilt University Press, 1968).

25. For the "primal horde," see Sigmund Freud, *Totem and Taboo*, trans. James Strachey (New York: Norton Paperbacks, n.d.), pp. 125–26. For the social contract theory, which posited the original and natural dignity of man in order to justify the improvement of man's lot in his present society, see Ernst Cassirer, *The Myth of the State* (New Haven: Yale University Press, 1946), "The Theory of the Social Contract," pp. 163–75. For the theory of evolution as an explanation of present human nature in terms of its animal ancestry, see the section on Charles Darwin in Stanley Edgar Hyman, *The Tangled Bank* (New York: Grosset's Universal Library, 1966), especially "The Origin of Species," pp. 26–43.

26. From *Claude Lévi-Strauss*, Modern Masters series, ed. Frank Kermode (New York: Viking Press, 1970), pp. 54–55. For Lévi-Strauss's own statement of his views, see the chapter, "Time Regained," in *The Savage Mind*, trans George Weidenfeld and Nicolson Ltd. (Chicago: University of Chicago Press, 1966), pp. 217–44.

For one "historical" culture which did succeed, by social, religious, and intellectual means, in the abolition of time and the construction of a temporally static universe, see Henry Frankfort, *Ancient Egyptian Religion* (New York: Columbia University Press, 1948).

27. *Myth and Reality*, trans. Willard R. Trask (New York: Harper Torchbooks, 1968), p. 31.

28. See Joseph Campbell, *Primitive Mythology*. The Masks of God, vol. 1 (New York: Viking, 1959), where anthropological evidence is used to establish the various chronological strata in myths, on a worldwide basis. For two scholars who are more archaeologically oriented, see Gertrude Rachel Levy, *Religious Conceptions of the Stone Age and Their Influence upon European Thought* (New York: Harper Torchbooks, 1963; originally *The Gate of Horn* [London: Faber and Faber, 1948]), E.O. James, *Prehistoric Religion* (New York: Barnes and Noble, 1957).

29. My statements reflect the chapter "Egypt: Cosmogonies of Rival Sanctuaries," in S.G.F. Brandon, *Creation Legends of the Ancient Near East* (London: Hodder and Stoughton, 1963), pp. 14–65; and R. Anthes, "Mythology in Ancient Egypt," in S.N. Kramer (ed.), *Mythologies of the Ancient World* (New York: Anchor Books, 1961), pp. 15–92.

30. For my remarks here on Sumerian mythology I follow Brandon's chapter, "Mesopotamia: Creation by Divine Invention or by Conquest of Primordial Chaos," *Creation Legends*, pp. 66–117. For a text in English translation of this myth of Enki I refer the reader to J.B. Pritchard (ed.), *Ancient Near Eastern Texts Relating to the Old Testament* 3d ed., with suppl., trans. S.N. Kramer (Princeton: Princeton University Press, 1969), pp. 37–41. For an interpretation, see G.S. Kirk, *Myth* (ch. 2, note 15), pp. 90–99.

31. *The Savage Mind* (ch. 2, note 26), pp. 13–16.

32. See the studies by Gertrude Levy and E.O. James (ch. 2, note 28); both these popular books include the Paleolithic in the scope of their comparativist speculations.

33. See John Pfeiffer, *The Emergence of Man* (New York: Harper and Row, 1969), pp. 164–72, esp. p. 167:

> Archaeological excavations rarely provide direct information about the feelings of our remote ancestors; usually we are reduced to guesses, shrewd or otherwise. But now and then the past leaves patterns whose significance cannot be mistaken. During the early 1900's such evidence was uncovered at Le Moustier about thirty miles west of La Chapelle-aux-Saints; it shows that *these people have developed a new way of thinking, a new attitude toward life and death* [my italics].
>
> A boy about fifteen or sixteen years old had been buried in a cave. He had been lowered into a trench, placed on his right side with knees slightly drawn and head resting on his forearm in a sleeping position. A pile of flints lay under his head to form a sort of stone pillow, and near his hand was a beautifully worked stone ax. Around the remains were wild-cattle bones, many of them charred, the remnants of roasted meat which may have been provided to serve as sustenance in the world of the dead. (The old man of La Chapelle-aux-Saints was also buried in a trench and surrounded by stone tools.)

34. See Jack Finnegan, *Light from the Ancient Past* (Princeton: Princeton University Press, 1959), vol. 1, p. 28.

35. This theory of myth too is now held in disrepute by most contemporary myth scholars. See Kirk, *Myth* (ch. 2, note 15), pp. 246–48; *Nature of Greek Myths* (ch. 2, note 22), pp. 280–86; G.E.R. Lloyd, *Polarity and Analogy* (Cambridge: Cambridge University Press, 1966), pp. 1–6; E.E. Evans-Pritchard, *Theories of Primitive Religion* (Oxford: Clarendon Press, 1965); Bidney, "Myth, Symbolism, and Truth," (ch. 2, note 1), pp. 6–19.

36. See Lévi-Strauss, *The Savage Mind* (ch. 2, note 26); Evans-Pritchard, *Theories of Primitive Religion*; and Ashley Montagu (ed.), *The Concept of the Primitive* (New York: Free Press, 1968).

37. *Nature of Greek Myths* (ch. 2, note 22), p. 90.

38. Ketterer, (ch. 1, note 13), p. 76. In my review of this book which appeared in *SFS* 1 (1974): 217–19, I gave credit to the author for his very real accomplishments as a critic of SF in this exciting book, and I believe that I learned a great deal about SF from it. However, I do have a basic disagreement with the author about mythological SF, and I registered my views in a symposium at the 1974 SFRA annual convention, now published as "On David Ketterer's *New Worlds for Old*," *SFS* 2 (1975): esp. pp. 136–37. Other participants included Robert H. Canary, Ursula K. LeGuin, and David Ketterer in reply (esp. p. 144); Robert Galbreath, chairman of the SFRA session, published his introduction to the symposium in *SFS* 3 (1976): 60–64.

Some of these ideas have also been published separately for an audience of classicists in "Science Fiction and the World of Greek Myths," *Helios* N.S.2 (1975): 1–22.

For Ketterer's references (pp. 76 and 333) to a recent trend in SF criticism to regard SF as a "new mythology" and as a secular displacement of the religious consciousness, see Bruce Franklin, Isaac Asimov, Frederik Pohl, and Darko Suvin, "Science Fiction: The New Mythology, MLA Forum," *Extrapolation* 10 (May 1969): 69–115. Also cf. my remarks at the Ketterer symposium, p. 135.

39. "Generic Discontinuities in SF" (ch. 1, note 19), p. 65.

40. White (ch. 1, note 28), esp. pp. 11–14.

41. The citation is from p. 172 of *The Fabulators* (New York: Oxford University Press, 1967), but my remarks on *Giles Goat-Boy* are in general indebted to the final chapter of the book, pp. 135–73. For Campbell's *Hero With a Thousand Faces* as the prefiguration of *Giles*, see "Having It Both Ways: A Conversation Between John Barth and Joe David Bellamy," *New American Review* 15 (1972): 134–50. My views of this kind of mythifiction from the literary mainstream have also been heavily influenced by Charles Altieri, "Ovid and the New Mythologists," *Novel* 7 (1973): 31–40.

42. In addition to White, I should give credit to Eric W. Herd, "Myth Criticism: Limits and Possibilities," *Mosaic* 2 (1969): 69–77, esp. 70, where the author remarks that far too much myth criticism "has produced work of dubious value, where the emphasis has been on the origin or the identity of the myth, and not on its function as the structural element in a work of literature." See p. 77, where Herd cites Charles Moorman:

> In literary scholarship, it has never been sufficient to delineate a source; the scholar must show how that source is used in the work at hand, how it itself becomes a tool of creation. To be able to show how the poet uses myth, and in doing so, to concentrate not on the identity of the myth, but on its function, not on its closeness to the known pattern, but on the changes which the poet effects in that pattern, not on origin, but on use would seem to me to constitute the proper aim of the myth critic.

(For this statement from Moorman himself, see his essay in Vickery, *Myth and Literature* [ch. 2, note 1], p. 175.)

43. "Science Fiction and the Genological Jungle," *Genre* 6 (1973): 261 and 266 respectively (in *Metamorphoses of SF* [ch. 2, note 6], pp. 25 and 31).

44. White, p. 3.

45. Interestingly, Ketterer, *New Worlds for Old* (ch. 1, note 13) pp. 44–46, also rejects Suvin's identification of myth-in-fiction as archaic metaphysics.

46. *Alternate Worlds* (ch. 1, n. 5), pp. 214–15. Much the same point is made in two reviews by Scott Sanders in *SFS* 2, no. 2 (July 1975), pp. 172 and 175–76. Cf. Robert J. Barthell, "SF: A Literature of Ideas," *Extrapolation* (henceforth, *Ex*) 13, no. 1 (December 1971): 56–63, who goes too far by eliminating literary, aesthetic possibilities for SF. The critical essays by Scholes, Suvin, Russ, and Ketterer listed in these notes rightly emphasize that the proper control of the cognitive-speculative element in a narrative can and does produce a satisfactory aesthetic effect.

47. The two articles are "On the Poetics of the Science Fiction Genre" (ch. 2, note 6) and "Science Fiction and the Genological Jungle" (ch. 2, note 43); they form chapters 1 and 2 respectively of *Metamorphoses of Science Fiction* (ch. 2, note 6). Ketterer explicitly acknowledges his debt to Suvin in *New Worlds for Old*, p. 26, note 1 (cf. Canary, "On Ketterer's *New Worlds for Old*" [ch. 2, note 38]: 145, note 4, and Joanna Russ, "Towards an Aesthetic of Science Fiction," *SFS* 2 [1975]: 112–19, esp. pp. 113, 117, and note 18). Stanislaw Lem anticipated Suvin's basic conception in "On the Structural Analysis of Science Fiction," *SFS* 1 (1973): 26–33. I again refer the reader to the journal *Science-Fiction Studies* where this theory of SF remains the subject of an ongoing critical discussion among the best SF scholars at work in the field today.

The earlier, more popularly oriented, and less academic phase of SF criticism—including the work of Sam Moskowitz and Damon Knight, for example—focused almost exclusively on the estrangement-effect in SF and fantasy, rather than on its cognitive sources; it was referred to as "the sense of wonder." See, e.g., Damon Knight, *The Sense of Wonder*, rev. ed. (Chicago: Advent, 1967), pp. 12–13.

A more recent attempt to point up the "subjunctivity" of speculative fiction has not taken hold as a model for further research, but the two major articles in which this notion is proposed are eloquent and do emphasize the validity of the non-naturalistic perspective in SF: see Samuel R. Delany, "About Five Thousand One Hundred and Seventy-Five Words," in Thomas Clareson (ed.), *SF: The Other Side of Realism* (Bowling Green, Ohio: Bowling Green University Popular Press, 1971), pp. 130–46; Joanna Russ, "Speculations: The Subjunctivity of Science Fiction," *Ex* 15, no. 1 (December 1973): 51–59. Cf. Ronald Munson, "SF: The Literature of Possibility," *Ex* 15, no. 1 (December 1973): 35–41.

48. "Poetics of SF Genre," p. 375 (his italics) (in *Metamorphoses* [ch. 2, note 6], pp. 7–8).

49. *Ibid.*, p. 374 (= *Metamorphoses*, p. 6).

50. *Structural Fabulation: An Essay on Fiction of the Future* (Notre Dame and London: University of Notre Dame Press, 1975), p. 47. I reviewed the book for *Ex* 17, no. 1 (December 1975): 49–51.

51. *Anatomy of Criticism* (Princeton: Princeton University Press, 1957), p. 49. "Romance" is Frye's term for that mythos of literature which is primarily concerned to portray an idealized world (for this term, also see his glossary, p. 367).

52. Used, passim, in both articles by Suvin, who is also my source for Lem's usage.

53. Cited from p. viii in Suvin's *Metamorphoses of Science Fiction*.

54. For Todorov's *The Fantastic* and his theory, see chapter 1, note 25.

55. *Structural Fabulation*, p. 70. Cf. pp. 134–35 (Fredericks) and 140–41(Ketterer) in the Ketterer Symposium cited above in note 38.

56. Eric Rabkin, *The Fantastic in Literature* (Princeton: Princeton University Press, 1976), pp. 37 and 78. For a more detailed discussion of Rabkin and other recent critics of Fantasy, see S.C. Fredericks, "Problems of Fantasy," *SFS* 5 (1978): 33–44 (includes bibliography).

57. I acknowledge two earlier articles: Stephen Scobie, "Different Mazes: Mythology in Samuel R. Delany's 'The Einstein Intersection,'" *Riverside Quarterly* 5, no. 1 (1971): 12–18; and David Samuelson, "New Wave, Old Ocean: A Comparative Study of Novels by Brunner and Delany," *Ex* 15, no. 1 (December 1973): 75–96, esp. 83–90. A shorter version of this interpretation appeared earlier in the essay "Revivals of Ancient Mythologies" (ch. 1, note 27).

58. *The Common Sense of Science* (New York: Vintage Books ed., 1967), p. 78. For a comparable explanation by the mathematician John von Neumann, founder of Game Theory, see Samuelson's article, p. 95, note 17:

> Gödel was the first man to demonstrate that certain mathematical theorems can neither be proved nor disproved with the accepted rigorous methods of mathematics. . . . Gödel actually proved this theorem, not with respect to mathematics only, but for all systems which permit a formalization, that is a rigorous and exhaustive description, in terms of modern logic: For no such system can its freedom from inner contradiction be demonstrated with the means of the system itself (from "Tribute to Dr. Gödel," pp. ix-x, in *Foundations of Mathematics; Symposium Papers Commemorating the Sixtieth Birthday of Kurt Gödel*, ed. Jack J. Buloff, Thomas C. Holyoke, S.W. Hahn [New York: Springer, 1969]).

59. Scholes and Rabkin, (ch. 1, note 6), p. 191.

60. *Billion Year Spree* (ch. 1, note 6), p. 8, author's italics. I can also concur with Ketterer, *New Worlds for Old*, p. 25, that "science fiction is not primarily valuable as prediction; rather, it teaches an adaptability and elasticity of mind in the face of change." Alvin Toffler's *Future Shock* (New York: Random House, 1970) remains a worthwhile exploration of "future shock" which has, unfortunately, fallen prey to the very phenomenon it studied—much of it is wildly out of date in less than a decade since its original publication.

61. *Future Shock*, p. 463.

62. In a non-fiction essay, "Death Warmed Over," published in the now defunct horror fanzine, *Cthulhu Calls* 3, no. 2 (October 1975): 43.

3. The Big Time

1. The story first appeared in serialized form in *Galaxy* magazine, March and April 1958, and won the Hugo Award for 1958. A popular account of Fritz Leiber's literary career appears in Sam Moskowitz, *Seekers of Tomorrow* (Cleveland: World Publishing Co., 1961), pp. 283–302.

Leiber's Change-War mythos has recently been revived by the author with a short story sequel told from the Snake rather than the Spider point of view: "Knight to Move," *The Book of Fritz Leiber* (New York: DAW Books, 1974).

I also refer the reader to Georges Dumezil's concept of "le Grand Temps" in "Temps et Mythes," *Recherches Philosophiques* 5 (1936): 235–51, i.e., that special, "eternal" time period set apart from ordinary human time in the ancient myths.

2. On the pre-Socratics, see Steven J. Dick, *Plurality of Worlds and Natural Philosophy: An Historical Study of the Origins of Belief in Other Worlds and Extraterrestrial Life* (Indiana University doctoral dissertation, 1976). For Plato, see the dialogues *Republic* (especially the Allegory of the Cave), *Phaedo*, *Phaedrus*, and (for Atlantis) *Timaeus* and *Critias*.

On Judeo-Christian eschatology, see Norman Cohn, *The Pursuit of the Millennium*, 2d ed. (New York: Harper Torchbooks, 1961), pp. 1–13; this book, subtitled "Revolutionary Messianism in Medieval and Reformation Europe and Its Bearing on Modern Totalitarian Movements," is a well-researched history of apocalyptic thinking in Western culture on the Judaic model.

In *Creation and Cosmology* (Leiden: E. J. Brill, 1969), an excellent introductory survey, anthropologist E. O. James emphasizes the continuity between ancient mythical and religious cosmologies and modern scientific (physical and astronomical) cosmologies like those of Samuel Alexander (*Space, Time, and Deity*) and Alfred North Whitehead (*Process and Reality*). Cf. the same author's *The Concept of Deity* (London: Hutchinson's Universal Library, 1950).

3. Ketterer, *New Worlds for Old* (ch. 1, note 13), p. 13. See p. 124, note 1, for a list of SF works based explicitly on the Judeo-Christian Apocalypse; p. 149 for the literary/imaginative relationship between Heaven in myth and "the heavens" of astronomy.

4. "On Fairy-Stories" (ch. 2, note 14).

5. An admission made by John White, *Mythology in the Modern Novel* (ch. 2, note 17), p. 69 and note 107, about the mainstream novel.

6. J. O. Bailey, author of modern SF's first scholarly history, after which the Science Fiction Research Association's annual Pilgrim Award is named, identifies *The Last Man* as the first of the world-catastrophe genre. See *Pilgrims Through Space and Time* (New York: Argus Books, 1947. Westport, Conn.: Greenwood Press, 1972), pp. 34–35. The best edition for contemporary readers is that edited by Hugh J. Luke, *Mary Shelley: The Last Man* (Lincoln: University of Nebraska Press, 1965). For an interpretation emphasizing the uniqueness of this novel as a work of narrative prose fiction, see Muriel Spark, *Child of Light* (ch. 1, note 7), pp. 150–65.

Ryszard Dubanski, "The Last Man Theme in Modern Fantasy and SF," *Foundation* 16 (May 1979): 26–31, identifies a few earlier examples of the last man theme in both poetry and prose fiction which did not become influential. This critic also emphasizes the impact of an alienated and isolated consciousness on all later SF.

W. H. G. Armytage, *Yesterday's Tomorrows* (Toronto: University of Toronto Press, 1968), obliquely mentions themes appropriate to this chapter: p. 34 on the "extinction of man" (cf. p. 229, n. 35, for three novels cited as instances of it); pp. 190–91 on the works of J. G. Ballard and William S.

Burroughs's *Nova Express* (1965), and all of the last chapter, "Operational Eschatologies."

7. Critical literature on H. G. Wells and *The Time Machine* is now substantial. For the mythical resonances of the work, I am most indebted to Robert Philmus, *Into the Unknown* (ch. 1, note 10), pp. 69–78; Wayne Connelly, "H. G. Wells's "The Time Machine": Its Neglected Mythos," *Riverside Quarterly* 5 (1972): 178–91; Scholes and Rabkin, *Science Fiction* (ch. 1, note 6), pp. 15–25 and 200–204; Darko Suvin, *Metamorphoses of Science Fiction* (ch. 2, note 6), ch. 9 and 10, pp. 208–42.

For another scholar who emphasizes the Sphinx-myth, see David J. Lake, "The White Sphinx and the Whitened Lemur: Images of Death in *The Time Machine*," *SFS* 6 (1979): 77–84.

8. *Pilgrims Through Space and Time* (ch. 3, note 6), p. 81. The italics are mine.

9. Joanna Russ, "Towards an Aesthetic of Science Fiction" (ch. 2, note 47), p. 115.

10. The time-traveler particularly raises this question about the delicate Eloi woman Weena. In the film version of 1960 starring Rod Taylor and Yvette Mimieux, the actress employed was simply too attractive, so time-traveler and Weena became romantically involved, which did not happen in Wells's book: in the original, time-traveler regards Weena and other Eloi as his *children*, a very Victorian sentiment.

The futuristic Sphinx was used as the cover illustration (by Virgil Finlay) to the publication of *The Time Machine* in *Famous Fantastic Mysteries* (August 1950). It is reproduced by Franz Rottensteiner, *The Science Fiction Book: An Illustrated History* (New York: New American Library, 1975), p. 21.

11. I have used the translation by Willis T. Bradley which appears in Sam Moskowitz's *Masterpieces of Science Fiction* (Cleveland and New York: World Publishing Co., 1966). This translation first appeared in Donald Wollheim's magazine, *Saturn*, in the first issue, March 1957. The novelette was first published posthumously in 1910 under the French title, "L'Eternal Adam" in the collection *Hier et Demain*, now in English as *Yesterday and Tomorrow* (London: Arco, 1965. New York: Ace, 1968).

There is the *merest* introduction to Verne's career in Moskowitz's *Explorers* (ch. 1, note 33), pp. 73–87, but I also refer the reader to Mark P. Hillegas, "An Annotated Biography of Jules Verne's *Voyages Extraordinaires*," *Ex* 3 (1962): 32–47, and I. O. Evans, *Jules Verne and His Work* (London: Arco, 1965). Cf. Armytage, *Yesterday's Tomorrows* (ch. 3, note 6), pp. 39–40.

12. For two famous novels that offer a contrast with Verne by asserting the theory of evolution as a temporal blueprint for the millennium, see Ketterer, *New Worlds for Old* (ch. 1, note 13), p. 104, on Edward Bellamy's *Looking Backward* (1888), and p. 129, on Jack London's *The Iron Heel* (1906). Also cf. W. H. G. Armytage, "Extrapolators and Exegetes of Evolution," *Ex* 7 (1965): 2–17.

For a history of the cultural theme of progress, see the classic study by J. B. Bury, *The Idea of Progress* (New York: Dover Publications, 1932).

13. Phillpotts was a prolific but little known minor writer; a number of his works are built upon Greek mythology. For a brief account of his work see Tuck's *Encyclopedia*; and for a bibliography of his works, Percival Hinton, *Eden Phillpotts* (Birmingham: G. Worthington, 1931).

14. *The Justice of Zeus* (Berkeley: University of California Press, 1971), p. 3.

15. Donald Wollheim, *The Universe Makers* (New York: Harper and Row, 1971), esp. pp. 42–44, a chapter entitled "The Cosmogony of the Future."

James Gunn, *Alternate Worlds* (ch. 1, note 5), p. 137, speaks of "the expanded vision that characterized the thirties."

16. *Explorers of the Infinite* (chapter 1, note 33), p. 270; cf. the same author's *Seekers of Tomorrow*, (ch. 3, note 1), p. 72. Moskowitz, *Seekers*, pp. 261–77, and Bailey (ch. 3, note 6), pp. 138–46, offer introductions to the work of Stapledon, but a more mature interpretation is offered in Curtis Smith's recent article, "Olaf Stapledon: Saint and Revolutionary," *Ex* 13 (1971–72): 5–15. Cf. the same author's bibliography, "The Books of Olaf Stapledon: A Chronological Survey," *SFS* 1 (1974): 297–99, and the later critical article, "Olaf Stapledon's Dispassionate Objectivity," in Thomas D. Clareson, *Voices for the Future* (ch. 1, note 18), pp. 44–63.

17. See Scholes, *Structural Fabulation* (ch. 2, note 50), pp. 62–67, who also cites (p. 63) Aldiss's quip from *Billion Year Spree*, p. 208.

18. The citations are from the undated Dover Books edition of *Star Maker* (bound with *Last and First Men*), pp. 398 and 429 respectively.

19. Moskowitz's *Seekers* (ch. 3, note 1) includes introductory accounts of Smith, Hamilton, Campbell, and Asimov.

20. In Fredric Brown's "Arena" (1944) a higher cosmic intelligence ("God") pits a human representative against an alien intelligent being in a single combat to the death to decide which species will survive, ultimately to join the cosmic intelligence, the other to be exterminated for good. In Brown's tale, the utter repulsiveness of the alien justifies the racial genocide as with Campbell's Teff-Hellani (the humans win in both tales, of course). In the *Star Trek* episode also entitled "Arena" the aliens have been converted into an intelligent saurian species, and though Captain Kirk wins the combat, the episode ends with the species co-existing. Brown's tale is a famous classic, most readily available in Silverberg's *Science Fiction Hall of Fame I* (New York: Avon Books, 1970), which is perhaps the best anthology of older SF, (it is mentioned in the following pages often enough), and in *The Best of Fredric Brown* (New York: Ballatine Books, 1977).

21. For a good survey of Campbell's contributions as writer, see Leon Stover, "Science Fiction, the Research Revolution, and John Campbell," *Ex* 14 (1972–1973): 129–48; includes a checklist of John Campbell's fiction. Cf. Wollheim, *Universe Makers* (ch. 3, note 15), chapter 17, pp. 74–79, "A Victorious Vernian"; Moskowitz, *Seekers* (ch. 3, note 1), pp. 27–46.

The story of *The Mightiest Machine* was continued in *The Incredible Planet*, which has appeared only in a very obscure edition from Fantasy Press (Reading, Pa., 1949).

22. "Twilight" and "Night" are among the most popular tales from the thirties among writers and fans alike. The first was selected to appear in Robert Silverberg's *Science Fiction Hall of Fame* and also appears in Patricia Warrick, Martin Harry Greenberg, and Joseph Olander (eds.), *Science Fiction: Contemporary Mythology (The SFWA-SFRA Anthology)* (New York: Harper and Row, 1978). The second tale appears in Sam Moskowitz's fine anthology, *Microcosmic God* (Cleveland: World Publishing Co., 1965).

Naturalist Loren Eiseley includes a very eloquent reading of "Twilight" by an environmentalist in *The Invisible Pyramid: A Naturalist Analyzes the Rocket Century* (New York: Charles Scribner's Sons, 1970), pp. 125–27.

23. The story is readily available in the Clarke anthology, *The Nine Billion Names of God*. Sam Moskowitz, *Seekers* (ch. 3, note 1), pp. 374–91, includes a chapter on Clarke that is out of date; a stronger general essay is that by Thomas D. Clareson, "The Cosmic Loneliness of Arthur C. Clarke," in *Voices for the Future* (ch. 1, note 18), pp. 216–37.

24. An intelligent discussion of this problem appears in Isaac Asimov, *Asimov's Guide to the Bible: New Testament* (New York: Doubleday, 1969), pp. 128–30: one speculation says that the star was a nova, as in Clarke's story, another that it was an astrological configuration, and a third that it was a comet.

25. This famous short story is published under the title of the entire collection, *The Nine Billion Names of God* (ch. 3, note 23), and in Robert Silverberg's *Science Fiction Hall of Fame* and Mayo Mohs' *Other Worlds, Other Gods* (ch. 1, note 12).

26. On this important novel, see the interpretation by Scholes and Rabkin, *Science Fiction* (ch. 1, note 6), pp. 216–20; and the contrasting views by David N. Samuelson, "Clarke's *Childhood End*: A Median Stage of Adolescence," *SFS* 1 (1973): 4–17, which is often too critical and fault-finding; a more balanced and positive view is offered by John Huntington, "The Unity of *Childhood's End*," *SFS* 1 (1974): 154–64.

27. My comments on the film are based on Jerome Agel (ed.), *The Making of Kubrick's 2001* (in paperback, New York: Signet, 1970), esp. script printed on pp. 165–68 and accompanying photos. In the novel version, *2001: A Space Odyssey, A Novel by Arthur C. Clarke Based on the Screenplay of the MGM Film by Stanley Kubrick and Arthur C. Clarke* (New York: Signet, 1968), the starchild is master of the planet *earth* which is identified as his "toy" and he can detonate at will a nearby nuclear device.

28. See S. G. F. Brandon, *Creation Legends of the Ancient Near East* (ch. 2, note 29), pp. 43–45; cf. Eliade, *Patterns in Comparative Religion* (ch. 2, note 2), pp. 413–16, for the general symbolism of the egg in myth and ritual.

29. The citation is from p. 24 of the only critical writing on this author I have found, in an insightful and refreshing article by Brian Earl Brown in the obscure fanzine, *Seldon's Plan* (#28, March 1976), pp. 19–24, edited by Cy Chauvin at Wayne State University in Detroit.

Stableford has also produced a substantial space opera on the Orpheus myth: *To Challenge Chaos* (N. Y.: DAW Books, 1972).

30. *New Worlds for Old*, (ch. 1, note 13), p. 300.

4. In Defense of Heroic Fantasy

1. *Anatomy of Criticism* (ch. 2, note 51), pp. 33–34: "If inferior in power or intelligence to ourselves, so that we have the sense of looking down on a scene of bondage, frustration, or absurdity, the hero belongs to the *ironic* mode. This is still true when the reader feels he is or might be in the same situation, as the situation is being judged by the norms of a greater freedom."

For a rigorous structuralist critique of Frye's interlocked categories of five heroic modes and four seasonal archetypal *mythoi*, see Todorov, *The Fantastic* (ch. 1, note 25), pp. 8-23.

2. Frye, as cited in note above; also cf. pp. 223-39, "The Mythos of Winter: Irony and Satire," and the glossary of terms, "ironic," p. 366. Cf. Charles I. Glicksberg, *The Ironic Vision in Modern Literature* (The Hague: Mouton, 1969), esp. pp. 3-24, where the author chronicles how verbal/rhetorical irony (a distinction between what is said and what is intended) turns into metaphysical irony in the nineteenth century: the quest for a meaning that we know is impossible—like the desire for an eternity when we know it is unattainable—leading to pessimism and nihilism.

3. All references to *Grendel* are from the Ballantine Books edition of 1972. Fantasy and science-fiction fans were immediately attracted to the novel. See the brief but valuable review by Veronica Kennedy in *SFRA Newsletter* #12 (June 1972), p. 4.

For a good English translation of *Beowulf*, including related texts from northern European epics and sagas, plus other valuable critical aids, see G.N. Garmonsway, Jacqueline Simpson, and H.R. Ellis Davidson, *Beowulf and Its Analogues* (New York: Dutton Paperbacks, 1971).

4. Robert Scholes, *The Fabulators* (ch. 2, note 41).

5. Grendel manifests two interrelated existential themes: (1) the encounter with nothingness: there are no absolute values; (2) Grendel wants *silence*, alienated as he is from a reality which he views as chaos: man, god, and society are all regarded as Nothing. See William Barrett, *Irrational Man: A Study in Existential Philosophy* (Garden City, N.Y.: Doubleday Anchor, 1962), esp. pp. 35-36 and 283 for confirmation of the view given above. On silence as the ultimate response to the black-humor (ironic) vision of the universe and an anti-heroic attitude toward human nature, see Ihab Hassan, *The Literature of Silence* (New York: Knopf, 1967) and Robert Scholes, "Stillborn Literature," *Bulletin of the Midwest Modern Language Association* 7 (1974), pp. 1-12. On the former, David Ketterer, *New Worlds for Old* (ch. 1, note 13), p. 10, writes: "In Hassan's vague terms, silent literature involves a sense of outrage at the void and an expression of the nullity or chaotic fragmentation of human existence."

6. Cf. p. 43 for Shaper's definition of Grendel as "the dark side" of man, as a representative of a "terrible race God cursed."

Gardner's interpretation of Grendel's role is closely paralleled in Joseph Fontenrose's comparative study of mythological monsters in *Python* (Berkeley: University of California Press, 1959), where it is noted at length that monsters are in general conceived of as opponents of human order. It is the monster's difference from men and his alien hostility that actually sanction and justify human society as a protector of man against dark, elemental forces. And in the combat motif common to many ancient mythologies, the side of mankind can be represented either by a human hero or a civilizing god. In other words, it is fear of the monster that provokes human society to greatness and creativity.

7. Frye, *Anatomy of Criticism*, p. 239.

8. Raymond M. Olderman, *Beyond the Waste Land: The American Novel in the Nineteen Sixties* (New Haven: Yale University Press, 1972), treats of

fabulist narratives that portray the dehumanized society and institutions of modern man in terms of T.S. Eliot's literary archetype, *The Waste Land* (*Grendel* was written too late for this book, but it fits its major concerns precisely). Olderman then explores attempts to transcend this hopeless arid literary vision in a new rebirth of the sense of wonder, as intimated by the final words cited from *Grendel*.

9. Published in the Ballard collection, *The Terminal Beach* (Penguin Books, 1966), and more recently in *Chronopolis and Other Stories* (New York: G.P. Putnam's Sons, 1971). For another critical reading, see Charles Nicol, "Ballard and the Limits of Mainstream SF," *SFS* 3 (1976): 150–53.

10. *Anatomy of Criticism*, p. 192: "*Sparagmos*, or the sense that heroism and effective action are absent, disorganized or foredoomed to defeat, and that confusion and anarchy reign over the world, is the archetypal theme of irony and satire." Note that in *Grendel*, however, the *sparagmos* of Grendel is an inversion of the usual anti-heroic dismemberment: Grendel is an anti-anti-hero.

11. The critical works referred to are Rabkin's *The Fantastic in Literature* (ch. 2, note 56), and W.R. Irwin, *The Game of the Impossible: A Rhetoric of Fantasy* (Urbana, Ill.: University of Illinois Press, 1976).

12. Throughout this chapter I am indebted to Jan De Vries, *Heroic Song and Heroic Legend*, trans. B.J. Timmes (London: Oxford University Press, 1963). The first seven chapters are a valuable survey of heroic sagas, myths, epics, and songs in their several cultures; the last six chapters describe the mythical atmosphere of the Heroic Age. Especially see chapter 12, pp. 227–41, for the author's insistence that the Heroic Age is indeed a *mythical* time. The seminal work on this subject is H. M. Chadwick, *The Heroic Age* (Cambridge: Cambridge University Press, 1912).

Cf. Robert Scholes' definition of "legendary time," *Structural Fabulation* (ch. 2, note 50), p. 12:

> Fictions of legendary time represent a stage in this growth of historical awareness. Legendary time has two stages, a "then" and a "now." Then, there were giants in the earth, or a paradise inhabited by man. Now, men are smaller and the conditions of existence are more constricting. Sometimes legendary time includes the notion of a future (a "then" in the other direction) in which lost greatness will be restored and paradise regained. Legendary time thus incorporates some notions of past, present, and future, but as distinct conditions—as beginning, middle, and end, rather than as a continuous process of change functioning through specific human actions.

Cf. G. S. Kirk, *Homer and the Epic* (Cambridge: Cambridge University Press, 1965; a shorter version of *The Songs of Homer*), p. 2:

> The main component of such an age, which tends to occur in the development of many different nations, are a taste for warfare and adventure, a powerful nobility, and a simple but temporarily adequate material culture devoid of much aesthetic refinement. In such conditions the heroic virtues of honor and martial courage dominate all others, ultimately with depressive effects on the stability of the society. It is usually during the consequent period of decline that the poetical elaboration of glorious deeds, deeds that now lie in the past, reaches its climax.

13. Both citations are adapted from medievalist and fantasy critic Charles Moorman. The first is from *A Knyght There Was: The Evolution of the Knight in*

Literature (Lexington: University of Kentucky Press, 1967), pp. 28-29 (for further authorities, cf. p. 156, note 4); the second is from "The Fictive Worlds of C. S. Lewis and J.R.R. Tolkien," in Mark Hillegas (ed.), *Shadows of Imagination* (Carbondale, Ill.: Southern Illinois University Press, 1969), p. 63.

14. For two popular accounts of Eddison's life and work, see Lin Carter, *Imaginary Worlds: The Art of Fantasy* (New York: Ballantine Books, 1973), pp. 32-38, and L. Sprague de Camp, *Literary Swordsmen and Sorcerers: The Makers of Heroic Fantasy* (Sauk City, Wis.: Arkham House, 1976), pp. 114-36. The *Worm* is the first novel in a famous trilogy whose second (*Mistress of Mistresses*) and third (*A Fish Dinner at Memison*) volumes belong to quite different genres of imaginative literature. It is regrettable that Eddison's works have not received the increased academic and analytical attention given to many other modern fantasists like Tolkien and C.S. Lewis.

15. For the mythological significance of *ouroboros*, see Erich Neumann, *The Origins and History of Consciousness*, trans. R. F. C. Hull (New York: Pantheon Books, 1954), pp. 5-38. Within Eddison's story, the ouroboros appears on the signet rings of the Witch kings to symbolize that each king, named Gorice, is really only his predecessor *reborn*. Cf. the reading of Robert Heinlein's "All you Zombies" in chapter 1.

16. See Lin Carter, *Imaginary Worlds* (ch. 4, note 14), pp. 32-37.

For an interesting retelling of Snorri for a juvenile audience there is Roger Lancelyn Green, *Myths of the Norsemen* (Puffin Books paperback, 1970).

The best introductory survey of Scandinavian mythology for the general reader is H. R. Ellis Davidson, *Gods and Myths of Northern Europe* (Penguin Books, 1964).

A number of other general works have constituted basic research for this mythology: John A. MacCulloch, *The Mythology of All Races*, Vol. 2, *Eddic* (Boston: Archeological Institute of America, 1930); E.O.G. Turville-Petre, *Myth and Religion of the North: The Religion of Ancient Scandinavia* (N.Y.: Holt, Rinehart and Winston, 1964); E. Haugen, "The Mythical Structure of the Ancient Scandinavians," in Michael Lane (ed.), *Structuralism: A Reader* (London: Cape, 1970), pp. 170-83 and 444-45 (notes). However, the latter essay is "structuralism" after the "tripartite social functions" formulated by Georges Dumézil and bears almost no resemblance to structuralisms like Claude Lévi-Strauss's or Jean Piaget's.

17. This is a thirteenth-century Icelandic handbook of traditional mythology and poetic kennings that its author had intended for educative purposes, as is indicated from its final section on "Poetic Diction." However, it is the first two sections, the "Prologue" and "The Deluding of Gylfi" (*Gylfaginning*), that make the *Edda* the most useful and popular source for Scandinavian (or "eddic") mythology. The best translation for English readers is Jean I. Young, *Snorri Sturluson: The Prose Edda* (University of California paperbacks, 1966), with a useful introduction by Sigurdur Nordal.

18. For the passage in "the Sybil's Song" (*Voluspa*) in the Elder (Poetic) Edda, see the translation by Paul B. Taylor and W.H. Auden, *The Elder Edda: A Selection* (New York: Random House, 1967), esp. pp. 152-3.

19. On Valhalla, Odin's warrior paradise, see Ellis Davidson, *Gods and Myths of Northern Europe* (ch. 4, note 16), pp. 149-53.

20. The critical literature on Tolkien's *Lord of the Rings* is not merely extensive: like every other instant classic of our consumer culture, much unnecessary fan writing has accumulated around what is actually, at heart, a real literary classic. However, some enlightening criticism has been written: in addition to Hillegas's anthology (ch. 4, note 13) and that by Isaacs and Zimbardo (ch. 4, note 21), I single out classicist Douglass Parker's review, "Hwast We Holbytla . . . ," *Hudson Review* 9 (1956–57), pp. 598–609, which in its brief span manages also to be one of the best general/theoretical essays on fantasy. Because it appears in so important a critical book from a prestigious university press, one must mention C.N. Manlove's chapter in *Modern Fantasy: Five Studies* (Cambridge: Cambridge University Press, 1975), pp. 99–151, but I have earlier recorded my judgment that, besides its overly hostile and negative complexion, the essay lapses too often into extraliterary irrelevance. See *SFS* (1978): 34–35. Another useful aid is Richard C. West, *Tolkien Criticism: An Annotated Checklist* (Kent, Ohio: Kent State University Press, 1970). There are easily another dozen books I could cite — biographies, guides, indexes — but space does not permit.

21. My remarks in this paragraph are based on W.H. Auden's brilliant essay on Frodo, "The Quest Hero," *Texas Quarterly* 4 (1961): 81–93; reprinted in Neil Isaacs and Rose Zimbardo, *Tolkien and the Critics* (Notre Dame, Ind.: Notre Dame University Press, 1968), pp. 40–61.

22. From "The Fictive Worlds of C.S. Lewis and J.R.R. Tolkien (ch. 4, note 13), p. 63; confirmed by Parker (ch. 4, note 20), p. 608.

23. Discussion in Carter, *Imaginary Worlds* (ch. 4, note 14), pp. 120–21.

24. See Carter, *Imaginary Worlds* (ch. 4, note 14), p. 66. Carter includes a valuable history of the genre, beginning with his description of Robert E. Howard's works, pp. 62–69, then dealing with later authors in his chapter, "Post-Howardian Heroica: The Swordsmen and Sorcerers' Guild of America, Ltd.," pp. 131–58. De Camp, *Literary Swordsmen and Sorcerers* (ch. 4, note 14), also contains a valuable chapter on Robert E. Howard, pp. 135–77, and on the later "Conan's Compeers," pp. 270–89.

Possibly the best anthology of s&s materials (reprinted from the fanzine *Amra*) is L. Sprague de Camp and George H. Scithers (eds.), *The Conan Grimoire* (Baltimore: Mirage Press, 1972).

25. My interpretation of *The Iron Dream*, especially as a parody of sword-and-sorcery, is indebted to the review of Ursula K. LeGuin in *Science Fiction Studies* 1 (1973): 41–44.

26. The Alpers article was printed in *SFS* 5 (1978):19–32; the citation is from p. 31. Manfred Nagl, "SF, Occult Sciences, and the Nazi Myths," *SFS* 1(1974):185–97, identifies the rise of Nazi barbarism with the rise of pseudoscientifically based science fantasy. Also, for this and other questions of Nazi mythology, Darko Suvin was good enough to recommend Hermann Glaser's study, *The Cultural Roots of National Socialism*, trans. Ernest A. Menze (Austin: University of Texas Press, 1978), esp. "Mythos against Logos," pp. 98–176.

27. Scholes and Rabkin, *Science Fiction* (ch. 1, note 6), p. 89; Alpers, revealingly, p. 30. For the various narratives that make up the series (including even a comic book story of *Elric* I encountered in *Star Reach* #6), see the article on Moorcock in volume 2 of Tuck's *Encyclopedia*. Most recently, cf.

Michael Moorcock, "Wit and Humor in Fantasy," *Foundation* #16 (May 1979): 16–22.

28. The title of the Ballantine Books edition (1976), *The Compleat Enchanter*, is a misnomer because the edition contains only the first three tales (plus an Afterword by de Camp, pp. 413–420), but it is still a valuable edition given its limits. For a survey of these and other stories by Pratt and de Camp, see Carter, *Imaginary Worlds* (ch. 4, note 14), pp. 77–83; de Camp, *Literary Swordsmen and Sorcerers* (ch. 4, note 14), pp. 178–94. Sam Moskowitz's chapter on de Camp in *Seekers* (ch. 3, note 1), pp. 151–66, is of course out of date for the last decade on this prolific writer.

As my own personal discovery, I add as a gloss on literary history that Pratt and de Camp seem to have been inspired in part by Frank Bellknap Long's "The Hounds of Tindalos" (1929), now reprinted in August Derleth's collection, *Tales of the Cthulhu Mythos*, vol. 1 (Ballantine Books, 1971); points of convergence include a character named Chalmers, recitation of mathematical formulas, and simultaneous universes.

29. There is an analogous scene, equally funny, in de Camp's later comic s&s novel, *The Goblin Tower* (Pyramid, 1968).

30. The last two novellas were published in one volume under the title, *Wall of Serpents* (New York: Avalon, 1960); Lin Carter revived the first in his *Great Short Novels of Adult Fantasy: I* (N.Y.: Ballantine, 1972).

A translation of the Kalevala is available in W. F. Kirby, *Kalevala: The Land of the Heroes*, 2 vols. (London: J.M. Dent & Co., 1907); for background and interpretation I follow Bjorn Collinder, *The Kalevala and Its Background* (Stockholm: Almvist and Wiksell, 1964), and De Vries (ch. 4, note 12), pp. 143–56. For Irish mythology, see the notes on Poul Anderson's *Broken Sword* later in this chapter.

I merely mention as one more evidence of my thesis about comic incongruity that the heroes of Kalevala speak in a sing-song poetry that mimics the worst failings of Kirby's translation, which itself was influenced by the rhythms of Longfellow's *Song of Hiawatha*.

31. I note that de Camp has added a story to this series as recently as "The Rug and the Bull" in Lin Carter's *Flashing Swords! #2* (Dell Books, 1974). Beyond any doubt, the Pusad tales develop perspectives by incongruity, too.

32. All references are to the Ballantine Books edition of 1971 which includes some minor revisions by the author. Anderson has attracted little attention from the academic community. The most valuable resource I've encountered so far is the Special Poul Anderson Issue of *F&SF* for April 1971; it includes appreciative essays by Gordon R. Dickson and James Blish and a most valuable bibliography of Anderson's writings. Cf. the analysis of "The Faun" in chapter 1 of this book.

For heroic mythology in the Icelandic sagas, see De Vries (ch. 4, note 12), pp. 92–98. For the Elves in Eddic mythology and in the Icelandic sagas, see J. A. MacCulloch, *Eddic Mythology* (ch. 4, note 16), pp. 219–27; for Trolls, pp. 285–87.

33. See De Vries, p. 101, for the theme in general; and p. 62 for its appearance in the *Niebelungenlied*. It is also a central tragic moment in the *Njal Saga*, the most monumental of all the Icelandic sagas (see the Penguin Books

translation by Magnus Magnusson and Hermann Palsson, p. 11, and chs. 128–30 in the saga itself). I wish to thank my friend and colleague William F. Hansen for explaining *brenna inni* to me.

34. The fundamental study is Otto Rank's *The Double: A Psychoanalytic Study* (1925), trans. Harry Tucker (Chapel Hill: University of North Carolina Press, 1971). More recent studies of this theme which is so popular in nineteenth- and twentieth-century literature are Ralph Tymms, *Doubles in Literary Psychology* (Cambridge: Bowes & Bowes, 1949), and Robert Rogers, *A Psychoanalytic Study of the Double in Literature* (Detroit: Wayne State University Press, 1970).

35. See the final chapter of John A. MacCulloch, *The Mythology of All Races*, Vol. 3, *Celtic* (Boston: Marshall Jones Co., 1918), part 1, pp. 206–13, especially p. 213 for the parallels drawn with the Mediterranean theme of "Great Pan is dead" (which are the exact words uttered by Anderson's Faun).

Snorri's "Prologue" to his *Prose Edda* clearly enunciates the theme of a pagan mythology that has vanished in the face of Christianity. For other references to Scandinavian traditions on the subject, see H. R. Ellis Davidson, *Gods and Myths of Northern Europe* (ch. 4, note 16), "The Passing of the Old Gods," pp. 211–23.

36. The comic-strip character Prince Valiant had a sword, the "Singing Sword," which itself became more and more berserk during battle; Moorcock's Stormbringer was mentioned earlier, but Thor's famous hammer, Mjollner, was a prototypical talismanic weapon which took on a life of its own. Skafloc's "broken sword" is of course still another doppelgänger. For the reforging of a magical broken sword as a theme of original Norse myth, see Ellis-Davidson, *Gods and Myths of Northern Europe*, p. 49.

37. *The Saga of Hrolf Kraki* (Oxford: Oxford University Press, 1933).

38. From the author's introduction in the edition cited, pp. xx, xviii, and xix respectively.

39. This novelette appears in Lin Carter's *Flashing Swords #1* (Dell Books, 1973). For Mermen, see MacCulloch on Eddic mythology (ch. 4, note 16), p. 210. The lore of the Kraken is described in Willy Ley's *Exotic Zoology* (Capricorn Books edition, New York, 1966), "The Curious Case of the Kraken," pp. 199–210.

5. Men like Gods

1. *Partisan Review* 32 (1965): 505–25. Especially see p. 508: "... the myth (of science fiction) is quite simply the myth of the end of man, of the transcendence or transformation of the human. ... fruitful artistically is the prospect of the radical transformation of *Homo sapiens* into something else; ..."

2. In addition to Fiedler's essay (cited in note 1), see his famous *Love and Death in the American Novel* (first published in 1960; Dell, revised ed., 1969); on the Divine Child archetype, see C. G. Jung and C. Kerényi, *Essays on a Science of Mythology* (ch. 2, note 17), pp. 70–100; on the Victorian child fantasy, whose very "real" influence is still seen in today's attitudes in America, see Charles Landrum Cornwell, *From Self to the Shire: Studies in Victorian Fan-*

tasy (University of Virginia doctoral dissertation, 1972; *Dissertation Abstracts* 33, no. 3, 1163–4A).

3. For a brief history, see Moskowitz's chapter in *Seekers* (ch. 3, note 1), pp. 101–17, "Superman," i.e., the comic book hero.

4. For a popular history, see Eric Bentley, *A Century of Hero-Worship: A Study of the Idea of Heroism in Carlyle and Nietzsche, With Notes on Wagner, Spengler, Stephan George, and D. H. Lawrence*, 2d. ed. (Boston: Beacon Press, 1957; 1st ed. published in London, 1947, as *The Cult of the Superman*). Emphasizing the role of individual creativity, Bentley groups these thinkers together as "heroic vitalists."

For Goethe, see William Barrett, *Irrational Man* (ch. 4, note 5), pp. 128–30 and 189–90. For a view of Carlyle's influence that is diametrically opposed to Bentley's, see Ernst Cassirer, *The Myth of the State* (New Haven: Yale University Press, 1946), pp. 189–223, who locates here the seeds of racist totalitarianism whereas Bentley defends the heroic vitalists against charges of being "proto-fascists." Also useful is R. J. Hollingdal's introduction to his English translation, *Thus Spoke Zarathustra*, 2d ed. (Penguin Books, 1969), pp. 11–35.

Charles Glicksberg, *The Ironic Vision in Modern Literature* (ch. 4, note 2), pp. 51–62, "The Dilemma of the Superman," interprets Nietzsche's Superman as a response to Schopenhauer's pessimism. Faced with the nightmarish vision of a totally meaningless cosmos which was destined to repeat itself cyclically ad infinitum (termed "Eternal Recurrence" in *Also Sprach Zarathustra*), the Superman (= the hero as philosopher *and* artist) can still satisfy his thirst for eternity—that is, for a cosmos in which contingent events have permanent value and meaning—by asserting his Will-to-Power, by loving and affirming that endless eternity of insignificance.

I am also indebted to an unpublished paper by B. R. Nagle entitled "Varieties of the Superman in Some Recent Science Fiction." The author takes Nietzsche's statements on the *Ubermensch* in *Also Sprach Zarathustra* and shows them as anticipations of A. E. van Vogt's themes of a more perfect mankind in *Slan* and of a superior educational system in *World of Null-A*; and of Theodore Sturgeon's theme of human, and humanizing, values in *The Synthetic Man* and *More Than Human*.

5. For the transition of the concept from philosophy to mainstream literature, see Armytage, *Yesterday's Tomorrows*, (ch. 3, note 6), pp. 99–111, "Superman and the System," which emphasizes D.H. Lawrence, H.G. Wells, Kurt Lasswitz, George Bernard Shaw, and William Butler Yeats (*A Vision*). The older science-fiction writers are described in the same author's "Extrapolators and Exegetes of Evolution," *Extrapolation* 7 (1965): 2–17, and in Richard Gerber, *Utopian Fantasy* (London: Routledge and Kegan Paul, 1955), pp. 15–26, "Man and Superman." Both these latter essays emphasize the close relationship between the theory of evolution and the concept of Superman.

6. See Lois and Stephen Rose, *The Shattered Ring* (Richmond, Va.: John Knox Press, 1970), pp. 48–54. One can, however, sympathize with critics of the Nietzschean Superman when real events like the Bobby Franks murder case or the rise of the Nazis are taken into account. As Bentley (ch. 5, note 2) has noted, the subject remains a deeply troubling one for twentieth-century ethical thought.

7. Also cf. the earlier discussions of Weinbaum in chapter 1, esp. note 33. Weinbaum also wrote a famous and popular short story about a sickly, dying young woman of the Depression Era who is converted by an experimental serum into a Superwoman: "The Adaptive Ultimate" (*Astounding Stories*, November 1935) refers to the woman's incredible adaptive abilities, but she is also "inhuman" by normal standards—a murderess, sexually uninhibited, a willful manipulator of other people. The story is now available in *The Best of Stanley G. Weinbaum* (ch. 1, note 33).

8. For "Literature of the Second Self," see the earlier citation of references in chapter 4, note 34.

9. A key fictional work on the theme of genetic atavism is Jack London's *Before Adam* (1907) which describes a modern man going back through his dreams into the consciousness of an almost human primate ancestor, Big-Tooth. A brief but valuable reading of the novel appears in Ketterer, *New Worlds for Old* (ch. 1, note 13), pp. 161–63. Inherited race memory accounts for the first-person narrator's ability to relive prehistoric events. The hero of London's *The Star Rover* (1915) jumps in consciousness from one of his earlier lives to another, reliving the past history of mankind. The narrative suggests a reversal of the embryological process, "ontogeny recapitulates phylogeny." Here the individual relives the race history in reverse order.

It is not possible to describe here every narrative that uses this theme. Poul Anderson's *Three Hearts and Three Lions* was mentioned earlier in chapter 4. Unfortunately, I must bypass Emil Petaja, an American writer of Finnish extraction, who wrote an interesting science fantasy tetralogy based on the *Kalevala*, the Finnish national epic (contrast de Camp and Pratt's "Wall of Serpents," the fourth Harold Shea story, mentioned earlier, chapter 4): the treatment of this mythology is unique and the Kuttnerian poetic prose style is attractive and appropriate for this particular mythology. These stories even make a nice popular, readable introduction to a rich and complex mythology which is hardly known in America, except perhaps through the symphonic tone poems of composer Ian Sibelius (e.g., *The Maid of Pohjola*, *The Swan of Tuonela*, *Lemminkainen*).

The four novels each center around one of the chief heroes of the *Kalevala*: Lemminkainen (*Saga of Lost Earths* [Ace, 1966]), Vainamoinen (*The Star Mill* [Ace, 1966]), Ilmarinen (*The Stolen Sun* [Ace, 1967]), Kullervo (*Tramontane* [Ace, 1967]).

Though there are many inconsistencies in the series, the tetralogy takes up four phases of the futuristic history of a people known as the "Vanhat." They are, of course, known to us today as the Finns, a race who are regarded as sorcerers in the popular folklore of northern Europe; in Petaja's fictive universe the cause of their extraordinary powers is ESP, which is part of their genetic make-up. Originally the Vanhat inhabited the world known as "Otava" in the constellation Ursa Major and were half of a much larger race. Then this other half, the "Valmis," abandoned their physical existence altogether and mingled with the very substance of the universe. Next, for reasons never explained, the Vanhat migrated to Earth where they submerged themselves, in early prehistoric times, with the nascent human population. It later results, to be sure, that many "men" bear Vanhat genes and are throwbacks to the alien race, though it is a still more important throwback characteristic that both full Vanhat and men with Vanhat genes can link minds in ESP fashion with their brethren, the Valmis, who are now one with the cosmos.

10. A. E. van Vogt has not yet received a fair critical evaluation from the academic community, but even in SF fandom he seems little appreciated for all the popularity his tales have maintained for some forty years, with many intelligent people today still surprised at their story-rich magic at first encounter. Moskowitz's chapter on him in *Seekers* (ch. 3, note 1), pp. 213–38, is far from complete; it may be supplemented by Damon Knight, *In Search of Wonder* (ch. 2, note 47), pp. 47–62, who is far too harsh and negative a critic.

Moskowitz, pp. 226–27, rightly recognizes in van Vogt a science-fiction transformation of the religious consciousness: "man has within himself Godlike powers if he will only work to discover and release them." Far too much criticism has been of a *personal* nature, attacking van Vogt as a man in two areas where he is certainly vulnerable: first, his susceptibility to pseudosciences like Ron Hubbard's Dianetics (in general, van Vogt overrates mind powers and believes in "the omnipotence of thoughts"); and, second, his well-known apology for his own habits of composition which involved a new idea every 800 words.

For a well-reasoned attack against van Vogt for his involvement with pseudoscience, see Martin Gardner (famous as a science popularizer and author of the mathematical games and puzzles in *Scientific American* and *OMNI*) *Fads and Fallacies in the Name of Science*, rev. ed. (New York: Dover Books, 1957), pp. 240, 287–88, and 346. On van Vogt's self-announced "rapid fire" approach to science-fiction plotting, see his essay in Lloyd Arthur Eshbach (ed.), *Of Worlds Beyond*, 2d ed. (Chicago: Advent, 1964), "Complication in the Science Fiction Story," pp. 53–66.

11. Originally published in *Unknown Worlds*, October 1943; 1st. ed. in book form, Fantasy Press, 1947. It has also appeared under the title, *Two Hundred Million A.D.* (as in the Paperback Library edition of 1964; often reprinted). All page references are to this last edition.

12. See James Gunn, "Henry Kuttner, C. L. Moore, Lewis Padgett *et al.*," in Clareson, *Voices for the Future* (ch. 1, note 18), pp. 185–215, esp. p. 212 on *Mask of Circe*. Moskowitz's chapter on Kuttner in *Seekers* (ch. 3, note 1), pp. 319–34, is inadequate and attempts to criticize him—wrongly, I believe—for the paucity of new scientific ideas in his stories. I tend, on the contrary, to agree with Damon Knight's more positive evaluation in *In Search of Wonder* (ch. 2, note 47), pp. 139–45, where Kuttner's verbal pyrotechnics and stylistic ingenuity are recognized. Kuttner's real skill, like that of so many other imaginative writers who are usually categorized as "science fantasy," lay in his exceptional ability to *poeticize* older fantasy and SF conceptions, to apply lavish details, gorgeous descriptions, and subtle linguistic nuances to the otherwise bare bones of a theme or narrative. Kuttner, like his wife C. L. Moore, makes us focus our attention on fine points and lets us dwell lovingly and at length on an imaginative theme whereas a van Vogt or a Heinlein seems to keep us ever racing along through new ones. If Kuttner too often seems to be imitative of earlier writers, I would credit it to his artistic intuition that those older ideas had not yet been exploited for their full literary and artistic potential.

Moskowitz's failures are catalogued in James Blish, "Moskowitz on Kuttner," *Riverside Quarterly* 5, no. 2 (February 1972): 140–43. For a bibliography of this author's works and some valuable popular essays see Karen Anderson (ed.), *Henry Kuttner: A Memorial Symposium* (Berkeley, Calif.: Senagram Enterprises, 1958).

13. For an account of other ancient sources and versions of Jason and the Argonauts, see J. R. Bacon, *The Voyage of the Argonauts* (London: Methuen & Co., 1925). In the genealogies, Circe was sister of king Aeetes of Colchis, hence aunt of Medea, and these two most famous witches of Greek antiquity seem in every way to be counterparts of one another (as Bacon remarks, p. 132).

14. Original script by Gilbert A. Ralston and Gene L. Coon. It is not to my purposes here to enter a lengthy discussion of the extensive literature on the TV series, nor of Trekkie fandom, nor of the obvious scientific implausibility of this and other plots in the series. For a Jungian reading of *Star Trek*, often superficial and never very convincing, though interesting, see Karin Blair, *Meaning in Star Trek* (Chambersburg, Pa.: Anima Books, 1977), esp. pp. 123–25, for the episode under discussion.

15. Indeed, much of the credibility of the character Zed is derived from our stereotyped response to Sean Connery's universally known role as James Bond. My colleague James Naremore of the English Department and Film Studies Program at Indiana University, is currently at work on a study of how major film figures affect our response to subsequent films in which they appear (e.g., Bogart, Gable, John Wayne).

16. For my essay on *Jack of Shadows*, see the earlier citation, chapter 2, note 18.

I have read with great interest a recent doctoral dissertation by John Rothfork, *New Wave Science Fiction Considered as a Popular Religious Phenomenon: A Definition and an Example* (University of New Mexico, 1973; *Dissertation Abstracts* 35–03A: 329). The author applies two metaphors to the understanding of Zelazny, one drawn from phenomenological philosophy and the other from Zen religion. See, *inter alia*, p. 179, where Rothfork emphasizes the Shadow theme in Zelazny: there is no ultimate, static Platonic noumenal world like Amber, only a phenomenal Heraclitean world of flux and becoming; Zelazny rejoices in the struggle within the fleeting world of appearances, rejects Zen enlightenment as an absolute goal, is constantly testing his own powers as well as that of the Shadow reality, and is dedicated to the power of words to enlighten the shadows. However, I must conclude that both of Rothfork's critical metaphors seem artificial and are applied to Zelazny's works in *a priori* fashion although they do lead to some interesting results.

17. All page references are to the Ace Books edition of 1967; a short, but quite distinctive version was serialized in *Fantasy and Science Fiction*, October and November 1965, under the title " . . . And Call Me Conrad."

Cf. White, *Mythology in the Modern Novel* (ch. 2, note 17), pp. 218–22, for an interpretation of Hans Erich Nossack's *Nekyia* (1947), a German novel which combines two features of *This Immortal*—a world after a major holocaust and prefigurations from ancient Greece—in a totally different vision.

18. For "Callicantzari" as trickster-ish hobgoblins of modern Greek

folklore, see John C. Lawson, *Modern Greek Folklore and Ancient Greek Religion* (Cambridge: The University Press, 1910), pp. 190–255; this book in general offers good background knowledge for *This Immortal*.

19. Rothfork (ch. 5, note 16), pp. 173–74, observes that all three novels under discussion here contain "open frames:" the reader is drawn into the fantasy by the narrator/hero who is every bit as confused (often amnesiac) as the reader, and a neat, orderly narrative is apparent only halfway into these novels.

20. New York: G. P. Putnam's Sons, 1969. This sophisticated literary work describes the ruined, post-holocaust earth in the language and images of St. John's Book of Revelation; its hero is supposedly the last of the Hell's Angels whose act of courage and generosity leads to his statue being set up in the Boston Common: a nice satire on the ultimate anti-establishment figure ending up as a hero in the bastion of the American establishment. Such intellectual merit and wit are both lacking in the recent film of the same name: Zelazny's lone hero now ends up as *two military types*! (played by Jan Michael Vincent and George Peppard) and after a series of trashy horror-type escapades (cannibalistic cockroaches, e.g.) conducted in praise of American military thinking and its technological hardware, the group of attractive Hollywood heroes reaches a sentimentally conceived paradise. The whole film is out of spirit with Zelazny's anti-establishment views.

21. All references are to the Avon Books edition of 1969 (original publication, Mercury Press, 1967).

In conversation, Zelazny informed me that Joseph Campbell's *Oriental Mythology*, The Masks of God, vol. 2 (New York: Viking, 1962), was fundamental reading matter for this novel. See specifically pp. 147–367. Other good introductory accounts are: A. B. Keith, *The Mythology of All Races, vol. 6. Indian* (Boston, 1917), part 1, or, very briefly, the article, "Mythology of India," in *New Larousse Encyclopedia of Mythology* (New York: Prometheus Press, 1959), pp. 339–92.

I am also generally indebted in these pages to an unpublished version of a paper by Robert L. Jones (Radford College, Va.), "Myth and Demythification in SF: Zelazny's *Lord of Light*." Especially suggestive is this author's view that Zelazny turns science into myth so that science itself may be demystified ("demythified").

22. "The Vitanuls" (*F&SF*, July 1967) now appears in the Mayo Mohs anthology, *Other Worlds, Other Gods* (ch. 1, note 12): the central Hindu myth concept is the recycling of souls; due to the twentieth-century population explosion and extended life span, the world runs out of souls, i.e., the animating principle has been exhausted and the babies born from now on lack the animating/vitalizing principles; they are "vitanuls." The living use all life up, there is none left over for the as yet unborn, and the saintly old doctor Kotiwala realizes how important his own impending death will be: there will be no new life without it. Ironically, the Indian doctor's generosity is played out against contemporary man's greed for more and more life; a new anti-senility drug has been discovered, making death even more remote for those now alive.

23. Original publication: New York: Doubleday, 1969. All page references are to the Avon Books edition of 1969. Portions of the novel appeared

as two distinct novellas: "Creatures of Light" (*If Science Fiction*, November 1968) and "Creatures of Darkness" (*If*, March 1969).

24. Typhon was the name the Greeks applied to Set; hence, Zelazny presents us with a split representation by making the two of them brothers.

Zelazny also inverts the intention of the original myth by characterizing Osiris and Horus as the traitors and rebels: in ancient Egyptian mythology they are the mythological prototypes respectively of the deceased and living king, father and son.

25. See ch. 2, note 18.

26. Since the appearance of the first two Amber novels, *Nine Princes in Amber* (Avon, 1970) and *The Guns of Avalon* (Avon, 1972), volumes have been appearing regularly from Avon Books: *Sign of the Unicorn, The Hand of Oberon,* and *The Courts of Chaos,* respectively.

27. On this Freudian concept, see the reference in ch. 2, note 25. The following brief explanation is provided by Werner Muensterberger and Christopher Nichols in their Introduction to R. Money-Kyrle's translation of Géza Róheim's *The Riddle of the Sphinx* (New York: Harper Torchbooks, 1974), p. xv, where the "primal horde" refers to:

> .... Freud's celebrated thesis that man's primeval social organization was a primal horde, a force-ruled harem where paternal strength dictated the father's sole possession of sexual rights over all females. There arose a time (so Freud's narrative continues) when the excluded males—the filial, fraternal band—joined together and slew and cannibalistically devoured their sire, only then, of psychic necessity, to form a sublimated father religion, totemism, which preserved the now internally established power of unconscious guilt and repression.

28. References to the publication and date of the first, fourth, and fifth volumes of the series are given in the text or in subsequent notes. The second and third novels are, respectively, *The Gates of Creation* (Ace, 1966), and *A Private Cosmos* (Ace, 1968).

For background on the career and writings of Farmer, I have used the chapter in Sam Moskowitz, *Seekers* (ch. 3, note 1), pp. 392–409. This essay is of course now over a decade out of date, but may be supplemented by an annotated bibliography by Thomas L. Wymer, "Speculative Fiction Bibliographies, and Philip José Farmer," *Extrapolation* 18 (1976–77):59–72; and two brief but insightful general studies: Russell Letson, "The Faces of a Thousand Heroes: Philip José Farmer," *SFS* 4 (1977):35–41; and Thomas Wymer, "The Worlds of Philip José Farmer," *Ex* 18 (1976–77):124–30. Discussion of essays by critics Leslie Fiedler and Franz Rottensteiner is reserved for chapter 6. For this and later observations on Farmer I am indebted to several conversations over the years with my friend and fellow SF fan Steve Lockwood.

29. By the time of the fourth novel, *Behind the Walls of Terra* (Ace, 1970), Kickaha realizes that all cosmologies are illusory, that all realities are equally artificial; the entirety of "creation" suggests a series of interlocked Chinese boxes which form an unresolvable cosmic riddle: if the Lords created Earth, *Who* created the Lords' home world, which is just as obviously an artificial creation?

30. Some examples: *Lord Tyger*, a Tarzan life based on the Campbellian heroic monomyth, taking place in an artificial universe as part of a scientific

experiment; *Lord of the Trees* (Ace, 1970), half of an Ace double where the other half, *The Mad Goblin*, has a hero modelled on Doc Savage, supposedly a sibling of the Tarzan-figure: the two books end at the same place, at the same scene; but otherwise both tales remain inconclusive, with the mysterious workings of a superhuman "primal horde" family in the background. *Tarzan Alive: A Definitive Biography of Lord Greystoke*, (New York: Doubleday, 1972); a clever piece of pseudoepigraphy.

Farmer is the most Burroughsian of modern storytellers, and the savage centaurs of Amerindia here closely recall the centaur-like beings who inhabit the moon in Edgar Rice Burroughs's *The Moon Maid* (New York: Frank A. Munsey Co., 1923).

31. Farmer is well known for his obsession with many kinds of ambivalence, including androgyny. The editors of *Stella Nova* (#1150) report Farmer's own ambivalent view that " . . . I tend to like heroes more than antiheroes. But not always." Much more remains to be said in my essay on *Flesh* in chapter 6.

6. The Return to the Primitive

1. The Johns Hopkins University Press (Baltimore), 1935. Cited from the Preface, p. ix. Cf. Northrop Frye's observation in *The Secular Scripture: A Study of the Structure of Romance* (Cambridge, Mass.: Harvard University Press, 1976), p. 29:

> We should note that the words popular and primitive mean essentially the same thing, except that "popular" has its context in class structure and "primitive" in history. If we define popular literature as what ignorant and vicious people read, the prejudice implied will make it impossible to understand what is going on in literature. Similarly, if we define the primitive only as the chronologically early, we create an illusion of literature gradually improving itself from naked savagery to the decent clothing of accepted cultural values. But actually the primitive is a quality in literature which emerges recurrently as an aspect of the popular, and as indicating also that certain conventions have been exhausted. The Greek romancers, for all their coyness, are more primitive in this sense than Homer or Aeschylus; the Gothic romancers, like many of the poets contemporary with them, are primitive in a way that Pope and Swift are not, and so are the folk singers and science fiction writers of our own day as compared with Eliot or Joyce.

2. For a valuable reading of this fable as an archetypal mythos (i.e., because of its impact on later SF), see Robert Philmus, *Into the Unknown* (ch. 1, note 7), "Jekyll and Hyde: A Faustian Mystery," pp. 90–99. Also see the earlier reference (chapter 4, note 34) to "literature of the second self."

3. Tuck's *Encyclopedia* contains an article on this author; also see H. P. Lovecraft, *Supernatural Horror in Literature* (original ed., Ben Abramson, New York, 1945; reprint with new Introduction by E. F. Bleiler, Dover, New York, 1973), pp. 89–90. The story is famous for its Chinese-box technique of narrative framing; the image of the Chinese box is cited explicitly in the text, too, to refer to a multi-layered mystery; and the image is reinforced by the variable mode of narration: from odd reportages in the voices of various persons to letters and testimonies. The same technique is used in the novel-

length work, *The Three Imposters* (1895)—see Lin Carter's edition of this obscure horror tale (Ballantine Books, 1972, with Introduction by Carter).

4. My remarks are derived from Barton Levi St. Armand, *The Roots of Horror in the Fiction of H. P. Lovecraft* (Elizabethtown, N.Y.: Dragon Press, 1977), pp. 47–58. My recent review in *SFS* 5 (1978):196–97, is far too harsh on Lovecraft, and the rejoinder by S. T. Joshi in defense of the horror master in *SFS* 7 (1980) 111–12, is well taken.

5. Burroughs's Tarzan, then, not only has affinities with the s&s figures considered in chapter 4, but also is an archetypal return-to-the-primitive hero (reverse evolution again). Tarzan is indeed a part of modern SF, but he is so large that he transcends the limits of any genre and seems downright mythical in his own right. See Leslie Fiedler, "Lord of the Absolute Elsewhere," *NY Times Book Review* (9 June 1974), p. 8; and Richard A. Lupoff, *Edgar Rice Burroughs: Master of Adventure*, rev. and enl. ed. (Ace Books, 1968), a valuable popular account of the prolific writer's many contributions to imaginative literature.

For more on this Stone Age mythos, see Aldiss, *Billion Year Spree* (ch. 1, note 6), pp. 151–52; Bailey, *Pilgrims* (ch. 3, note 6), pp. 88–90. Mainstream writer and classicist William Golding has achieved status as a master of primitivist philosophy (*Lord of the Flies*) and a primitive, early human mentality (Neanderthal Man's in *The Inheritors*).

6. L. Sprague de Camp is remembered for "The Gnarly Man" (*Unknown*, June 1939; often reprinted, most recently in *The Best of L. Sprague de Camp* [Ballantine, 1978]), a science fantasy tale of the last surviving Neanderthal man, who is 50,000 years old!; and for his collaboration with P. Schyler Miller, *Genus Homo* (Reading, Pa.: Fantasy Press, 1950), prototype of the "Planet of the Apes" fantasy where humans "evolve" into apes. For Farmer, see the discussion of his Tarzan in chapter 5. Almost any of his works contain appearances by Burroughs-style protohumans (e.g., in the Riverworld series especially).

7. On this tale, see Sam Moskowitz, *Seekers of Tomorrow* (ch. 3, note 1), p. 284.

Walter M. Miller's *A Canticle for Leibowitz* (1959) is probably the single most successful SF fable on a specific religious model: after atomic world-cataclysm, a new Roman Catholic Middle Ages rises, ultimately struggles to a new Industrial Age, only to fall back once again into major atomic disaster. See David Ketterer, *New Worlds for Old* (ch. 1, note 13), pp. 140–48, and Russell Griffin, "Medievalism in *A Canticle for Leibowitz*," *Ex* 14(1972–73):112–25.

Closely allied to these works are the Dying Earth science fantasies of Jack Vance (*The Dying Earth* [1950] and its sequel *The Eyes of the Overworld* [1966]) which portray a decadent world at the end of our sun's life and where science has degenerated into effete, playful magic; a world "burned out" in more than one sense.

8. The positive value given primitivism and simplicity is important to Boas and Lovejoy's study (ch. 6, note 1). Graeco-Roman antiquity provides many important exemplars, from the archaic poet Hesiod's *Works and Days*, to the life-style and philosophy of the Cynics, to Roman satirists like Varro and Juvenal.

9. See Victor Turner, *The Ritual Process: Structure and Anti-Structure* (Chicago: Aldine Pub. Co., 1969).

10. All page references for *Flesh* are to the expanded Doubleday version of 1968 (in paperback, reprinted by Signet Science Fiction in 1969). Beacon Press published a shorter version in 1960. Also see *Ex* 18 (1976–77): pp. 66–67.

For Graves's *Whie Goddess*, I have used the "Amended and Enlarged Edition" published by Noonday Press, 1966. John B. Vickery, *Robert Graves and the White Goddess* (Lincoln: University of Nebraska Press, 1972) is a readable survey of this theme throughout Graves's corpus. One work that Vickery does not even mention in passing is *Watch the North Wind Rise* (1949; also published as *Seven Days in New Crete*), an explicit novelistic treatment of the White Goddess which should now be read closely with Robert H. Canary's excellent analysis, "Utopian and Fantastic Dualities in Robert Graves's *Watch the North Wind Rise*," *SFS* 1 (1973–74): 248–55.

It is important for background to this paper to note that Sigmund Freud anticipated this view of triune woman in his essay, "The Theme of the Three Caskets" (1913), published in vol. 12 of James Strachey's standard edition of the *Complete Works* (London: Hogarth Press, 1958), pp. 290–301 (see specifically the last page of the essay).

Finally, I must add the proviso that the concept of the White Goddess, being so essential to Graves's personal myth, may have inspired Farmer by any number of routes, not necessarily from the book of that title, though the latter is the definitive statement of it.

11. In this and many other of his mythological ideas, Graves is indebted to Frazer's *Golden Bough* (for details, see Vickery, pp. 1–25), where one repeated and essential image is that of a vegetative deity whose career of birth, waxing powers, waning potency, death, and rebirth is modeled on the annual cycle of seasons. Graves retains the Dying God as his own central masculine symbol but the male is secondary to the female, the latter remaining the inexhaustible repository of power, fertility, and immortality. Graves's major treatment of the Dying God as such is in his novel, *King Jesus* (for which, see Vickery, pp. 47–53).

I have consulted two important general studies of Frazerian ideas and themes: Stanley Edgar Hyman, *The Tangled Bank* (New York: Atheneum, 1962), pp. 187–291, and John B. Vickery, *The Literary Impact of the Golden Bough* (Princeton: Princeton University Press, 1973).

12. Northrop Frye, "Graves, Gods and Scholars," *Hudson Review* 9 (1956):298–302, recognizes that much of what Graves has to say is sly, obscure satire against the modern world—and his readers.

13. "Thanks for the Feast," in *The Book of Philip José Farmer*. (DAW Books, 1973), esp. pp. 238–39.

14. Fiedler, "Thanks for the Feast," pp. 236–37; Rottensteiner, "Playing Around with Creation: Philip José Farmer," *SFS* 1 (1973–74): 97. Unfortunately the latter article is almost solely the author's expression of his distaste for Farmer precisely in the three areas under discussion, and it is prescriptive criticism rather than analysis. For further criticism of Rottensteiner, see Damon Knight's comments registered in *SFS* 1 (1973–74): 219–20; and *SFS* 2 (1974–75): 89.

15. *Love and Will* (New York: Norton, 1969), esp. pp. 163–64 and 170–72; cf. *Power and Innocence: A Search for the Sources of Violence* (New York: Norton, 1972), for the transforming power of violence.

16. I would further speculate that the "crudity" in style and plot construction which Fiedler, Rottensteiner, and Knight (ch. 6, notes 13 and 14) have all recognized as typical throughout even the best of Farmer's works is isomorphic with the demonic atmosphere: the direct, frenzied, Burroughsian pace of Farmer's adventures mirrors the demonic passions of his heroes.

17. He turns up in Frazer's *Golden Bough*, and it is there that Farmer seems to have found him and not in Graves. See vol. 5 (vol. 1 of *Adonis Attis Osiris*), 3rd ed. (London: Macmillan and Co., 1914), pp. 230–31.

However, the figure of Tom Tobacco, who is clearly a doublet of Barleycorn, seems to be solely Farmer's conception and is a neat Frazerian imitation.

18. *Love's Body* (New York: Random House, 1966), p. 15 (the ancient reference is Livy 1.4–5).

I should at least mention Susan Brownmiller, *Against Our Will: Men, Women, and Rape* (New York: Simon and Schuster, 1975), a recent feminist work that regards rape as a sustained political mechanism by means of which men intimidate women and keep them in their place; she regards rape as the *sine qua non* of male-oriented Western civilization.

INDEX OF AUTHORS AND THEIR WORKS

Italicized numbers refer to major discussions.

Aldiss, Brian: 5, 10, 22, 23, 78; *Frankenstein Unbound*, 7, 63
Alpers, Hans Joachim: 104–5, 120
Ancient Astronauts: 180
Anderson, Poul: 4, 113–20; "The Faun," 28–29, 119; *The Broken Sword, 113–16,* 117, 118, 119; *Hrolf Kraki's Saga, 116–18,* 119; *The High Crusade,* 118, 119; "The Longest Voyage," 118; *Three Hearts and Three Lions,* 118; *The Merman's Children,* 118–19
Apollonius of Rhodes: *The Voyage of the Argo,* 129
Arabian Nights: 110
Ariosto: *Orlando Furioso,* 110
Aristophanes: 171
Asimov, Isaac: 29, 79; "Nightfall," 74; *The Gods Themselves,* 82, 83

Ballard, J. G.: 74, 119; "The Drowned Giant," *95–96*
Barbour, Douglas: 61
Barth, John: 12, 92; *Giles Goat-Boy, 49–50*
Battlestar Galactica: 78, 174
Baum, L. Frank: *The Wizard of Oz,* 133
Blake, William: 25
Blish, James: 74
Bond, Nelson: 15, 54; "The Cunning of the Beast," *8–10*
Boorman, John: *Zardoz, 133–35*
Boucher, Anthony: 80; "Balaam," *52–53;* "The Quest for St. Aquin," *53–54*
Borges, Jorge Luis: 178
Bradbury, Ray: 4, 64
Broch, Hermann: 49, 54, 174
Brown, Fredric: 4–5, 79

Brunner, John: 170; "The Vitanuls," 141
Bulwer-Lytton, Edward: 122
Bunyan, John: 99
Burgess, Anthony: 86, 92; *M/F,* 174
Burroughs, Edgar Rice: 127, 148, 152, 155, 164
Burroughs, William S.: *Naked Lunch,* 26
Butler, Samuel: 179

Cabell, James Branch: 51
Campbell, John W.: 83; *The Mightiest Machine, 78–79;* "Twilight," 79; "Night," 79
Campbell, Joseph: 36, 65; *The Hero With a Thousand Faces,* 17, *49–50,* 172
Camus, Albert: *Sisyphus,* 8
Capek, Karel: 178
Carlyle, Thomas: 122
Carroll, Lewis: 106
Carter, Lin: 101, 102
Clarke, Arthur C.: 79–82, 83, 173; "The Star," *79–80;* "The Nine Billion Names of God," *80–81;* *Childhood's End,* 81; *2001: A Space Odyssey, 81–82*
Close Encounters of the Third Kind: 31
Coleridge, Samuel Taylor: "Kubla Khan," 110

Davidson, Avram: 4
de Camp, L. Sprague: 4, 5, 102, *106–13,* 119–20, 152; *The Incomplete Enchanter, 106–10;* *The Castle of Iron,* 110; "The Wall of Serpents," 110–11; "The Green Magician," 110–11; *The Carnelian Cube,* 111; *Land of Unreason,* 111; *The Tritonian Ring,* 111; *The Fallible Fiend, 112*
Delany, Samuel R.: 4, 48, 133, 173; *The Einstin Intersection, 58–62,* 137, 174

[225]

Index of Authors

del Rey, Lester: 79
De Vries, Peter: 92
Dick, Philip K.: 23, 55; *A Maze of Death*, 20–22, 57; *Deus Irae* (with Zelazny), 179–80
Donleavy, J. P.: 92
Doyle, Arthur Conan: *The Lost World*, 152

Eddison, E. R.: 101; *The Worm Ouroboros*, 97–99, 119; *Styrbiorn the Strong*, 98; *Egil's Saga*, 98
Eliot, T. S.: "The Waste Land," 151
Ellison, Harlan: 4, 23, 133; "The Place With No Name," 26–28, 95; *The Beast That Shouted Love at the Heart of the World*, 28; "A Boy and His Dog," 28; *Deathbird Stories*, 28
Euripides: *Medea*, 129

Farmer, Philip José: 4, 56, 127, 136, 146–48, 152, 155–69; World of Tiers Series: *146–48*, 164; *The Lavalite World*, 146; *The Maker of Universes*, 146–48; "Son," *157–58*; "Father," *158–59*; *The Lovers*, 158; *Flesh*,158, *159–69*; *Strange Relations*, 155–59; "Mother," *156*, 157; "Daughter," *157*; "Riders of the Purple Wage," 165
Fox, Gardner F.: 102
Frazer, James George: 108, 160, 173
Friedman, Bruce J.: 92

Gardner, John: 12, 119; *Grendel*, *91–95*, 96, 112
Gernsback, Hugo: 56
Goethe, J.W. von: 122
Graves, Robert: 49, 169; *The White Goddess*, *159–60*, 166, 167, 168
Gunn, James: 5, 54–55

Haggard, H. Rider: *She*, 152
Hamilton, Edmund: 78
Harness, Charles L.: 15, 54; "The New Reality," *11–12*, 20, 74
Harrison, Harry: 22, 23; *Captive Universe*, *18–20*
Hawthorne, Nathaniel: 7
Heinlein, Robert: 29, 54, 79; "All You Zombies," *15–16*, 174; *Glory Road*, *17–18*, 50, 95
Heller, Joseph: 92
Holocaust: 175
Howard, Robert E.: 102, 108, 112
Hrolfs Kraka Saga: 116
Huxley, Aldous: *Ape and Essence*, 153

In Search of Ancient Mysteries: 180

Jakes, John: 102
Joyce, James: 49, 54, 138
Jung, Carl: *Flying Saucers*, 180

Kuttner, Henry: 89, 124, 146; *The Mask of Circe*, 125, *128–31*

Le Guin, Ursula K.: 4; *Rocannon's World*, 99; *The Left-Hand of Darkness*, 169
Leiber, Fritz: 101, 105, 112, *119–20*; *The Big Time*, 66–68, 83, 145; *Gather, Darkness!*, *152–53*
Lem, Stanislaw: 34, 55, 56, 178; *Cyberiad*, 179
Lewis, C. S.: 52
Lockridge, Ross: 49
Lovecraft, H. P.: 51, 151; "The Rats in the Walls" (Cthulhu series), *151*
Lucian: 171; *True History*, 5, 7

Macdonald, George: 52
Machen, Arthur: "The Great God Pan," *151*
Mann, Thomas: 49, 54
Merritt, Abraham: 152
Miller, Walter M.: *A Canticle for Leibowitz*, 53, 74
Mohs, Mayo: *Other Worlds, Other Gods*, 8, 52
Moorcock, Michael: 4, 23, 54, 105, 133; *Behold the Man*, 23–26, 47, 95
Moore, Catherine L.: 129
Morris, William: 98, 99

Nietzsche, Friedrich: 122, 128; *The Birth of Tragedy*, 122, 129
Njal Saga: 117
Norton, André: 4, 153

Orwell, George: *1984*, 153
Ovid: *Metamorphoses*, 110

Petaja, Emil: 4
Phillpotts, Eden: *The Miniature*, 74–76, .82, 86
Plato: 171
Poe, Edgar Allan: 7, 55
Pound, Ezra: *Guide to Kultur*, 159
Pratt, Fletcher: 106–11; *The Well of the Unicorn*, 111; also see L. Sprague de Camp

Index of Authors

Rand, Ayn: *Anthem*, 153
Renault, Mary: 49
Russ, Joanna: *The Female Man*, 169

Sartre, Jean-Paul: *Flies*, 8
Shakespeare, William: *Macbeth*, 168
Shelley, Mary: *Frankenstein*, 6–8, 10, 29, 32, 62, 69, 72, 171; *The Last Man*, 69
Shelley, Percy Bysshe: "Prometheus Unbound," 7
Shirer, William L.: 104
Silverberg, Robert: 22; "After the Myths Went Home," *1–4*; "Breckenridge and the Continuum," 174; *Tower of Glass*, 179
Smith, E. E. "Doc": 78
Spenser, Edmund: 99; *The Faerie Queene*, 109–10
Spinrad, Norman: 119, 120; *The Iron Dream*, *102–4*, 175
Stableford, Brian M.: 4; *Dies Irae* trilogy, *83–90*
Stapledon, Olaf: 76–77, 79, 83, 122, 123; *Last and First Men*, 76–77; *Star Maker*, 77
Star Trek: 31, 78; "Who Mourns for Adonais?", *132–33*
Star Wars: 5, 78, 174
Stevenson, Robert Louis: "Dr. Jekyll & Mr. Hyde," *150–51*
Sturgeon, Theodore: 122, 123
Swann, Thomas Burnett: 4, 153

Tenn, William: 4, 16; "Medusa Was a Lady!", *12–15*, 74, 95
Tolkien, J. R. R.: 38–39, 69, 97, 119; *The Lord of the Rings*, 39, *99–101*; *Silmarillion*, 51, 100, 101, 116
Twain, Mark: 108, 118

Updike, John: 49

van Vogt, A. E.: 50, 122, 123, 124, 131; *The Book of Ptah*, *125–28*, 131
Verne, Jules: 63, 170; "The Eternal Adam," *71–73*, 74
Von Daniken, Erich: 174; *Chariot of the Gods?*, 180
Vonnegut, Kurt: 55, 56, 92

Wallis, G. McDonald: *Legend of Lost Earth*, *153–54*
Weinbaum, Stanley: 50, 54, 122, 123; "A Martian Odyssey," *29–31*, 125; "The Lotus Eaters," 30; "Proteus Island," 30; *The New Adam*, *124–25*
Wells, H. G.: 50, 63, 76, 77, 79, 82, 83, 122, 123; *The Time Machine*, *69–71*, 73, 74, 150
Whitman, Walt: 162
Williams, Charles: 52
Williamson, Jack: 29
Wilson, Gahan: 28
Wylie, Philip: 122

Yeats, W. B.: 61; *A Vision*, 159

Zelazny, Roger: 4, 48, 50, 56; *This Immortal*, 135, *136–38*, 145, 173; *Lord of Light*, 135, *138–41*, 145, 173; *Creatures of Light and Darkness*, 135, *141–44*; Amber series, 135; *Isle of the Dead*, 135; *Jack of Shadows*, 135, 145; "A Rose for Ecclesiastes," 135–36; *Damnation Alley*, 138; *Deus Irae* (with Dick), 179–80

INDEX OF MYTHOLOGIES

Amerindian: 147–48, 155, 165
Anglo-Saxon. *See Beowulf*, Old Norse
Archetypes. *See* Modern myths
Atlantis: 5, 47, 73–74, 78, 148, 152, 171, 173, 174, 181
Aztec: 18–20

Beowulf: 91–95, 100
Bible/Biblical. *See* Hebrew, Judeo-Christian, New Testament
Buddhism: 139–41. *See also* Hindu

Celtic: 3, 108–10, 110–11, 114, 115
Christian. *See* Judeo-Christian, New Testament
Eddic/Eddas. *See* Old Norse
Egypt, ancient: 2, 41, 44–45, 50, 82, 126–27, 135, 141–44
Euhemerism: 173

Finnish: 110–11, 115

Greek, ancient: 2–3, 4–5, 17, 28–33, 39, 40, 41, 47, 50, 51, 60–61, 65, 74–76, 77, 82, 96, 111, 114, 128–33, 135–38, 145, 146–48, 151, 153, 164, 165, 170, 171, 173; Apollo, 129–31, 132; Jason and the Argonauts, 129–31; Midas ("The Golden Touch"), 4–5; Odysseus (Homer's *Odyssey*), 8, 29–33, 81–82, 86–88, 98, 129, 131; Oedipus and the Sphinx, 70–71, 179–80; Perseus and the Medusa, 12–15; Prometheus, 6–8, 26–28, 42, 47, 145; Trojan War (Homer's *Iliad*), 2–3, 17 (Helen), 75–76, 83–90, 97–98, 100, 122, 147, 151 (Helen). *See also* Atlantis
Greek, modern: 136–38

Hebrew: 2, 41, 47, 49, 52–53, 65, 70–71, 75, 111, 146–47, 170, 171–72; Adam and Eve (Genesis/Paradise/Eden), 2, 8–12, 36, 67, 71–73, 124–25, 147, 150, 155, 170–71; *Book of Job*, 25
Hindu: 3, 27, 50, 135, 138–41; cf. 80–81

Irish. *See* Celtic

Jesus Christ. *See* New Testament
Judeo-Christian: 125, 150–51, 152–53, 158–59, 165, 166. *See also* Hebrew, New Testament

Kalevala. See Finnish

Magic: 152–53
Modern myths: androgyny, 169, 179; Billy the Kid, 60–61; Dying God (J. G. Frazer), 2, 3–4, 132, 159–69; Faust, 6, 7, 130; Frankenstein, 6–11, 20, 32–33, 76, 127, 130, 131, 138, 146, 150–51, 163, 171, 174, 176, 178, 179; Mu, 181; Nazism, 36, 47, *102–5*, *175* (cf. 124, 128); Odysseus, 31–33, 127, 146, 171, 174, 176, 178; Prometheus, *see* Frankenstein; Tarzan, 148, 152, 155, 164. *See also* Atlantis

Near Eastern, ancient: 40, 41, 44–45, 51, 65, 146; Adonais, 132
New Testament: 23–28, 49, 60–61, 80, 114, 134–35, 170
Northern Europe. *See Beowulf*, Celtic, Finnish, Old Norse

Old Norse (Eddic): 2–3, 42, 74, 98–99, 107–9, 111, 113–19, 145, 154–55, 170–172, 173; Valhalla, 17, 98–99; cf. *Beowulf*
Old Testament. *See* Hebrew
Ouroboros: 16, 97–99, 149

Roman: 28–29, 51, 148, 167; Rape of the Sabine Women, 167

Scandinavian. *See* Old Norse
Sumerian. *See* Near Eastern, ancient

[229]